New Jersey

Crossroads of Commerce

HELEN-CHANTAL PIKE

Newark at night, with the illuminated Prudential Center arena, center

New Jersey

Crossroads of Commerce

HELEN-CHANTAL PIKE

This book was produced in cooperation with the New Jersey Chamber of Commerce. Cherbo Publishing Group gratefully acknowledges this important contribution to *New Jersey: Crossroads of Commerce*. The publisher would also like to thank the New Jersey Historical Society for their assistance with this publication.

 cherbo publishing group, inc.

president	JACK C. CHERBO
chief operating officer	ELAINE HOFFMAN
editorial director	CHRISTINA M. BEAUSANG
managing feature editor	MARGARET L. MARTIN
senior feature editor	TINA G. RUBIN
senior profiles editor	J. KELLEY YOUNGER
profiles editors	NEVAIR KABAKIAN
	LIZA YETENEKIAN SMITH
associate editors	SYLVIA EMRICH-TOMA
	JENNY KORNFELD
editorial assistant/proofreader	MARK K. NISHIMURA
profiles writers	SYLVIA EMRICH-TOMA
	NEVAIR KABAKIAN
	JENNY KORNFELD
	JO ELLEN KRUMM
	STAN ZIEMBA
creative director	PERI A. HOLGUIN
senior designer	THEODORE E. YEAGER
designer	NELSON CAMPOS
senior photo editor	WALTER MLADINA
photo editor	KAREN MAZE
digital color specialist	ART VASQUEZ
sales administrator	JOAN K. BAKER
client services supervisor	PATRICIA DE LEONARD
senior client services coordinator	LESLIE E. SHAW
client services coordinator	KENYA HICKS
executive assistant	JUDY ROBITSCHEK
administrative assistant	BILL WAY
regional development manager	GLEN EDWARDS
eastern regional manager	MARCIA WEISS
publisher's representative	LINDA SPROEHNLE

Cherbo Publishing Group, Inc.
Encino, California 91316
© 2008 by Cherbo Publishing Group, Inc.
All rights reserved. Published 2008.

Printed in Canada
By Friesens

Subsidiary Production Office
Santa Rosa, CA, USA
888.340.6049

Library of Congress Cataloging-in-Publication data
Pike, Helen-Chantal
A pictorial guide highlighting New Jersey's
economic and social history.

Library of Congress Control Number 2008929202
ISBN 978-1-882933-89-1
Visit the CPG Web site at www.cherbopub.com.

The information in this publication is the most recent available and has been carefully researched to ensure accuracy. Cherbo Publishing Group, Inc. cannot and does not guarantee either the correctness of all information furnished it or the complete absence of errors, including omissions.

To purchase additional copies of this book, contact Joan Baker at Cherbo Publishing Group: jbaker@cherbopub.com or phone 818.783.0040 ext. 27.

Composite of New Jersey Devils hockey fans, October 2007

ACKNOWLEDGMENTS

The author would like to thank James Amemasor and Beth Mauro from the New Jersey Historical Society; Bonita Craft Grant from New Jersey Special Collections at the Alexander Library, Rutgers University–New Brunswick; Dr. Marc Mappen, executive director of the New Jersey Historical Commission; Dr. Alex Magoun, director of the Sarnoff Library; Margaret Martin and Tina Rubin of Cherbo Publishing Group; fellow writer and author Pamela J. Waterman of Mesa, Arizona; and the reference staffs at the Monmouth County Library–Eastern Branch in Shrewsbury and the Newark Public Library.

George Washington Bridge over the Hudson River, New York City skyline in background

TABLE OF CONTENTS

From left to right: Wading at the beach; Donald Trump's Taj Mahal Casino Resort, Atlantic City; shops at the Tropicana Casino and Resort, Atlantic City.

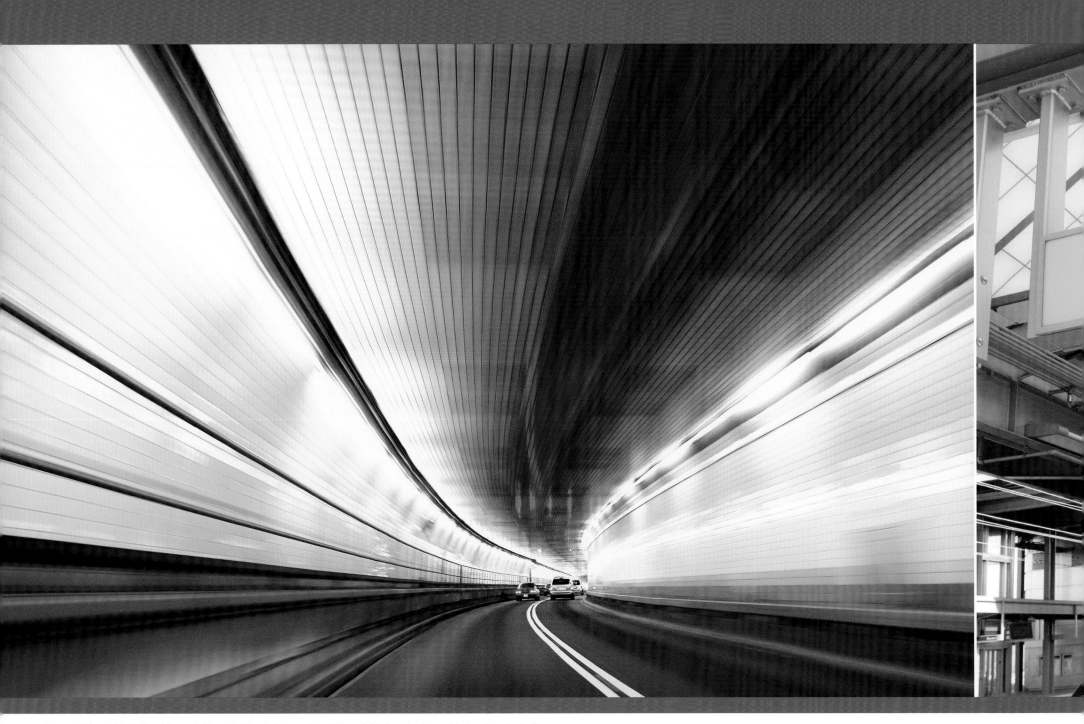

From left to right: Holland Tunnel; Newark Liberty International Airport Station; tanker aside loading dock, Bayonne.

From left to right: Richard Serra sculpture, *The Hedgehog and the Fox,* Princeton University, Princeton; Lawrence T. Babbio, Jr. Center, Stevens Institute of Technology, Hoboken; New Jersey Transit station lobby, Secaucus.

From left to right: Camden Riversharks home game at Campbell's Field; Prudential Center arena, Newark; fans rushing Rutgers University wide receiver Kenny Britt at Rutgers Stadium, October 18, 2007, Piscataway.

CORPORATIONS & ORGANIZATIONS PROFILED

The following organizations have made a valuable commitment to the quality of this publication.

Historic Colgate clock with Goldman Sachs tower in background, Jersey City

BUSINESS VISIONARIES

The following companies and organizations are recognized as innovators in their fields and have played a prominent role in this publication, as they have in the state. The New Jersey Chamber of Commerce gratefully acknowledges their participation in *New Jersey: Crossroads of Commerce*.

at&t
Your world. Delivered.

AT&T
One AT&T Plaza, Dallas, TX 75202
Contact: Bill Strawderman, Executive Director
Phone: 908-234-6770
E-mail: bstrawderman@att.com
Web site: www.att.com
Use of the AT&T logo is granted under permission by AT&T Intellectual Property

Burlington County Department of Economic
Development and Regional Planning
50 Rancocas Road, Mount Holly, NJ 08060-6000
Contact: Mark A. Remsa, Director
Phone: 609-265-5055 / Fax: 609-265-5006
E-mail: edcoordinator@co.burlington.nj.us
Web site: www.co.burlington.nj.us/departments/economic/
"Balanced . . . Beautiful . . . Burlington"

Delta Dental of New Jersey
1639 Route 10, Delta Dental Plaza, Parsippany, NJ 07054
Phone: 973-285-4000 / Fax: 973-285-4139
E-mail: smile@deltadentalnj.com
Web site: www.deltadentalnj.com
"Everyone Deserves Good Oral Health"

BASF Corporation
100 Campus Drive, Florham Park, NJ 07932
Phone: 800-526-1072 or 973-245-6000
Web site: www.basf.com/usa

Camden County, New Jersey
520 Market Street, 15th Floor, Camden, NJ 08102
Phone: 856-751-2242 / Fax: 856-751-2247
E-mail: justask@camdencounty.com
Web site: camdencounty.com
"Making It Better, Together."

George Harms Construction Co., Inc.
62 Yellowbrook Road, Howell, NJ 07731
Mailing Address: P.O. Box 817, Farmingdale, NJ 07727
Tom Hardell, President and COO
Phone: 732-938-4004 / Fax: 732-938-2782
E-mail: thardell@ghcci.com
Web site: www.ghcci.com
"Building New Jersey the American Way . . ."

Bristol-Myers Squibb
345 Park Avenue, New York, NY 10154-0037
Web site: www.bms.com
"Together we can prevail™"

Capital One Bank
710 Route 46 East, Suite 306, Fairfield, NJ 07004
Douglas L. Kennedy, President, New Jersey Division
Phone: 973-439-7600 / Fax: 973-882-5018
Web site: www.capitalonebank.com

Horizon Blue Cross Blue Shield of New Jersey
Making Healthcare Work®

Horizon Blue Cross Blue Shield of New Jersey
3 Penn Plaza East, Newark, NJ 07105
Web site: www.horizonblue.com
"Making Healthcare Work."

Jersey Central Power & Light
A FirstEnergy Company

Jersey Central Power & Light
300 Madison Avenue, Morristown, NJ 07962-1911
Contact: Ron Morano, Senior Public Relations Representative
Phone: 973-401-8097 / Fax: 330-315-8941
E-mail: rmorano@firstenergycorp.com
Web site: www.firstenergycorp.com

NAI James E. Hanson
Commercial Real Estate Services, Worldwide.

NAI James E. Hanson
235 Moore Street, Hackensack, NJ 07601
William C. Hanson, President
Phone: 201-488-5800 / Fax: 201-488-0246
Web site: www.naihanson.com
"Performance Driven, Tradition Bound"

New Jersey Education Association
180 West State Street, P.O. Box 1211, Trenton, NJ 08607-1211
Joyce Powell, President
Phone: 609-599-4561 / Fax: 609-392-6321
Web site: www.njea.org
"Making public schools great for every child!"

NOVARTIS

Novartis Pharmaceuticals Corporation
One Health Plaza, East Hanover, NJ 07936
Contact: Gina Moran, Executive Director, External Communications
Phone: 862-778-5000
E-mail: gina.moran@novartis.com
Web site: www.pharma.us.novartis.com

Raritan Bay Medical Center
Advancing care every day

Raritan Bay Medical Center
Information / Physician Referral: 800-DOCTORS (800-362-8677)
Web site: www.rbmc.org

Perth Amboy Campus
530 New Brunswick Avenue, Perth Amboy, NJ 08861
Phone: 732-442-3700

Old Bridge Campus
One Hospital Plaza, Old Bridge, NJ 08857
Phone: 732-360-1000

RUTGERS
THE STATE UNIVERSITY OF NEW JERSEY

Rutgers, The State University of New Jersey
83 Somerset Street, New Brunswick, NJ 08901-1281
Contact: Office of the Vice President for University Relations
Phone: 732-445-INFO (4636)
E-mail: AskUs@rci.rutgers.edu
Web site: www.rutgers.edu
"Jersey Roots, Global Reach"

STEVENS
Institute of Technology

Stevens Institute of Technology
Castle Point on Hudson, Hoboken, NJ 07030
Contact: Patrick A. Berzinski, Director, University Communications
Phone: 201-216-5000 / Fax: 201-216-5520
E-mail: media@stevens.edu
Web site: www.stevens.edu
"Per aspera ad astra—'Through adversity to the stars'"

WACHOVIA

Wachovia Bank, N.A.
301 South College Street, Suite 4000, Charlotte, NC 28288-0013
Contact: Fran Durst, Corporate Communications Manager
Phone: 908-598-3062
E-mail: frances.durst@wachovia.com
Web site: www.wachovia.com

Wakefern Food Corporation/ShopRite
5000 Riverside Drive, Keasbey, NJ 08832-1209
Phone: 908-527-3300 or 800-746-7748 / Fax: 908-527-3397
Web site: www.shoprite.com
"Always Fresh . . . Always for Less!"

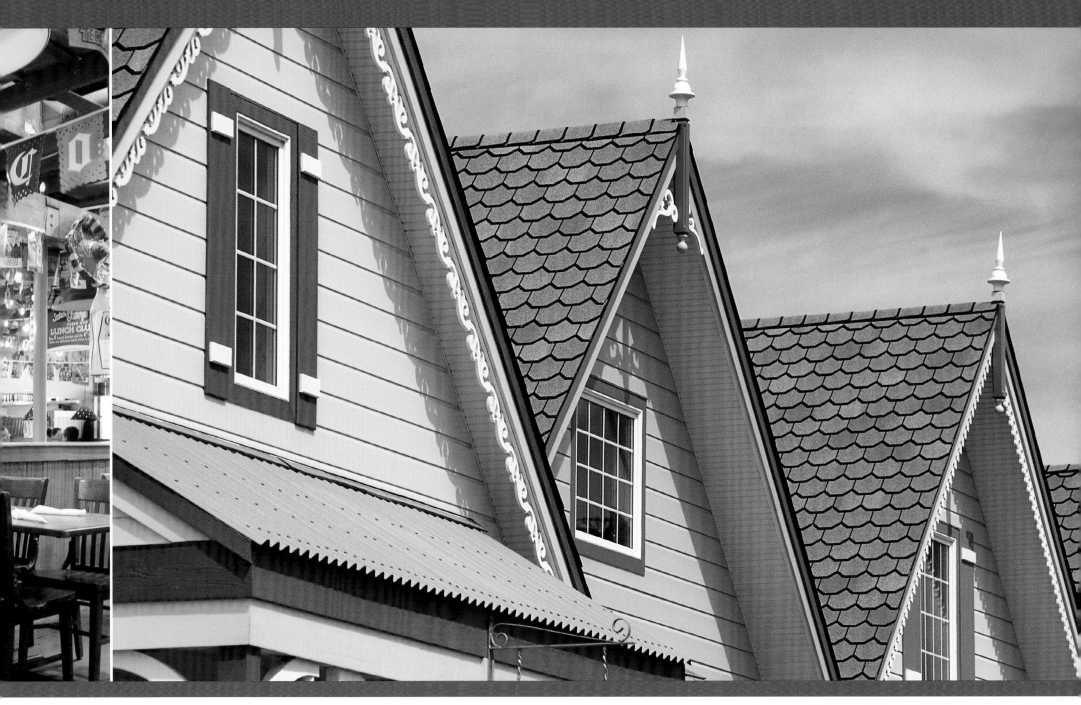

From left to right: Kruise Nite classic car show, Freehold; chow time at Chevys Fresh Mex, Clifton; colorful commercial Victorians, Cape May.

From left to right: Hiker on Mt. Tammany, Delaware Water Gap National Recreation Area; Great Falls of the Passaic River, Paterson; Mullica River, Pinelands National Reserve.

From left to right: Riding home with the catch of the day; superb surfing in Belmar; a sign of the past in Cape May.

From left to right: Ready for takeoff at the Quick Chek Festival of Ballooning, Readington; up close with a hippo at Adventure Aquarium, Camden; pecan pie—not what she expected at the Annual Crawfish Fest, Augusta.

From left to right: John Mayer in concert at Susquehanna Bank Center, Camden; Giant Wheel at Gillian's Wonderland Pier, Ocean City; high-speed tubing at Mountain Creek Waterpark, Vernon Township.

Rotunda of the New Jersey State House, Trenton

FOREWORD

New Jersey is a revolutionary state in every sense of the word. It sits at the crossroads of the American Revolution, site of turning points in the war such as the battle of Trenton. Our state welcomes Revolutionary War buffs to a variety of sites, from Washington's Headquarters and Fort Nonsense in Morristown to the Barracks Museum in Trenton, along the banks of the famously crossed Delaware River. Moving forward from the American Revolution, New Jersey is known for innovation and sheer brain power. Thomas Edison and Albert Einstein—who lends his name and reputation to the technology corridor dubbed Einstein's Alley—come to mind immediately. New Jerseyans have revolutionized the world.

Located between New York and Philadelphia, the Garden State has a flavor all its own. Our highly educated workforce is the reason that 24 Fortune 500 companies are headquartered here. Add to that a quality of life that includes great universities, a sparkling shore, and access to the arts, and you begin to understand why high achievers call New Jersey home. Those not lucky enough to live here spend close to $40 billion annually to enjoy our shore, ski our mountains, and explore our historic sites.

Medicine chest to the world, our state's pharmaceutical community continues to innovate and revolutionize the industry with the development of life-saving and life-enhancing drugs. The sciences, whether genomics, biotechnology, or information technology, provide the country's highest wages to Garden State workers. And speaking of the "Garden" State, we are among the nation's top producers of blueberries, eggplant, and, of course, the famous Jersey tomato. If New Jersey were a country, it would rank as the 17th-largest economy in the world.

I hope that you enjoy this book, which provides a taste of what New Jersey has to offer, and I invite you to explore further this exceptional state.

Joan Verplanck

Joan Verplanck
President
New Jersey Chamber of Commerce

NEW JERSEY TIMELINE

1524   1758   1776   1789

GIOVANNI DI PIER ANDREA DI BERNARDO DA VERRAZZANO PATRIZIO FIOR. GRAN CAPIT. COMANDANTE IN MARE PER IL RE CRISTIANISSIMO FRANCESCO PRIMO, E DISCOPRITORE DELLA NUOVA FRANCIA.

Giovanni da Verrazzano (1485–1528)

1524
The first European to explore the region, Giovanni da Verrazzano arrives in New Jersey.

1609
Henry Hudson explores Hudson Bay, claiming New Jersey for the Dutch.

1642
America's first brewery is established in Hoboken.

1746
British North America's fourth college, the College of New Jersey, is granted a charter. It will be renamed Princeton University at its sesquicentennial in 1896.

1758
New Jersey creates the country's first Indian reservation, Brotherton, for the Lenni Lenape tribe.

1766
Queen's College, known later as Rutgers, the State University of New Jersey, is granted a charter.

1776
George Washington and his troops make a surprise attack on Hessian mercenaries in Trenton. The Battle of Trenton proves to be a turning point in the Revolutionary War.

1783
Princeton serves as the nation's capital for a short period of time. The following year, Congress moves to Trenton for a few months.

1789
After being the third state to ratify the Constitution, New Jersey is the first state to ratify the Bill of Rights.

1792
Alexander Hamilton, the first Secretary of the Treasury, establishes the country's first industrial park at the Great Falls in Paterson.

The College of New Jersey (later Princeton University), depicted circa 1763

1793   1811   1848   1858

1793

Jean Pierre Blanchard makes the first hot-air balloon flight in North America, landing in Gloucester County, and delivers the first "airmail" letter.

The Burr and Hamilton Duel, 1804

1804

Founding Fathers and archrivals Alexander Hamilton and Aaron Burr duel in Weehawken, resulting in Hamilton's death.

1811

Developed by John Stevens, the world's first steam ferry goes into service between Hoboken and Manhattan. Stevens will also create America's first locomotive on his estate in Hoboken.

1825

Born in Maplewood and a leader of the Hudson River School, Asher Brown Durand helps found the New York Drawing Association, later known as the National Academy of Design.

1838

Samuel Morse and Alfred Vail make the first successful public demon-stration of the telegraph at the Speedwell Iron Works in Morristown.

1846

The first organized baseball game to be played under the modern rules established by Andrew Cartwright is played on Hoboken's Elysian Fields.

1848

Trenton Psychiatric Hospital opens. Dorothea Dix, advocate for the humane treatment of the mentally ill, founded the hospital and considered it her "firstborn child."

1858

William Foulke discovers the first nearly complete dinosaur skeleton, which is named *Hadrosaurus foulkii*, in Haddonfield.

Lithograph, *The American National Game of Baseball*, published by Currier & Ives in 1866 illustrating championship match at Hoboken's Elysian Fields

NEW JERSEY TIMELINE

1869   *1870*   *1876*   *1885*

Rutgers vs. Princeton in the first intercollegiate football game, 1869

1869
Rutgers and Princeton universities play each other in the country's first intercollegiate football game, in New Brunswick. Rutgers wins, 6–4.

1870
Thomas Mundy Peterson votes in Perth Amboy, becoming the first African-American in the United States to vote after the passage of the 15th Amendment.

1870
The first section of Atlantic City's boardwalk, which will be the birthplace of saltwater taffy, opens.

1875
In Newark, John Fairfield Dryden founds the Prudential Friendly Society, the first company in the United States to offer life insurance to the working class.

1876
Thomas Alva Edison opens his first full-scale laboratory, in Menlo Park. He will invent the carbon transmitter, phonograph, and incandescent electric lighting here.

1884
The only president to serve two non-consecutive terms and be married in the White House, Grover Cleveland, a Caldwell native, is elected to his first term of presidency.

Atlantic City boardwalk and Steel Pier, undated photo

1885
Alice Stokes Paul, a leading suffragist and founder of the National Women's Party, is born in Moorestown.

1896
The first professional basketball game is played in Trenton between the Trenton and Brooklyn YMCAs. The "Trentons" will become champions of the National Basketball League, the sport's first professional association.

1897
Dr. John Dorrance of the Joseph Campbell Preserve Company, which was founded in Camden and is a predecessor of the Campbell Soup Company, develops condensed soup.

1898
Paul Robeson, son of an escaped slave, is born in Princeton. He will become a Rutgers valedictorian, an exceptional athlete, an internationally renowned actor and singer, and a controversial activist against fascism and racism.

The 1,621-foot-long Steel Pier, the first pier supported by a steel framework, opens in Atlantic City.

1902   *1920*   *1927*   *1933*

1902
Future New Jersey governor and U.S. president Woodrow Wilson becomes president of Princeton University, which he will turn into an influential institution while accomplishing higher education reform.

1907
Fort Lee becomes the motion picture capital of the world, with more than a dozen major studios filming here over the next two decades.

USS *Shenandoah* moors on the USS *Patoka*, 1925

1933
America's first drive-in theater opens outside Camden. The featured film is *Wife Beware*.

After accepting a position at the Institute for Advanced Study, Albert Einstein arrives in Princeton, where he will live and work for the remainder of his life.

1915
Frank Sinatra is born in Hoboken. Over his lifetime, the acclaimed singer/actor's awards will include 21 Grammys, three Oscars, two Golden Globes, and an Emmy.

1916
Contributing land and resources, Elizabeth Coleman White collaborates with Frederick Coville and develops a commercial variety of blueberries at her home in the Pine Barrens.

1920
Earle Dickson, an employee of New Brunswick–based Johnson & Johnson, creates the first Band-Aids for his new wife, so she can bandage her cuts while he is at work.

1921
Lakehurst Naval Air Station becomes headquarters for lighter-than-air flight. It is where America's first dirigible, the USS *Shenandoah*, is built; a zeppelin begins and ends its 12-day, round-the-world trip; and the *Hindenburg* crashes.

1927
Construction begins on the George Washington Bridge, which will be the world's longest suspension bridge at its completion, while the Holland Tunnel, the first long underwater tunnel designed for cars, is completed downriver.

1932
Landing in Newark, Amelia Earhart, record-breaking and record-setting aviation pioneer, is the first woman to fly solo across the country.

Vince Lombardi, undated photo

1939
Vince Lombardi, who will make football history coaching the Green Bay Packers, begins his career at St. Cecilia High School in Englewood, staying here for eight years.

NEW JERSEY TIMELINE

1940   1954   1958   1962

Brainy Weather Machine at
Fort Monmouth, undated photo

1940
The beauty pageant that started in Atlantic City as a swimsuit competition is officially named the Miss America pageant, and the Miss America Organization is incorporated.

1946
Fort Monmouth, where the electronic study of weather, radar, and radio communication has been developed, establishes radar contact with the moon.

1947
A team of scientists at Murray Hill's Bell Laboratories invents the world's first transistor.

1952
Rutgers professor Selman A. Waksman—who first used the term "antibiotic"—wins the Nobel Prize in medicine for his discovery of the first antibiotic that is effective against tuberculosis.

1954
On the Waterfront, a Columbia Pictures production starring Marlon Brando, opens. Filmed in Hoboken and based on actual events occurring on the docks, it will win eight Oscars.

1956
Revolutionizing the shipping industry, the SS *Ideal X*, the first ship that is designed for containerization, leaves Port Newark for Houston, Texas, carrying 58 containers full of freight.

1958
Mary Roebling, a West Collingswood native and the first female president of a major commercial U.S. bank (the Trenton Trust Company), is the first woman to be appointed a governor of the American Stock Exchange.

1962
Newark's Frankie Valli and the Four Seasons record the megahit "Sherry," beginning their reign at the top of the pop charts. Over nearly four decades, they will sell 100 million records and have a Broadway hit, *Jersey Boys*, based on their story.

From left to right: Tommy DeVito, Frankie Valli, Bob Gaudio, and Nick Massi of the Four Seasons, circa 1965

Marlon Brando in *On the Waterfront*, 1954

1963   1965   1975   1977

Buzz Aldrin, 1969

1975
Lauryn Hill, whose 1998 solo debut album, *The Miseducation of Lauryn Hill*, will win the singer five Grammy Awards, is born in West Orange.

1976
New Jersey becomes the nation's second state to legalize gambling but limits it to Atlantic City. The first casino, Resorts International, will open here in two years.

1977
Meryl Streep, who was born in Summit, begins her film career as Ann Marie in *Julia*. She will earn two Academy Awards and more nominations for the award than any other actor.

1978
Montclair State University's record-setting basketball player Carole Blazejowski, a native of Elizabeth, receives the inaugural Wade Trophy, awarded annually to the top female college basketball player.

1963
Tom Sims, a 13-year-old student in Haddonfield, creates a "ski board," an early model of the snowboard, in woodshop class.

1964
Teaneck is the first community in the country to voluntarily integrate its schools.

1965
In his final basketball game for Princeton University, future New Jersey senator Bill Bradley scores 58 points against Wichita State University, setting an NCAA Division I single-game record (until 1970) and a Final Four record.

1969
Montclair native and lunar module pilot for *Apollo 11*, Edwin Eugene Aldrin Jr.—"Buzz" Aldrin—is the second man to set foot on the moon (after mission commander Neil Alden Armstrong).

Meryl Streep, undated photo

NEW JERSEY TIMELINE

1982   1983   1984   1995

Bruce Springsteen, 1985

1984
Musician Bruce Springsteen, of Freehold, releases *Born in the U.S.A.*, which, with seven top-10 singles and 15 million copies sold, becomes Columbia Record's best seller and is the number-one album for seven weeks.

1995
The New Jersey Devils hockey team wins the Stanley Cup, becoming the first professional sports champions in the state.

1989
After winning the Pulitzer Prize for fiction for her novel *Beloved*, Toni Morrison begins teaching at Princeton University, where she will establish the Princeton Atelier, a collaborative workshop for writers and performers.

1982
Sarah Vaughan, whose five-decades-long singing career started at Mount Zion Baptist Church in her hometown of Newark, wins a Grammy Award for her album *Gershwin Live!*

1983
Figure skater Dick Button, the Englewood native who won the U.S., North American, European, world, and Olympic championships in 1948, is included in the inaugural class of the U.S. Olympic Hall of Fame.

New Jersey Devils celebrating Stanley Cup win, 1995

1996　1998　2001　2006

Jack Nicholson with Oscar for Best Actor, 1998

1998

In a Supreme Court case between the states of New Jersey and New York, most of Ellis Island is declared to belong to New Jersey.

1999

Johnson & Johnson, founded and headquartered in New Brunswick, merges with Centocor, which makes it one of the world's largest biotechnology companies.

2001

After improving New Jersey's environment, Governor Christine Todd Whitman is appointed EPA administrator in President George W. Bush's administration.

2004

New Jersey's budget includes $9.5 million for the new Stem Cell Institute of New Jersey, making the Garden State the first state to fund stem cell research.

2006

The New Jersey Nets finish the NBA 2006 postseason with two 10-game winning streaks, their fourth Atlantic Division title in five years, and their fifth consecutive playoff appearance.

Merck & Co., whose global head-quarters is located in Whitehouse Station, is ranked among the top 20 employers in the biotechnology and pharmaceutical industries by *Science* magazine.

1996

Legendary Yankees hitter Lawrence Peter Berra—"Yogi" Berra—a long-time resident of Montclair, is granted an honorary doctorate degree from Montclair State University.

1998

Jack Nicholson, who was born in Neptune, wins his third Oscar, this time for portraying Melvin Udall in *As Good As It Gets* (1997).

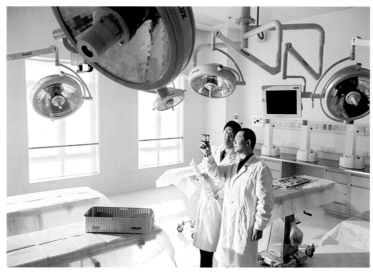

A professional exchange at Johnson & Johnson Medical (China) Ltd. Science Center

2007

Pollstar magazine recognizes Continental Airlines Arena (now Izod Center) and Giants Stadium at Meadowlands Sports Complex as among the most popular venues in the world in terms of ticket sales.

2008

First Lady Laura Bush awards the Ocean County Library a National Medal for Museum and Library Services, recognizing it as one of the top 10 such institutions in the nation.

The Atlantic City Convention and Visitors Authority partners with Pepco Energy Services to install the largest single-roof solar panel in the nation at the Atlantic City Convention Center.

PART ONE

A LEGACY OF OPPORTUNITY:

New Jersey, Fertile Ground for Advancement

Working the harvest at Theodore Budd's bog near Pemberton, September 1910.

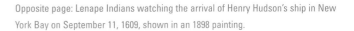

CHAPTER 01

FROM COLONIZATION TO REVOLUTION

1524–1776

New Jersey has represented economic opportunity ever since Florentine explorer Giovanni da Verrazzano sighted its coastline as part of his discovery of a new continent in 1524. Eighty-five years later, in 1609, English navigator Henry Hudson charted the land for one of the 17th century's more prominent import-export firms, the Dutch East India Company. The region seemed ideal: geographically diverse and teeming with plants and wildlife, it had two long rivers, two protected bays, and an extensive oceanfront, all of which offered the promise of trade. Too, there was the possibility of bargaining for animal pelts and grain with the indigenous Indians, an established civilization of seminomadic Lenapes.

Writing in his log as they lay at anchor in the North River (which would later be named for Hudson), Robert Juet, Hudson's first mate on *de Halve Maen* (the *Half Moon*), observed:

> The people of the country came aboard brought green tobacco they go in deer skins loose, well dressed. Some in mantles of feathers and sorts of good furs the women came to us had red copper tobacco pipes and other things of copper they did wear about their necks. The people are civil and desire clothes. The country is full of great tall oaks.

SETTLING NEW NETHERLAND

With investors to satisfy, the Dutch East India Company created the New Netherland Company in 1614 to oversee the construction of trading

posts and the development of permanent villages in the new territory, called New Netherland. That same year, cartographer Cornelis Hendrickson piloted the treacherous shoals of Barende-gat (today's Barnegat) Inlet and claimed for Holland the islands on either side, as well as all the forested land that fronted the Great Bay to the south and the rivers that emptied into it. In time, the Dutch established a small whaling hamlet at the northern tip of the longer island. It would also serve as a final checkpoint for the export of timber, a valuable commodity to the lowland Dutch.

Finally, sailing for the Dutch West India Company in 1623, Cornelis Mey led settlers up the Delaware River to the mouth of a tidal creek surrounded by trees. There he oversaw the construction of Fort Nassau, a trading post in the vicinity of today's Westville. The following year, he went further upriver and delivered Belgian Wallons to Burlington Island, where they, too, built an outpost for trade, though later they moved to the mainland.

The Dutch soon began importing cattle, horses, sheep, chickens, and pigs as provisions for their settlers. Their strategy to protect as well as expand their territorial investment extended to paying doctors, craftsmen, and soldiers to relocate to the New World.

The development expenses for the new territory were more than the Dutch West India Company had anticipated. To increase its profit, the company turned to patroonship, a concept of real estate development whereby an investor bought land and populated it with colonists, who settled it at their own expense. In 1630 company director Michael Pauw purchased a tract across the Hudson River from the capital of New Amsterdam, on Manhattan Island, and hired a subcontractor to sign up 50 pioneers interested in settling the property. The subcontractor was unsuccessful, and the land reverted to the company. Moreover, a misunderstanding with the Lenapes led the initial settlers to decamp to New Amsterdam. It would take the persuasive efforts of

German immigrant Thielman van Vleck to convince the provincial governor of New Amsterdam to allow for a return across the river to restart a trade center on the river's

A View from Paulushook, of Horsimus on the Jersey shore & part of York Island

west bank. Granted in 1660, the charter created Bergen, a fortified—but New Jersey's first—permanent European settlement.

Under the auspices of the New Sweden Company, Swedish settlers and a few Finns arrived in 1638 and built the hamlet of Nya Sverige, south of Fort Nassau on the Delaware River. They later erected Fort Nya Elfsborg, closer to where the river meets the bay, to better protect their trade in furs. In 1697 Finnish immigrant Eric Mullica led a group from Raccoon (today's Swedesboro) east along the state's third-largest river (which now bears his name), setting up a homestead in the area where the river empties into Little Egg Harbor. The Mullica River became an alternate transport route to the sandy roads of the coastal plain. Fifty-one years later, botanist Peter Kalm would arrive to collect and identify plant species that could be of economic benefit to Sweden.

Intent on solidifying their worldwide leadership in the production of whale oil, soap, and baleen, the Dutch established a commercial port on the peninsula where the Atlantic Ocean meets the Delaware Bay. The name of the port honored Captain Mey; later it was anglicized to Cape May. When whaling faded,

the ocean harvesting of clams, oysters, and saltwater fish replaced it. Between fishing seasons, many of the seamen earned their living as farmers along the bay's vast, nutrient-rich, low-lying coastal plain. Long, warm summers contributed to the budding agricultural success of the region, nurturing such crops as salt hay and vegetables—especially corn for cattle and hog feed.

The healthy, salt-air breezes blowing across Cape May would help launch another industry more than a century later. In the summer of 1766, overworked Philadelphians would begin sailing to the peninsula to escape the city's oppressive heat and airborne germs, wading ashore to rustic accommodations in canvas tents scattered along the beachfront.

While the Dutch regarded most of New Netherland as a collection of trading ports, the British eyed the region as an extension of their empire. Having already launched colonies in Virginia and Massachusetts Bay, they set their sights on the geographic linchpin they needed. In 1664 they seized control of all Dutch-owned lands. It took three more years and the signing of the Treaty of Breda, however, for the English to drive out the Dutch.

The English renamed their new possession New Jersey to acknowledge the role played by the Channel Isle of Jersey, where King Charles II and his brother, James, Duke of York, had lived in exile during the English Civil War (1642–51). The island's royal governor, Sir George Carteret, had granted the brothers asylum. When Charles gave James the New Netherlands property between the two rivers, James turned the land over to Sir Carteret

and Lord John Berkeley to manage. In turn, they sent Captain Philip Carteret, a cousin, to increase the revenue potential from the colony.

RISE OF RIVER CITIES

Expansion followed. Puritan Robert Treat and other settlers left the larger colony of Connecticut in 1666 to settle land bounded by Newark Bay, the Passaic River, and the Watchung Mountains. They created Newark, soon to become one of the largest cities in the colonies. The settlers organized a town-meeting form of government, a militia, and an official religion in the form of the Congregational Church. Membership was necessary for white male property owners to vote. This church-based government lasted nearly 70 years, until Josiah Ogden harvested his wheat on a Sunday rather than lose it to rain.

A variety of industries arose in Newark. Here and there, settlers in small cottages along Broad Street began making finished goods for trade, starting with shoes, which they made from animal hides.

Across the colony, on the Delaware River just south of Assiscunk Creek, 230 Quakers from London and Yorkshire founded New Beverly in 1677. A couple of name changes later, the town was called Burlington and was garnering a reputation as a shipbuilding center and a market for produce from

outlying plantations such as the 300-acre Peachfield, in Westampton. Given the shortage of settlers, helping to till and harvest those large fields were African slaves brought by the Dutch and indentured white laborers, who worked off their contracts while gaining the kind of knowledge that

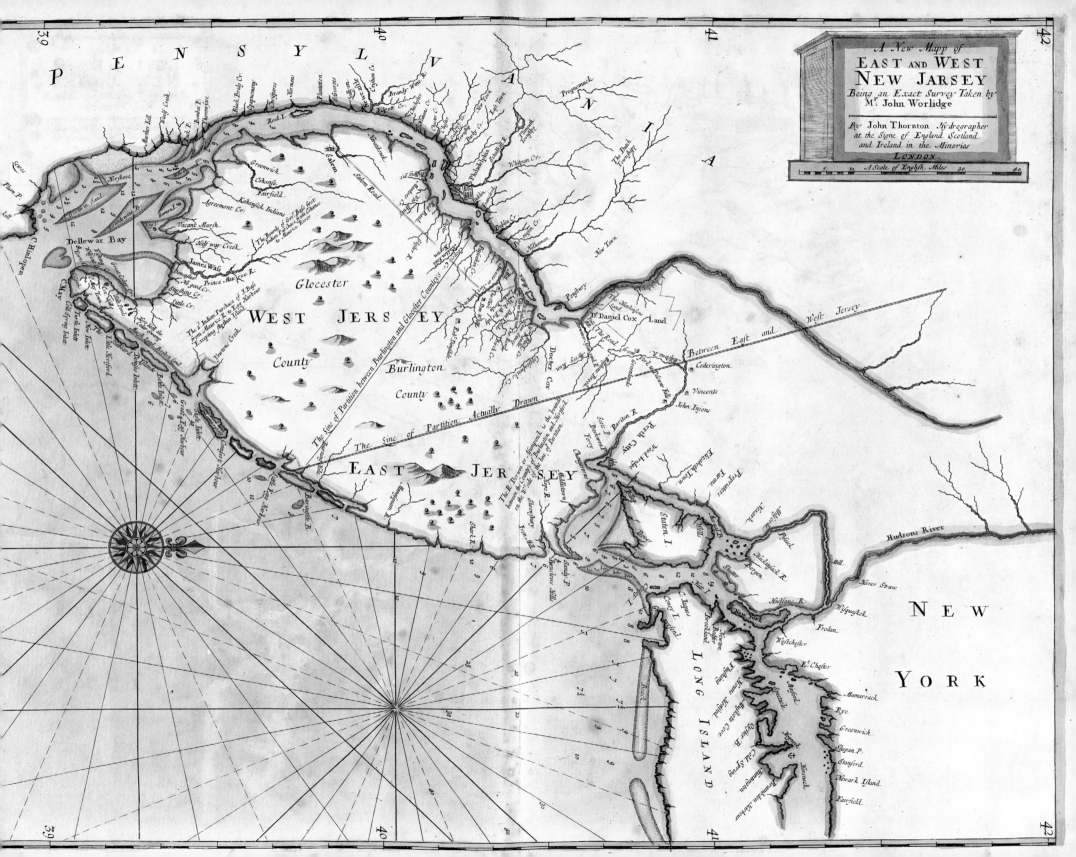

P E N S Y L V A N I A

A New Mapp of
EAST AND WEST
NEW JARSEY
Being an Exact Survey Taken by
Mr. John Worlidge

By John Thornton Hydrographer
at the Signe of England, Scotland
and Ireland in the Minories
LONDON.

A Scale of English Miles

Pregnemuck

The Dutch Township

Brandy Wine R.
New Town
East Town
Plimoth Longpt.
Whitpan Cr.
Philadelphia
Skoolkill R.
Dublin
Frankford
Dublin Cr.
Poaquesin Cr.
Nshamon
New Town

Greenwich
Cohanse
Fairfield
Agreement Cr.
Kahansick Indians
Half way Creek
Vacant Marsh
James Wals
Prince Maurice R.
No good Cr.
Stephint Cr.
Little Cr.

Salem
Salem Road

Glocester

WEST JERSEY
County

Pensbury
Dr. Daniel Cox Land

The Hudson's
Read
The Road from N. York to Groundwad.

Cederington

Between East and West Jersey

Docter Cox

Vincents
John Insons

Dellewar Bay
C. Hinlopen
C. May

Newtons Creek

Burlington
County

The Line of Partition between Burlington and Glocester Countys

The Line of Partition Actually Drawn

Falls
South Bariton. R.
Scots P.
Perth Gaty.
Wood bridge
Elizabeth Town
Proprietors Farm
Mart
Mush

EAST JERSEY

The R. Derwen or Assinpinck is the bound between the Countys of Burlington and Horford on the West side of the line of Partition.

Shark R.
Shrewsbury Hills

Chingarowa
Middletown
Amboy R.
Topefatcong
Iron Hill

Staten I.

Barnegate B.

Little Egg Harbour
Great Egg Harbour
Absekon Beach
Cedar Inlet

Sandy P.

Aquackanonk
Passaik
Bergen
Hackinsack R.

Hudsons River

Shutter
Hudsons R.
New York

Nover Straw
Wilquayfick
Frodan
Westchester

NEW
YORK

LONG ISLAND

Hudson Cove
Oyster B.
East Spring
Huntington
Brandon Harbour

Mamaroack
Rye
Greenwich
Shepan P.
Stanford
Newark Ysland
Fairfield

CITY OF TRENTON.

would prepare them to start their own businesses. The bountiful yields from Burlington farmland prompted settler John Crips to write:

I do not remember that ever I tasted better water in any part of England, than the springs of this place do yield; of which is made very good beer and ale; and here is also wine and cyder.

A considerably smaller group of English Quakers, led by Mahlon Stacy, made their way farther up the river in 1679, to the Falls of the Delaware. There Stacy built a log mill and a clapboard house. In 1714 a well-connected and well-financed Philadelphia merchant, Scots-born William Trent, arrived and bought out the family's holdings, including 800 acres on Assunpink Creek. More entrepreneurs followed, and the ensuing transformation made "Trent's Towne" (Trenton) into a second commercial center on the Delaware. A steady fleet of schooners transported produce, flour, stoneware, and other finished goods to Philadelphia, while cut timber from the forests that grew thickly along the upper river valley came downstream to mills that turned the logs into board lumber for the construction trades. Trenton boasted a directory of craftsmen, a courthouse, and military barracks built during the French and Indian War. A ferry service to Philadelphia added to the town's role as an overnight destination on the Kings Highway between Boston, Massachusetts, and Charleston, South Carolina. In 1790 Trenton would become New Jersey's capital.

In 1683 English, Scottish, and French merchants founded Perth Amboy on land where the Raritan River empties into Lower New York Bay. Their goal was to establish a port city to control the burgeoning commerce in bread, cider, beef, dairy products, and leather, all of which came from colonial farms in the Raritan valley.

REVOLUTIONARY THINKING
Its roots intertwined with religious precepts, the colony's rising merchant class extended its influence beyond trade with a foray into higher education. Sparked by the Great Awakening, which encouraged introspection and a commitment to a new standard of morality, Scottish

Presbyterians and Dutch Reformed ministers each created a college in the years before the American Revolution—a distinction for New Jersey that was unique among the 13 colonies. In 1746 the Scottish Presbyterians established the

College of New Jersey in Elizabeth; in 1766 the Dutch Reformed ministers received a charter from the court of King George III for Queen's College, which they built on the rolling hills overlooking the Raritan River in the farming community of

New Brunswick. The curricula of both schools focused on arts and sciences: philosophy reinterpreted for Christianity; Latin and Greek; and, as part of the increasing interest in science that characterized the 18th century, the study of mathematics.

In 1756, 10 years after its founding, the College of New Jersey was relocated to the more centrally situated village of Princeton; in 1896 it would be renamed Princeton University.

In 1825, nearly 60 years after Queen's College was established, its trustees would honor Revolutionary War hero and philanthropist Colonel Henry Rutgers by renaming the school after him.

Like the Dutch, the British noted the escalating expense of territorial expansion. Settlers, imbued with a growing sense of self-determination and independence, had stopped paying rent on the land they farmed for their English landlords. Moreover, the cost to maintain troops in the colonies was

climbing. To help mitigate expenses, in 1765 the British Parliament passed the Stamp Act, a tax on all legal and commercial documents, newspapers, and pamphlets produced in the colonies.

On December 22, 1774, colonists staged a tea party in the port town of Greenwich, on the Cohansey River near Delaware Bay. After breaking into a house in which recently imported tea leaves had been stored, a group of patriots hauled the leaves to the public square and burned them in a bonfire. Twenty-three participants were twice brought to trial and twice declared innocent.

By summer 1775, volunteers had started military preparations for a confrontation that seemed more and more inevitable. In June 1776, New Jersey's provincial congress removed William Franklin from his office as royal governor. A month later, colonists wrote their first constitution and declared New Jersey an independent state. But the battles that followed cost residents dearly. Nowhere in the 13 colonies was the American Revolution more prolonged, nor fought with such intensity, as on this strategic ground that was the crossroads of commerce.

CHAPTER 02

TRANSFORMING THE WORLD

1790–1890

With relative political peace in the decades following the Revolutionary War, New Jersey attracted inventors and entrepreneurs eager to test their theories and respond to the growing nation's industrial and leisure needs. Military leaders who had distinguished themselves during the Revolution used their considerable tactical skills to start a new revolution of industry. Two men in particular, Lieutenant Colonel Alexander Hamilton and Colonel John Stevens, made significant contributions that accelerated the state's reputation as an ideal location for commerce.

An early proponent of urban planning, Hamilton—the new nation's first Secretary of the Treasury—chose Paterson in 1791 as the place to develop the country's first planned industrial city. Eighteen miles from Newark Bay, Paterson was blessed with the natural resource of the Passaic River, a swift-moving body of water that thundered over a 77-foot drop at an estimated 12,000 cubic feet per second. The hydropower inherent in the Paterson Falls, when later coupled with the invention of electricity, would propel the mass production of such diverse products as textiles, engines, and firearms. Hamilton's confidence in Paterson's potential attracted Vernon Royle, a prolific inventor who would register almost 200 patents in his lifetime.

EXPANSION ON ALL FRONTS

A breakthrough in transportation technology occurred in 1791 when Stevens, of Hoboken, received a patent for an improved steam engine; he installed the finished product in a paddle wheeler, the *Phoenix*. His sons, Robert and Edwin, took his propulsion blueprints further with their successful design of the first American-built steam locomotive. Together with Robert's patent for a T-rail form of track, the Stevens family's inventions led to explosive growth in rail transport in the young country while solidifying New Jersey's reputation as a national crossroads.

The new rail network helped a number of south Jersey communities flourish; in particular Camden, which already had established its geographic importance with regular ferry service across the Delaware River to Philadelphia, Pennsylvania. Tracks radiated northeast to Trenton and South Amboy and southeast to Atlantic City. Traveling to the seashore in 1879, poet Walt Whitman recorded his observations of the New Jersey landscape from a window on the Camden–Atlantic City train:

> What a place the railroad plays in modern democratic civilization! . . . [providing] direct means of making a really substantial community—beginning at the bottom, subsoiling as it were—bringing information and light into dark places opening up trade, markets, purchases, newspapers, fashions, visitors, etc.

Atlantic City was not the only resort whose popularity grew because of the railroads. Nolan's Point, a

mountain resort on Lake Hopatcong, in the northwestern part of the state, was another, thanks to the Central Railroad of New Jersey. Meanwhile, the Raritan and Delaware Bay Railroad linked Port Monmouth to Vineland and Bridgeton, helping to spur both recreational and residential development in southern Jersey.

As leisure pursuits flourished in the 19th century, so did the quest for academic excellence. In 1853 a group of educators formed the New Jersey State Teachers Association with that goal in mind, holding their first convention that same year in New Brunswick. The organization, which would be renamed the New Jersey Education Association, was also influential in the establishment of colleges to fully prepare teachers. In 1855 the state legislature funded construction of New Jersey's first three teachers' colleges in Trenton, Paterson, and Newark; by the 21st century they would be known, respectively, as the College of New Jersey, in Ewing; William Paterson University, in Wayne; and Kean University, in Union. In 1856 Bishop James Roosevelt Bayley opened the doors to the first diocesan college in the United States, the private, Roman Catholic Seton Hall College, in South Orange. (It would gain university status in the next century.) And in 1870, descendents of the Stevens family donated their 55-acre Hoboken estate to create the Stevens Institute of Technology.

New Jersey's Revolutionary War heroes also established the state's first financial institutions to help boost industrial growth. In 1804 a group of patriots led by Elisha Boudinot deposited an estimated $100,000 of their own money to open the Newark Banking and

Across the state, industry was equally diverse in the capital city. Trenton's factories turned out steel, rubber, wire, rope, linoleum, cigars, and pottery, especially high-end porcelain dinnerware graced by the Lenox name. Colonel Isaac Smith, a Supreme Court justice, took the lead in opening the Trenton Banking Company in 1804, the same year Boudinot's group opened the Newark bank. The Trenton Banking Company's most important customer was the state government. The bank also financed the state's participation in the War of 1812 and the Civil War.

In 1812 the State Bank at Camden incorporated as New Jersey's third financial institution from which new enterprises could receive backing.

Barely into the second decade of the new century, New Jersey faced new combat with the British as U.S. forces attempted to expel them, once and for all, from the continent. For three years, the War of 1812 raged on land and at sea. Raids on merchant ships in the all-important cargo channel (which still parallels the Jersey coast in the Atlantic Ocean) and on oyster schooners in Delaware Bay disrupted trade. The Jersey Blues, the state militia that had been called up during the Revolution, reenlisted to protect Sandy Hook Lighthouse, at the entrance to Raritan Bay. The Ringwood Ironworks, comprising five forge-and-furnace complexes, made shot for this war just as it had for the Revolution. The Hazard Powder House, located in Bayonne—the peninsula port between Newark Bay and Upper New York Bay—stored gunpowder for the U.S. Navy and surrounding forts.

Though the United States ratified the Treaty of Ghent in 1815 to end the war, New Jersey's military role was far from over. In 1880 the U.S. War Department bought land in Dover, eventually encompassing 6,500 acres, for the Picatinny Powder Depot. The army would build the first powder factory there in 1907 and change the depot's name to Picatinny Arsenal, after which the facility would rapidly develop into a critical center for munitions research and development. Around the same time the War Department was buying land in Dover, Lammot duPont built a dynamite plant in Gibbstown for the manufacture of gunpowder.

Insurance Company. Newark's population had reached 4,000 that year, and the city boasted seven shoe manufacturers along with several hat and clock makers, jewelers, silversmiths, and sheet-iron workers. The following year it would welcome its first brewery.

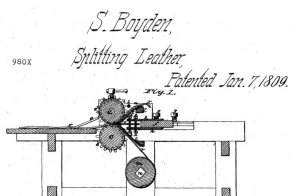

S. Boyden,
Splitting Leather,
980X
Patented Jan. 7, 1809.

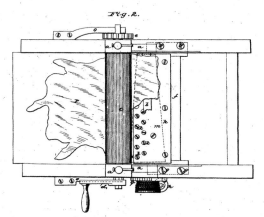

Eventually named the Repauno Chemical Works, duPont's company would soon become the world's largest producer of dynamite.

CREATIVE MINDS AT WORK

At the close of the War of 1812, blacksmith and mechanic Seth Boyden arrived in Newark, a city poised for postwar expansion and eager to welcome more manufacturers. More interested in inventing products than mass producing them, Boyden let others use his creations to open factories that put Newark at the forefront of the Industrial Revolution.

Most far-reaching was Boyden's invention of a machine for splitting hide into thin strips; by 1879 the city's factories would claim almost 90 percent of the country's leather market. An experiment with a linseed oil–based lacquer led to Boyden's creation of a process for making patent leather, which became another Newark staple. He also improved the method of silver-plating buckles and harness ornaments.

Boyden didn't stop there. He invented a machine for making nails that spurred the construction trade.

He discovered how to make malleable iron castings, zinc oxide for furnaces, and an inexpensive process of manufacturing sheet iron, supporting factories that produced steam engines, locomotives, and furnace grates. He even improved on a hat-forming machine.

Boyden retired to the suburb of Maplewood and began tinkering in plant organics, breeding a large hybrid strawberry that drew the praise of local farmers. Boyden was, in the words of Thomas A. Edison, "one of America's greatest inventors."

Edison picked up the mantle when Boyden died in 1870. That was, in fact, Edison's defining year, when he perfected the Universal stock printer for Wall Street. With his $40,000 fee, he opened a small factory in Newark, where he worked on improving the speed and efficiency of assorted devices relating to the nascent telegraph industry. In 1876 he moved to Menlo Park, where he laid out New Jersey's first fully equipped research lab, which many regard as the forerunner of modern corporate research and development campuses. Here he invented the light bulb, the phonograph, the electric trolley, the electric power source, better telephone transmitter technology—in all, receiving more than 400 patents. In 1887 he moved to West Orange, where he launched the motion picture and sound recording industries. In 1892 all of Edison's enterprises would be consolidated into the General Electric Company.

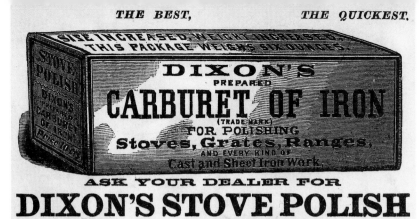

If Edison's defining year was 1870, fruit merchant Joseph Campbell and his business partner, Abraham Anderson, found 1869 to be auspicious. Taking advantage of advances in food processing and the abundance of produce grown in the temperate climate and fertile soil of south Jersey, the pair formed the Joseph A. Campbell Preserve Company in Camden, where workers canned tomatoes, vegetables, condiments, and minced meats. In 1895 the company began selling ready-made, canned tomato soup for 35 cents. When company chemist Dr. John T. Dorrance would discover, in 1897, how to eliminate water from the canning process and thereby condense the can's volume, sales of the soup (at the newly reduced price of a dime) would soar. In 1922 the firm's new name would become the Campbell Soup Company.

Both Campbell and Edison shone at America's first world's fair, staged for the centennial year of 1876. Held in Philadelphia, the International Exhibition of Arts,

Manufactures and Products of the Soil and Mine showcased the best that the United States had achieved. Not only did Campbell and Edison receive medals, but so did such other New Jersey enterprises as the Dixon Crucible Company, maker of graphite pencils, in Jersey City, and Camden-based R. Esterbrook & Company, the first U.S. maker of steel pens.

The centennial exposition also paid homage to New Jersey's growing stature in the world: August 24, 1876, was proclaimed Jersey Day. Abraham Browning, former state attorney general from Camden County and the proprietor of the extensive Cherry Hill Farm orchards, made a rousing speech that touted the state's agricultural wealth. In his oration, Browning bestowed the "Garden State" moniker on New Jersey, which has been part of the state identity ever since.

The Industrial Revolution was picking up momentum, and New Jersey was clearly playing an important part. One businessman who recognized that fact was John D. Rockefeller, of Cleveland, Ohio. In 1874 Rockefeller leased the Erie Railroad docks in Weehawken, on the Hudson River, for use by his Standard Oil Company. Three years later he bought a refinery in Bayonne, and four years after that, another in Jersey City. Pipelines brought crude oil from as far away as Oklahoma and Illinois. In 1882 the company reorganized as Standard Oil of New Jersey; it would go through several more name changes before becoming known as Exxon Corporation.

Alfred Vail was another visionary investor. In 1837 New York University professor Samuel F. B. Morse headed west across the Hudson River at the invitation of Vail, a former student. Looking for a financial backer and supporter in order to perfect his rudimentary electromagnetic telegraph, Morse found both in Vail, whose family owned the Speedwell Iron Works, a manufacturing compound in Morristown. In addition to the use of

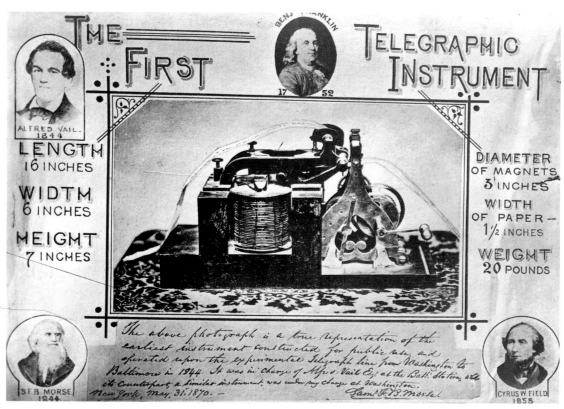

Speedwell's laboratory-like setting, Vail offered to write the code of dashes and dots that would convert the alphabet into electromagnetic impulses and to provide Morse with a cash advance. In 1838 workers wrapped two miles of conductive wire about the Speedwell barn and Vail tapped out a message that Morse successfully received: "A patient waiter is no loser." Vail supported Morse for six more years, until the long-distance transmission between Washington, D.C., and Baltimore, Maryland, proved the telegraph's commercial potential.

HEALTH, WEALTH, AND PROTECTION

Another noteworthy partnership to emerge in 19th-century New Jersey involved three brothers: James Wood Johnson, Edward Mead Johnson, and Robert Wood Johnson. James discovered a way of mass-producing an early form of bandages known as medicated plasters, and his brother Edward set up a modest sales office in New York. They called their partnership Johnson & Johnson. Their older brother, Robert, then joined them, investing his profits

from a previous business into the manufacture of surgical equipment. In 1886, retaining the name Johnson & Johnson, they relocated to a former wallpaper factory in New Brunswick and refocused the company to establish the ready-to-use surgical dressings industry.

The Johnsons began their business in an era when hospital health care and the insurance industry were developing. During both the American Revolution and the Civil War, military field hospitals had been primitive affairs, and only the

wealthy could afford home visits by doctors. In 1862 Newark was reported to have had a military hospital for Civil War casualties brought north by ship, but apparently it was discontinued when the war ended in 1865. Several civilian hospitals, however, did open during the era and remained so. In 1863 the Sisters of the Poor of Saint Francis established St. Mary's Hospital in Hoboken. In 1865 the Episcopal Church founded the Hospital of Saint Barnabas in a private home in Newark; two years later Saint Barnabas became New Jersey's first incorporated hospital. In 1877 the Coopers, Camden's leading philanthropic family, funded the 30-bed Camden Hospital, which opened a decade later as the Cooper Hospital.

The new concept of life insurance as a safety net for survivors made sense to Robert Livingston Patterson, who established the

Mutual Benefit Life Insurance Company in Newark in 1845. Policies for the working class came from John F. Dryden, who created the Prudential Friendly Society in Newark in 1875; its name would later be changed to the Prudential Insurance Company of America. In the next century (in 1932–33), the Associated Hospitals of Essex County—the forerunner of Horizon Blue Cross

Blue Shield of New Jersey—would write the state's first policies for hospital and medical insurance from a small office in Newark.

The idea of property insurance arose even earlier, in the 19th century. Wood was not only the primary building material but also a cheap source of heat. The combination of the two often proved catastrophic, resulting in the loss of property as well as life. In 1810 attorney Joseph C. Hornblower became secretary of the Newark Mutual Assistance Fire Assurance Company (later the Newark Fire Insurance Company), the state's first firm to insure property against fire damage. Other companies followed, in Camden and New Brunswick. In 1855 the Newark Firemen's Insurance Company was founded; in the 20th century, it would become part of the giant CNA Financial Corporation.

This Gilded Age, which brought unprecedented economic opportunities, was to continue for some time to come.

CHAPTER03

EMERGENCE OF A MODERN SOCIETY

1890–1929

As the 19th century became the 20th, the Atlantic seaboard experienced a blossoming of culture and the economy, even as expansion to the Pacific Ocean opened new doors of westward settlement. The Columbian Exposition of 1893, held in Chicago, heralded the City Beautiful movement, and commercial and residential architecture found a new vocabulary in the classical models of Greece and Rome. As slogans around the state highlighted New Jersey's economic strength, a distinct consumer society emerged.

On the Upper New York Bay, banners exhorted "Everything for Industry," and in Jersey City, "industry" ran the gamut, from General Pencil, American Pottery, and C. F. Mueller (pasta) to Detwiller & Street Fireworks Manufacturing, Lembeck & Betz Eagle Brewing, and Colgate-Palmolive, the soap makers whose dockside clock would remain a harbor fixture.

In Hoboken, food processing factories churned out Tootsie Rolls, Hostess cakes, Lipton tea, and Maxwell House coffee. Industrial

providers included Bethlehem Steel Corporation and the Reedy Elevator Manufacturing Company, as well as Keuffel & Esser, makers of drawing materials and drafting tools for architects and engineers.

In Trenton, Eugenius Outerbridge founded Agasote Millboard Company in 1909 to make high-density fiberboard. The company's name would be changed in 1936 to Homasote Company to better reflect the weather-resistant, recycled paper compound that replaced millboard. In

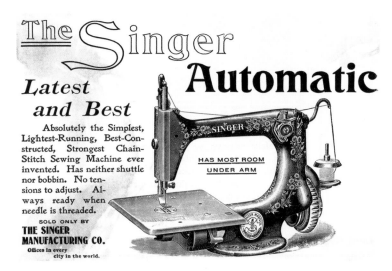

The Singer Automatic

Latest and Best

Absolutely the Simplest, Lightest-Running, Best-Constructed, Strongest Chain-Stitch Sewing Machine ever invented. Has neither shuttle nor bobbin. No tensions to adjust. Always ready when needle is threaded.

SOLD ONLY BY
THE SINGER MANUFACTURING CO.
Offices in every city in the world.

HAS MOST ROOM UNDER ARM

Fort Lee, J. Fletcher Creamer & Son started a contracting company in 1923 that would eventually serve businesses, government, and utilities nationwide. In Bayonne, Ida and William Rosenthal established the Maidenform Brassiere Company in 1926. Clothing factories, equipped with sewing machines made by the Singer Manufacturing Company in Elizabeth, turned out ready-to-wear garments that filled department stores, the new trend in shopping.

Nowhere was this trend more evident than in Newark. For those of modest means, L. S. Plaut had built a five-and-dime store in 1870 that S. S. Kresge Company, the forerunner of Kmart Corporation, bought in 1923. Louis Bamberger opened the L. Bamberger and Company department store in 1892, offering middle-class families good value, and sold it to Macy's in 1929. Julius Hahne catered to the upper class at Hahne and Company, which dated to 1858. In Camden, Sears, Roebuck and Company constructed a dramatic, Greek Revival–style department store on Admiral Wilson Boulevard that resulted in a bustling new neighborhood.

The trend of selling many different items under one roof also emerged in the food industry. The first supermarket in the nation, the Great Atlantic & Pacific Tea Company (A&P), opened in Manhattan in 1859 and incorporated in New Jersey in 1900. Seven years later, the company relocated its headquarters to Jersey City.

Supermarkets owed much of their success to agricultural advances that enabled large-scale farming operations, which produced not only more quantity but also more variety. One of those advances was overhead irrigation. Among the first in the Garden State to implement it was Seabrook Farms, a 57-acre vegetable business started in Cumberland County in 1893 by Arthur Seabrook. His son, Charles F. (C. F.), who put in the new watering system, also expanded the farm's scope with an on-site canning and freezing facility and additional acreage. At the same time, he subcontracted with independent farmers for still more of the produce that grew so well in south Jersey's temperate climate and

loamy soil. C. F. also built modern greenhouses for the winter cultivation of such summer produce as roses and radishes and oversaw the construction of a freight spur from his enterprise south to the Central Railroad of New Jersey line that passed through Bridgeton. By 1939 Seabrook was the largest farming operation in New Jersey. It would continue to grow throughout the century under the Seabrook Farms name, until the current generation would rename it Seabrook Brothers and Sons.

Market Street from Broad St. Newark, N.

Two bog farmers also made agricultural history in the state. Following in the footsteps of his grandfather, who began farming cranberries in Chatsworth in 1895, William S. Haines planted more than 700 acres of vines on his way to becoming the state's largest cultivator; he was one of the first farmers to join the Massachusetts-based Ocean Spray cranberry cooperative after its launch in 1930. Elizabeth White of Browns Mills earned acclaim in 1916 as the co-cultivator of the edible blueberry,

which extended the bog farmers' growing season from the September harvest of cranberries to the July harvest of blueberries.

CHEMICAL REACTIONS

Processed foods received a healthy boost from the growing interest in whole grains. The National Gum and Mica Company, established in New York City in 1895, made a vegetable paste sought after by the Quaker Oats Company and National Biscuit Company (Nabisco). In 1912 National

Gum and Mica established manufacturing operations in Dunellen and moved the company there in 1920. National Gum and Mica's innovative research in bonding agents for noncomestible use would prompt a name change to the National Starch and Chemical Company in 1959 and the construction of a modern headquarters in Bridgewater in 1975.

In the broad field of industrial chemistry, smaller firms that had found the state attractive were themselves appealing acquisitions for larger, more well-financed companies looking to diversify. In 1920 General Chemical Corporation's sulfuric acid plants in Edgewater and Camden became part of a merger that resulted in the Allied Chemical & Dye Corporation; in 1943 Allied would open a research laboratory in a former umbrella factory in Morris

Township. In 1929 American Cyanamid, a fertilizer manufacturer in Linden, bought the Calco Chemical Company, a maker of organic-based dyes in Bound Brook. Intending to expand their market share in consumer goods, E. I. Du Pont de Nemours and Company leaders acquired the Grasselli Chemical Company's Linden plant in 1928, adding to their inventory 25 different base compounds found in such products as cellophane, detergent, shampoo, rayon, paint, pigment, and flashlight batteries.

As more new products emerged to meet the needs of consumers, European companies seized their chance to gain an international market for their products within America's highly versatile chemical industry. Their most dynamic development was the creation of

Among the earliest commercial entities was the German company Hoechst, which opened a sales office in Newark in 1890 to market consumer drugs. In 1903 another German firm, Merck & Company, built an organic chemistry laboratory and plant in the river city of Rahway. By 1929 even the Swiss firm of Hoffman–La Roche had relocated from cramped offices in Manhattan to a spacious country campus in Nutley, where it built a vitamin research laboratory, North American sales office, and company headquarters.

American pharmaceuticals entrepreneurs also found the state appealing. Lowell M. Palmer and Theodore Weicker, for example, bought Brooklyn drug company E. R. Squibb & Sons in 1905 and opened an ether production plant in

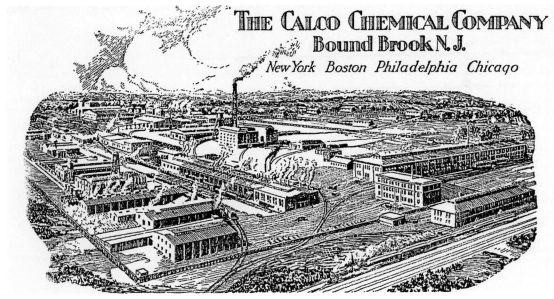

pharmaceuticals, whose fundamental chemistry benefited from the process used to create nondrug formulations. German and Swiss entrepreneurs, eager to sell to Americans, began arriving on the East Coast and soon made their way to New Jersey. They found the state desirable for both its abundant supply of freshwater rivers and its proximity to consumer markets and foreign shipping ports.

Jersey Natural Gas Company emerged to serve north and central Jersey customers. A 1910 merger between Atlantic City Gas and Water Company and Atlantic City Gas Company became the first of the mergers that would create South Jersey Gas, on Absecon Island, in 1947. As early as 1886, the Electric Light Company of Atlantic City powered the resort with two generators from the Edison Manufacturing Company. These ran everything from the outdoor billboards that lined the famous boardwalk to hotel rooms, street lights, and the electric trolley system.

In 1927 the state's northern and southern telephone networks merged, resulting in New Jersey Bell Telephone Company, which opened its headquarters in Newark two years later. The new statewide utility incorporated technological advances in transmitting sound.

Indeed, the 1920s were heady times for sound waves, with the advent of radio broadcasting.

Looking for content to fill those airwaves, in 1929 David Sarnoff, executive vice president of the Radio Corporation of America (RCA), purchased the Camden-based Victor Talking Machine Company, the world's largest producer of recorded music. Camden inventor Eldridge Johnson had launched Victor in 1901 to make phonographs.

the Raritan River town of New Brunswick to supply the growing field of surgical anesthesiology.

THE POWER OF CONNECTION
To meet the burgeoning needs of industry, utility companies sprang up near developing cities. The largest to flourish during this period was the Newark-based Public Service Corporation of New Jersey. The company began in 1903, when Thomas N. McCarter Jr. left his family's well-established law firm to amalgamate more than 400 gas, electric, and trolley companies throughout much of the northern half of the state. Along New Jersey's northern border, businesses found their power needs met by New York utility Rockland Light & Power Company.

After a round of turn-of-the-century mergers and divestitures, Jersey Central Power & Light and New

This page, clockwise from left: Woodrow Wilson, 1911, prior to his inauguration as New Jersey governor; construction of the Holland Tunnel, 1920; a Jersey City train shed in the 1890s. Opposite page, counterclockwise from bottom left: The newly opened Benjamin Franklin Bridge, 1926; the New York entrance to the Holland Tunnel, opening day, 1927; Newark Airport, 1929.

BUSINESS ON A GRAND SCALE

Trenton and Camden took advantage of marketing slogans to further their long-standing industrial rivalry, taking it international in the 20th century with "Trenton Makes, the World Takes" and "On Camden's Supplies, the World Relies." But behind the jingles, the state's economic reach was expanding. At his 1911 inauguration as New Jersey's governor, Woodrow Wilson observed:

> The whole world has changed within the lifetime of men not yet in their 30s; the world of business, and therefore the world of society, and the world of politics. The organization and movement of business are new and upon a novel scale. . . . Corporations are . . . merely organizations of a perfectly intelligible sort which the law has licensed for the convenience of extensive businesses. . . . The gate of opportunity stands wide open.

Wilson's remarks about the new scale of business reflected an academic trend that had begun taking shape in the mid 19th century: the creation of formal schools of commerce. The Trenton Business College, which had opened in 1865, incorporated in 1897 as Rider Business College (for its first president, Andrew Jackson Rider), and in 1929 the Seth Boyden School of Business opened in Newark. Nearly a century after Rider's 1865 debut, the school would acquire university status. In 1934 the Seth Boyden School would merge with the University of Newark, becoming part of Rutgers University 12 years later. It would eventually become the Rutgers Business School.

Transportation and distribution systems, likewise, experienced unique changes during this era.

The first breakthrough occurred in 1908, with the Hudson and Manhattan Railroad's construction of tunnels through the Hudson River bedrock in order to link the Hoboken station to the 19th Street train yards in New York City. The next change took place in 1915, with the formal creation of Port Newark and its modern terminals for ocean, rail, and truck containers, which helped launch the era of intermodal transport. But it was advances in flight technology that gave New Jersey the regional lead when, in 1928, Newark Airport opened as a regional distribution center for the U.S. Postal Service. Passenger service was inaugurated two years later.

Another transportation "first" in the state was the 1926 opening of the Benjamin Franklin Bridge over the Delaware River, linking Camden to Philadelphia. It was the first vehicular bridge to connect New Jersey to another state. The following year, the opening of the Holland Tunnel under the Hudson River enabled delivery trucks to shuttle between Jersey City's industrial waterfront and lower Manhattan. And in 1928, the Goethals Bridge and Outerbridge Crossing were completed, allowing finished goods to make their way from factories in Elizabeth and Perth Amboy, respectively, across the Staten Island Expressway to marine terminals in Brooklyn.

New Jersey's industrial rise tapped into another new trend: conventions. Businesspeople now had a professional reason to travel. All along the state's Atlantic coastline, large public auditoriums were built, but none so spacious as Convention Hall, a seven-acre, concrete facility that opened in 1929 on the Atlantic City boardwalk. The building would host numerous events besides trade shows, including the annual Miss America beauty pageant and ice sports. The hall's versatile floor could be flooded with water and frozen. Along the boardwalk, majestically named hotels such as the Claridge, the Chalfonte-Haddon Hall, and the Ritz-Carlton, the latter designed by famed New York architect Whitney Warren, were erected. Restaurants touted fresh bounty from local farms and fishing fleets. Piers with myriad venues for entertainment stretched out into the ocean. Was it any surprise, then, that Atlantic City became known as the Nation's Playground?

The nascent travel and tourism industry also took root in other parts of the state. In 1916 the elegant, $1 million Robert Treat Hotel opened on Park Place in Newark, and among its first overnight guests were the new U.S. president, Woodrow Wilson, and his wife. Nine years later, Shriners built the $2 million Salaam Temple on Newark's Broad Street, where it would serve double duty as a performance venue. In New Brunswick, renowned architect Thomas W. Lamb designed the State Theatre in 1921 for movies and vaudeville. In 1923 avid naturalists Anthony R. and Susie Dryden Kuser, of Newark, donated their 11,000-acre estate in the mountains of rural Sussex County to the state to create High Point State Park. Its landscaped gardens were designed by the Olmsted Brothers firm, which in 1900 had helped to plan Branch Brook Park in Newark as part of the City Beautiful movement. The Kusers also donated money in 1928 to build an obelisk within High Point State Park, both to mark the state's highest elevation and to honor World War I veterans.

Despite the period's optimism and sloganeering, dramatic change lay on the horizon.

CHAPTER 04

PRAGMATISM AND DETERMINATION

1930–1949

The gush of prosperity during the Roaring Twenties evaporated in the stock market crash of October 29, 1929. New Jersey's various industries, from agriculture to banking, from the construction trades to the canal and railroad networks, struggled to remain solvent. Federal legislation helped. The Emergency Banking Act of 1933 gave assistance to private banks. The National Recovery Act of the same year enabled big businesses to use self-governance to protect their profits. The Agriculture Adjustment Administration paid large landholders to take acres out of production, while the Home Owners' Loan Corporation not only helped those of modest means hold on to their houses but also kept mortgage institutions afloat.

Among the banks to survive the Great Depression, two were managed by women. The Susan B. Anthony Building and Loan Association had been founded in Newark in 1923 by attorney Jennie E. Precker, who kept her bank for women going by mandating a higher cash reserve than necessary. The Trenton Trust Company was run by one-time stockbroker and business student Mary Herbert Roebling, who took over as president in 1937, a year after her husband died. Roebling brought customer-friendly innovations to the company, such as merchandising, public relations, and drive-in banking, to attract and hold depositors.

MOVING FORWARD

The pragmatism demonstrated by these two women characterized the state's can-do attitude of the 1930s. Transportation projects started in the

This page, clockwise from left: Newly opened Ford Edgewater plant, December 1930; test run through the new Lincoln Tunnel, December 1937; Works Progress Administration (WPA) crew filling in the Morris Canal, 1936. Opposite page: Relief workers in Ewing Township carry food for distribution to needy families, 1936.

previous decade, for example, were now completed. The most notable was the George Washington Bridge, which opened on October 25, 1931. An engineering feat of steel suspension, the 3,500-foot span across the Hudson River between Fort Lee and upper Manhattan was designed by Bergen County's Othmar Ammann, whom the Port Authority hired as chief engineer. The bridge had another local connection, too: Trenton's John A. Roebling's Sons Company received the contract to make its formidable 107,000 miles

of steel cable. The George Washington Bridge was part of a much larger national roads initiative to better connect the eastern seaboard states. The advantage to New Jersey's economy was obvious: trucks now had a faster route by which to deliver products to New York City and the Northeast.

Just one month after the George Washington Bridge opened, the Bayonne Bridge did too, providing a new commercial link between New Jersey and Staten Island. And within

six years, commuters to Manhattan had two new routes by which to get to work. One was by train from the art deco–neoclassical Pennsylvania Station, which opened in 1935 on Market Street in Newark. Another was from the Weehawken waterfront via the Lincoln Tunnel, which opened in 1937. And on the state's western riverfront, the new, steel Easton-Phillipsburg Toll Bridge across the Delaware connected Pennsylvania and New Jersey in 1938.

Federal agencies helped fund other major transportation projects in the state during the Depression. The Public Works Administration financed the construction of the art deco ferry terminal on Ellis Island, across from the Jersey City waterfront, in 1934.

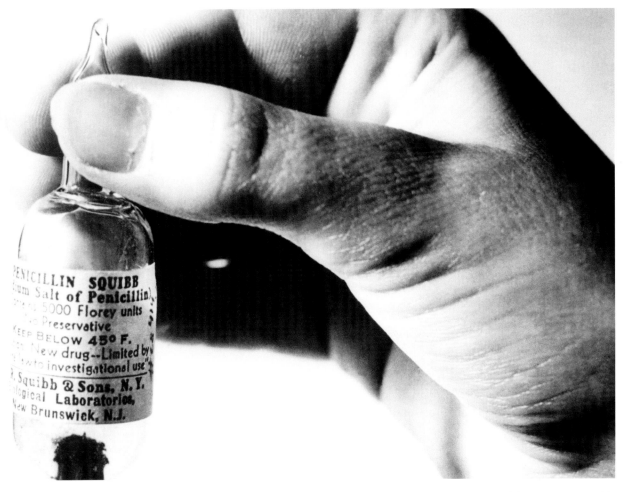

Nutley had developed the first commercially viable methods of synthesizing vitamins B1, B2, and C.

But the most important scientific breakthrough of the era happened in 1943, in the Rutgers laboratories of microbiologist Selman A. Waksman. Working with a grant from Merck, Waksman's research team developed the antibacterial agent streptomycin, the cure for tuberculosis—a highly contagious disease that had responded only sporadically to fresh-air treatment.

While Rutgers excelled at practical investigations, in the town of Princeton a new, independent, 800-acre campus for theoretical exploration opened in 1933. The Institute for Advanced Study, which would focus on theoretical studies in history, mathematics, and the natural and social sciences, was founded in 1930 by department store heirs Louis Bamberger and his sister Caroline Bamberger Fuld, of Newark, with a donation of $5 million. Almost immediately the institute attracted the attention of the world's leading

The Works Progress Administration (WPA) funded the conversion of two canals, in Newark and Trenton. First, the Morris Canal bed in Newark was covered over as part of its 1935 incorporation into a trolley system. In a similar move in 1936, after the Pennsylvania Railroad abandoned the Delaware and Raritan Canal in Trenton, WPA workers filled it in and paved it over. In both cases, the

reclaimed mileage became new additions to the state's diverse and expanding transportation network.

Pragmatism also filtered through the pharmaceuticals industry during the 1930s and 1940s, resulting in notable medical advances. Schering Plough Corporation, incorporated in 1935 in Madison, witnessed the first synthesis of steroid drugs, and in

1943, under a joint arrangement with Merck & Company of Rahway, produced the hugely successful anti-inflammatory steroid cortisone. In 1944 E. R. Squibb and Sons opened the nation's largest penicillin plant in New Brunswick to meet the antibiotic needs of thousands of soldiers wounded in World War II. On the preventive front, by 1939 Hoffman–La Roche chemists in

physicist, Nobel Prize–winner Albert Einstein, who joined the faculty in 1933 and remained on it until his death in 1955. In 1947 J. Robert Oppenheimer, a member of the Manhattan Project—which developed the atomic bomb—became the institute's director.

As the 20th century progressed, the state became increasingly known for groundbreaking research, surpassing even its 19th-century reputation as the prime address for manufacturing. Nowhere was this more evident than in the field of communications. In December 1947, six years after AT&T

Corporation built Bell Laboratories on former farmland in Murray Hill, three Bell scientists—Walter Brattain, John Bardeen, and William Shockley— developed the transistor, which would turn out to be the fundamental building block in radios, televisions, computers, cell phones, MP3 players, and virtually all future forms of communications equipment.

ECONOMIC CATALYSTS

The September 1939 outbreak of war in Europe triggered a dramatic rise in defense contracts, giving various New Jersey enterprises a way out of the economic slump of the Depression. The New York Shipbuilding Corporation, located in Camden, drew on its success building ships for the navy during World War I to supply 70 vessels at the start of the new war and 148 landing craft three years later. Picatinny Arsenal in Dover expanded, as did the Gibbstown munitions facility of E. I. Du Pont de Nemours Company. The Wright Aeronautical plant in Paterson also increased its production of aircraft engines, employing workers, many of them women, in three daily shifts. Former

custom clothing designer Elizabeth Hawes, of Ridgewood, was one of them. She wrote about her experiences in her 1943 book, *Why Women Cry; or, Wenches with Wrenches*:

> We polished off the long, round part of the gears and also the flat surfaces of the flanges. A

This page: One of the first American merchant ships to be armed under the revised U.S. Neutrality Act, Hoboken, November 1941. Opposite page, left: Mechanic John Murphy with a stack of Cyclone aircraft engines, Wright Aeronautical Corporation, Paterson, 1942. Opposite page, right: Lola Boyle assisting the war effort at Brewster Aeronca Corporation, Newark, 1943.

gear is apt to look quite like a candlestick in its early states. You later discover that most of the stick part is there merely so you can hold the piece in your machine and gets cut off in the end. . . . Most of the women who are going to the machines . . . used to be sandwich makers, telephone operators, servants, salesgirls, secretaries, or housewives. Their jobs, though they might have been vital, were uncreative in the extreme. When you work the machine that makes the bit that turns the motor that raises the plane that's going to soar in the clouds or a piece of the Frigidaire, for that matter, that's going to keep the food from rotting—when you do that, you feel creative.

Despite the economic downturn of the Depression, the business of creating cultural traditions for leisure enjoyment continued. Utility mogul Thomas N. McCarter Jr. donated funds to build a stage at his alma mater, Princeton University. Called the McCarter Theatre, it opened in 1930 as a home for the university's musical comedy troupe and soon became a pre-Broadway venue. Another stage, the War Memorial Theater, opened in Trenton in 1932. Handsomely designed in the Italian Renaissance style, it was dedicated to opera, ballet, and classical music

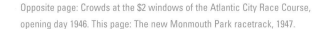

1942 erected Garden State Park, a thoroughbred track, on 223 acres of land along Marlton Pike in rural Delaware Township. Its surprising success prompted Mori to acquire Cherry Hill Farm, across the highway, on which he built a hotel to accommodate overnight visitors to his track. Mori named his luxury hotel the Cherry Hill Inn, paying homage to the farm that had been owned by 19th-century Camden County politician Abraham Browning.

Buoyed by Garden State Park's success, investors built two thoroughbred tracks at the shore as part of a larger initiative to stimulate tourism along the Atlantic coast. The new Monmouth Park, in Oceanport, and the Atlantic City Race Course, in Hamilton Township, both opened in 1946.

Throughout the rest of the century, real estate development and the slow but inexorable transition from manufacturing to research and development would redefine not only the Garden State landscape but also its economy.

and brought performers, as well as patrons, to the capital. The state's third notable venue, the Paper Mill Playhouse, in Millburn, was founded in 1934 as a stage for musical theater and offered its first show four years later.

Less grandiose forms of entertainment also found an audience. Betting on horse races had been banned since 1894 but experienced renewed interest in the late 1930s, when watching professional sports was identified as a separate leisure industry. New legislation was passed to allow for state-regulated wagers.

The first developer to build a racetrack was Eugene Mori, who in

CHAPTER 05

THE BOOM YEARS

1950–2000

The second half of the 20th century saw exciting opportunities, far beyond what Dutch explorer Henry Hudson could have imagined in 1609, when he first sighted New Jersey. The state surged forward with groundbreaking research and fortified its leadership in foreign trade by implementing a sophisticated intermodal transportation network. On the corporate front, North Jersey's proximity to the financial resources of Wall Street resulted in attractive zip codes for new or expanding companies.

South Jersey's open land, suitable for spacious offices, was a convenient and appealing alternative for Philadelphia-based firms needing to modernize and expand beyond the city's historic confines. Moreover, New Jersey's spreading suburbs, filled with new ranch, split-level, and two-story homes, lured young families out of aging cities and created a growing retail market for new products and services. The setting where corporate expansion, residential construction, and retail development intersected most

dramatically was in South Jersey's rambling Delaware Township.

Following the public's extraordinary response to the launch of Eugene Mori's Garden State Park and the Cherry Hill Inn in the previous decade, Delaware Township experienced successive waves of farm conversions, resulting in neighborhoods of well-appointed homes. New homeowners made the short commute to Philadelphia or the suburbs for well-paying research and management

This page: Symbols of Cherry Hill success, clockwise from left: Subaru of America headquarters building, erected in 1986; jars of pickles produced by locally headquartered Vlasic Foods International; Cherry Hill Mall, the first enclosed shopping center on the East Coast. Opposite page: E. J. Korvette discount department store across from Bergen Mall, Paramus, 1960s.

positions. Among the many employers tucked into this corner of Camden County were defense contractor Lockheed Martin Corporation, pharmaceuticals maker A. H. Robbins, media conglomerate Gannett Corporation, and Cherry Hill Hospital (which would become part of the Kennedy Health System).

In 1961 Mori built the East Coast's first enclosed shopping center, Cherry Hill Mall, at the regional crossroads of Route 38 and Haddonfield Road. This area—including Route 70, which bisected both highways—was nicknamed the Golden Triangle. Even as Mori was christening his latest real estate project, on other developers' drawing boards lay blueprints for the upscale shopping plazas, movie multiplexes, restaurants, luxury-automobile dealerships, and hotels managed by Hilton and Holiday Inn that would soon follow.

By the time Cherry Hill Mall opened in October 1961, a distinctive, 24-square-mile community had emerged within Delaware Township, and with it came the need for a new zip code to handle the mail for the area. By voter referendum, Cherry Hill seceded from the township and set up an independent municipality, complete with an economic development office to further encourage corporate relocation. Subaru of America, Vlasic Foods International, and Commerce Bancorp put corporate offices in Cherry Hill. New Jersey American Water, the largest investor-owned water utility in the Garden State, opened its headquarters in nearby Voorhees.

The emergence of the retail industry was no less spectacular in the borough of Paramus, a settlement in northeastern New Jersey once known for its celery farms. During the late 1950s–early 1970s, shopping malls proliferated along Routes 4 and 17 and the Garden State Parkway. High-end retailers Lord & Taylor, B. Altman & Company, and FAO Schwarz followed their Fifth Avenue

customers out of Manhattan to Paramus's Fashion Center. Department stores Abraham & Straus and Sears, Roebuck and Company, which catered to the middle class, opened the Paramus Park Shopping Center. Bamberger's, Gimbels, and J. C. Penney Company anchored Garden State Plaza in Paramus. Their competitors, Stern Brothers Department Store, Orbach's, and J. J. Newberry Company, signed leases for the borough's Bergen Mall, which also featured a playhouse for Broadway shows that presaged the arrival of mall-based movie theaters.

While retail and residential construction was replacing the farmland that once fed the colonists, the Garden State food business was expanding. Supermarkets replaced mom-and-pop grocery stores. Intending to make bulk purchases at lower costs and pass their savings along to shoppers, a group of independent grocers in 1946 formed the cooperative Wakefern Food Corporation, based in Elizabeth. The grocer-owners, seeing the advantages of operating their stores under one name, began using "Shop-Rite" in 1951 to attract price-conscious

consumers. The strategy worked, and by the end of the century Wakefern had become a chain of regional supermarkets operating in five states.

Wakefern found itself competing with a breakaway group of grocers who formed Supermarkets General Corporation. In 1968 they launched the Pathmark stores, featuring one-stop shopping. Pathmark inventory included such nonfood items as small appliances, and the stores even offered the opportunity to shop 24 hours a day—a boon to shift workers in the growing health care, hospitality, and transportation sectors. Supermarkets General executives chose Carteret as the location of their headquarters for its

proximity to the Newark and Elizabeth cargo terminals and its easy access to the state's network of highways.

Both co-ops were up against the historical dominance of the Great Atlantic & Pacific Tea Company (A&P). After a series of mergers and divestitures throughout much of the second half of the century, A&P emerged in the 1990s as a supermarket powerhouse, acquiring grocery chains ranging from the low-end Waldbaum's to the high-end Food Emporium and eventually purchasing the Pathmark stores. A&P's corporate growth required larger headquarters than its Jersey City address allowed, and in 1974, the supermarket titan followed other companies to the bucolic Pascack Valley town of Montvale, in northern Bergen County at the New York State border.

ATTRACTIVE SUBURBAN HUBS

Montvale offered entry to the Garden State Parkway, which—via its northern connection to the New York State Thruway—provided businesses easy access to New York's wealthy Westchester County and the Connecticut cities of Stamford and Greenwich, farther east. A commuter train also ran between Montvale and Manhattan. This combination of factors influenced numerous companies, from Mercedes-Benz and BMW to equipment maker Ingersoll-Rand Company and medical device manufacturer Datascope Corporation, to build offices in Montvale.

Researchers and retailers alike discovered, too, that by following the horseshoe-shaped, tree-lined Interstate 287, they could find rewarding work and a countrified way of life. From New York's Westchester and Rockland counties, I-287 comes west into Mahwah, in the Ramapo Valley, and then wends its way south through the rolling horse-and-winery country that characterizes the outlying areas of Parsippany–Troy Hills, Morristown, Bedminster, Far Hills,

and Bridgewater. Its exits provide access to such businesses as AT&T, BASF Corporation, Bristol-Myers Squibb, Delta Dental of New Jersey, Honeywell International, Siemens Corporate Research, National Starch and Chemical Company, and Bridgewater Commons, a luxury shopping mall.

Going south, I-287 ends in Edison Township, a 32-square-mile municipality along the Raritan River

that developed into a pivotal transportation hub during this period. Not only does an active Conrail line run through Edison, but so do the major intrastate routes 1, 27, 440, and 202/206, as well as the New Jersey Turnpike and Garden State Parkway.

When manufacturing declined in Edison during the postwar decades, industrial properties were converted to warehouses, giving the township new vigor as an integral distribution center between the Newark and Elizabeth marine terminals and central New Jersey's prosperous Middlesex, Monmouth, and Mercer counties. Companies such as Etienne Aigner, Fujifilm USA, Revlon Consumer Products Corporation, Aramark Corporation, and Cablevision Systems Corporation (News 12 New Jersey) opened offices in Edison. The New Jersey Convention and Exposition Center went up with more than 150,000 square feet of exhibition space, making it the largest trade-show compound in north Jersey. In the new millennium, a shuttle service would begin taking

Edison commuters to a New Jersey Transit train station to facilitate access to offices in Newark, New York City, New Brunswick, Trenton, and Philadelphia.

Joining Cherry Hill, Montvale, and Edison, the fourth desirable region to

emerge in the postwar decades was along the Route 1 corridor southeast of Princeton University and the Institute for Advanced Study. Speaking at the 25th anniversary dinner for RCA Laboratories in 1967, David Sarnoff, the founder of both RCA and the National Broadcasting

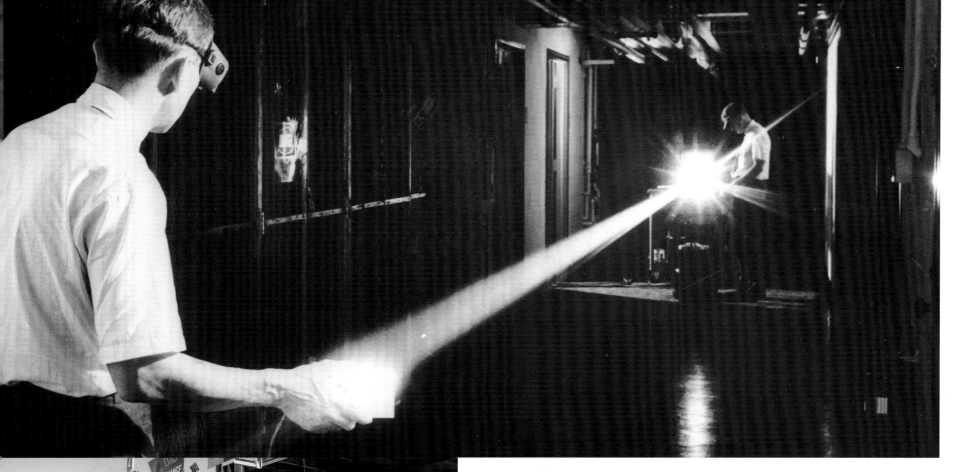

Corporation (NBC), remarked that Princeton had become "the nucleus of one of the nation's foremost scientific communities" as scores of research laboratories followed RCA into the area.

PAVING THE WAY

Without a doubt, roads and bridges made it easier to do business in the Garden State. In 1951 the Delaware Memorial Bridge, which crossed the Delaware River between Pennsville and New Castle, Delaware, was dedicated. Two years later, the 118-mile, northeast/southwest New

Jersey Turnpike opened, accelerating the use of the new bridge. A second span would be added in 1968. In 1956 the Delaware River–Turnpike Toll Bridge at Burlington opened, connecting truck traffic between the New Jersey and Pennsylvania turnpikes.

Meanwhile, the principal north/south corridor along the state's eastern profile became the 173-mile Garden State Parkway. Initial construction began in 1947 and was picked up again in late 1954, after the New Jersey Highway Authority had been

created. The parkway's Cape May terminus was finished in 1956, and the northern extension that linked to the New York State Thruway was ready the next year.

Commuters between south Jersey and greater Philadelphia also experienced more options as three key bridges were erected across the Delaware during the latter half of the century. The first to open, in 1957, was the Walt Whitman Bridge, between Gloucester City and south Philadelphia. (Two decades later, an extension would be built to the newly constructed Atlantic City Expressway, which would prove particularly helpful in easing the flow of summer traffic from Philadelphia to the Jersey shore.) The Commodore Barry Bridge (named for Irish-born Philadelphia naval officer John Barry, who fought in the American Revolution) was next, opening between Bridgeport and Chester, Pennsylvania, in 1974. The Betsy Ross Bridge, between Pennsauken and north Philadelphia, opened in 1976, the nation's bicentennial year.

Further cementing New Jersey's pivotal role in moving products to and from the mid-Atlantic and New England regions was the 1953 opening of the I-80 bridge through the remote Delaware Water Gap, on the state's northwestern border with Pennsylvania. South of the Delaware Water Gap, the I-78 Toll Bridge between Phillipsburg and Easton opened in 1989.

This last bridge over the Delaware proved critical in handling the surge of truck traffic along I-78 that resulted from upgrades in the 1960s–70s by the Port Authority of New York and New Jersey to its facilities at the eastern end of the interstate. Indeed, during this period, the Port Newark–Elizabeth Marine Terminal became the largest container dock in the eastern United States, attracting such companies as shipping giant A. P. Moller-Maersk Group and global automobile processing company Dependable Auto Shippers (DAS). In addition to modernizing its marine and truck facilities, the Port Authority updated the logistics for

Monmouth engineers developed the first night-vision goggles in 1968, and in 1972, working with doctors at the installation's Patterson Army Hospital, they designed the lifesaving defibrillator-pacemaker that regulates heart rhythms.

its ship-to-rail links to the Canadian Pacific Railway, CSX Transportation, and Norfolk Southern Corporation.

The Port Authority didn't stop there. In 1973 it opened new passenger terminals at Newark International Airport, part of a long-term strategy to serve global travelers. In 1987 Continental Airlines chose Newark as one of its U.S. hubs. Also in the 1980s, both Federal Express Corporation and United Parcel Service opened air cargo terminals at Newark International to handle the transfer of expedited material

between their delivery trucks and freight planes.

The revitalized Delaware River Port Authority also made improvements. In 1991 construction began on AmeriPort, a regional intermodal transfer facility to be shared by Camden and Philadelphia. Completed two years later, AmeriPort anticipated the new era of double-stack containers, inaugurated there in 1996.

RESEARCH "FIRSTS"
After World War II, military electronics research continued. The

Army Electronics Command (ECOM) was formally established at Fort Monmouth in 1962, four years after President Dwight D. Eisenhower's Christmas message was broadcast via historic "talking satellite." The satellite transmission technology had originated at the base. Base engineers also developed the antenna to receive weather pictures taken by the Tiros-1 satellite. Both advances in satellite communications laid the groundwork for the high-volume commercial transmission of voice, data, and images that would be enjoyed in years to come. Fort

At various New Jersey research campuses owned by AT&T's Bell Laboratories, engineers pioneered work on lasers, solar cells, and the telephone touch-tone pad. They also wrote the code for the UNIX operating system that led to the creation of the Internet and designed computer modems for the military that were later adapted for the consumer marketplace.

The aftermath of the Second World War generated another first for the state with the introduction of rehabilitative medicine. In 1948

Opposite page, left: Maher Terminals container facility, Port Newark. Opposite page, right: Continental Airlines hub, Newark Liberty International Airport, with Manhattan skyline in background. This page, left: Bell Labs' Executive Planning Information and Communication (EPIC) system, late 1970s–early 1980s. This page, right: Ortho Dialpak birth control pill dispenser by Ortho-McNeil Pharmaceutical, Raritan, 1999.

The last 50 years of the 20th century also witnessed the pharmaceutical industry taking the lead as New Jersey's top revenue producer, the commercial result of various ground-breaking discoveries. One notable partnership in the area of synthetic hormones was that of Merck & Company and Schering-Plough Corporation, whose scientists teamed up in 1950 to manufacture cortisone. That decade, too, researchers at Ortho Pharmaceutical Corporation, a Raritan-based division of Johnson & Johnson, discovered a low-dosage combination of synthetic hormones that would be ideal for oral contraceptives. Ortho scientist Carl G. Hartman, who led the research, was honored for his contributions with the Margaret Sanger Award from the Planned Parenthood Federation of America in 1966. By the 1980s, Ortho had developed the multiphasic birth control pill, which in the 21st century would become the most prescribed type of birth control pill in the nation.

At Hoffman-La Roche in Nutley, Dr. Leo Sternbach's research into psychotropic drugs brought relief to thousands of anxiety sufferers when it resulted in the tranquilizers Librium (1957) and Valium (1963).

Speaking to the *New York Times* in 1998, Dr. Daniel O. Hauser, director of preclinical research for Novartis, the global pharmaceutical company then located in Summit, praised the fraternity of highly educated and innovative chemists in New Jersey, noting that the state was "the place where you find the talent."

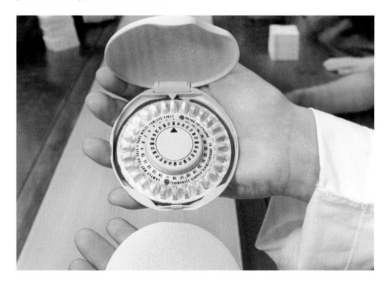

orthopedic surgeon and naval physician Henry H. Kessler, a Newark native, opened the Kessler Institute for Rehabilitation, a 16-bed hospital in West Orange, to address the needs of maimed veterans and civilians with a wide variety of physical afflictions, including polio and, a decade later, the effects of the sedative Thalidomide. In 1975 the hospital added a residency training program in physical medicine and rehabilitation in cooperation with the nearby College of Medicine and Dentistry of New Jersey. The Kessler Institute would become one of the nation's leading centers for spinal cord injury research and treatment, designated a model system by the National Institute on Disability Rehabilitation and Research.

ROBUST RECREATION INDUSTRY

While New Jersey's diverse business base and sophisticated infrastructure were transforming the economy, the travel and tourism industry in the Garden State was changing the way people spent their leisure time.

The opening in 1960 of the Latin Casino, in Cherry Hill, signaled a new era of arena-styled entertainment in the state. National headliners such as Frank Sinatra and the Temptations bypassed Philadelphia's smaller stages to perform in this enormous amphitheater before south Jersey's growing population. The arena trend continued outdoors when the New Jersey Highway Authority opened the saucer-shaped Garden State Arts Center, at the Garden State Parkway in Holmdel, in 1968. Musical acts as varied as the New York Philharmonic Orchestra and singer-guitarist James Taylor came to perform at the futuristic-looking building designed by architect Edward Durrell Stone. Three decades after its opening, the structure was renamed the PNC Bank Arts Center after the Pittsburgh-based bank that had entered the New Jersey market.

In the 1970s, the New Jersey Sports and Exposition Authority oversaw construction of the 750-acre Meadowlands Sports Complex in East Rutherford. In 1976 the 80,000-seat Giants Stadium was the first venue to open on the site, as the new home of the New York

Giants and, in 1984, New York Jets, both of the National Football League. The Meadowlands Racetrack, designed for harness racing, opened next, in 1977. Its seating capacity of 40,000 made it the largest track in the state. The 1981 relocation of the Hambletonian, the sport's most prestigious trotters competition, to the Meadowlands Racetrack further boosted the track's stature among national racing fans. The 20,000-seat Brendan Byrne Arena also opened at the Meadowlands in 1981, welcoming the National Hockey League's New Jersey Devils and the National Basketball Association's New Jersey Nets. The arena, which hosts such diverse acts as Mary J. Blige and New Jersey native son Bruce Springsteen, would be renamed the Izod Center in 2007. In 2005 the Meadowlands sports complex would begin a dramatic addition in the form of Meadowlands Xanadu, a two-million-square-foot entertainment-shopping-indoor skiing destination slated for completion in 2009.

Just as Anthony R. and Susie Dryden Kuser were attracted to the northwestern part of the state earlier in the century, lifestyle mogul Hugh Hefner was drawn there in the latter half of the century. He found the tiny village of McAfee, at the base of Appalachian Trail, to be an ideal location for an alpine-styled resort. Opened in 1971, that resort—the Great Gorge Playboy Club—put Sussex County on the nation's radar as a winter getaway for skiing enthusiasts. The region's economic potential grew as savvy entrepreneurs added opportunities for vacationers to golf, fish, hike, and balloon.

For its part, Atlantic City underwent a significant transformation in the late 1970s and 1980s after voters statewide agreed, in 1976, to permit legalized casino gambling in the Queen of Resorts. The aim was simple: Make the oceanfront destination competitive with its desert rival, Las Vegas, Nevada. In 1978 the first hotel-casino opened with the conversion of the historic Chalfont–Haddon Hall Hotel into the glitzy Resorts International. Two years later, gaming impresario Steve Wynn

replaced the Strand Motel with the towering Golden Nugget hotel casino; and on it went. Whether by renovation or new construction, the frontage of the famous Boardwalk experienced a striking change. And inside the new venues, large showrooms for nightclub-style entertainment could seat 1,000 or more patrons, while ballrooms attracted the notice of corporate events planners.

These changes were just the beginning. In the 21st century, the entire state would experience a history-making metamorphosis that would propel its commerce in new directions.

CHAPTER 06

SETTING THE PACE FOR THE FUTURE

2001–

Economic opportunity in New Jersey has revolved around one enduring quality: resilience. Throughout 300 years, in which business cycles boomed and waned, visionary leaders made decisions that enabled companies to adapt and stay the course. Even before the terrorism attacks that destroyed the World Trade Center on September 11, 2001, industry executives and state policy makers were working to improve the business climate in the Garden State. The goal was straightforward: Prepare the state, which had been the nation's 19th-century manufacturing trailblazer, to meet 21st-century challenges. The initiatives they developed acknowledge New Jersey's historic strengths, emphasizing renewable resources, urban revitalization, scientific research, and luxurious new ways to relax.

GOING GREEN

Just as 17th-century Dutch and English traders had seen the possibilities of the Garden State's natural assets, modern investors recognized the potential of New Jersey's two abundant renewable resources: wind and solar power.

In 2006 the state made history when it became the site of the United States' first coastal commercial wind project, funded by public and private sources. The Jersey-Atlantic Wind Farms produces enough electricity for more than 2,000 homes from its five turbines at a wastewater treatment facility operated by the Atlantic County Utilities Authority in Atlantic City.

THIS HOUSE USES
80% LESS ENERGY
THAN THE AVERAGE HOME

The BASF Near-Zero Energy Home-Paterson, N.J.

Built as part of the BASF Better Home, Better Planet Initiative, this house demonstrates the benefits of high-performance materials using chemistry. It is stronger, faster to build, more affordable to own and has a lower impact on the environment.

After the demonstration phase, this home will be donated to St. Michael's Housing Corporation

www.betterhomebetterplanet.com

Helping Make Buildings Better

□ · BASF

As part of a plan to have 20 percent of the state's energy come from renewable sources by 2020, the New Jersey Board of Public Utilities (BPU) in 2008 began reviewing proposals for a grant of up to $19 million for construction of an offshore wind farm that would serve as a test site.

New Jersey made history again in 2007, when Ferreira Construction, in Branchburg, was recognized as having the first known commercial building in the United States to go "net zero electric"—that is, to produce more electricity than it uses—thanks to the installation of 1,276 solar panels on the roof of its new, 41,500-square-foot warehouse. Company officials estimate Ferreira will save $75,000 a year in energy costs while earning income for surplus energy sold to the local utility.

The BPU is among numerous state agencies offering programs that encourage communities to go green, as well. In Highland Park, the town hall has solar panels, and a solar-powered environmental education center is under construction. Highland Park also participates in a larger initiative in which 11 municipalities to date, from the seashore town of Belmar to the state capital of Trenton, have adapted green building methods into their redevelopment plans and land-use ordinances. They follow the Leadership in Energy and Environmental Design (LEED) rating system established by the U.S. Green Building Council.

The greening of the Garden State goes even beyond wind and solar power. In 2007 Rutgers's New Jersey Agricultural Experiment Station assessed the state's biomass and its potential for bioenergy production for the BPU's energy master plan. The appraisal resulted in the creation of a ground-breaking bioenergy calculator that estimates potential biopower and biofuel generation from current and projected biomass feedstocks.

Rutgers's pioneering work in the 21st-century renewable energy field is multifaceted. At Rutgers's EcoComplex, an environmental research center in Bordentown, the university supports various forward-thinking projects related to water resources, solid waste management, renewable energy, and controlled agricultural activities, such as hydroponics and genetic engineering. As a business incubator, the EcoComplex assists start-up companies seeking to tap New Jersey's diverse renewable energy opportunities. Acrion

Technology, for example, cleans landfill gas, converting it to methane for energy use; HydroGlobe removes metals from water; Terracycle converts worm castings into fertilizer; and Garden State Ethanol is designing what may become the East Coast's first ethanol facility.

The green movement in New Jersey is also taking place in the growing health care field, and one pioneering facility in particular has brought the state national recognition: the Sarkis and Siran Gabrellian Women's and Children's Pavilion at Hackensack University Medical Center (HUMC). Features such as organic meals, mercury-free medical devices, and nontoxic cleaning products earned the pavilion a spot on the 2006 Top 10 Green Hospitals ratings compiled

statewide policies focusing on mass transit development, corporate tax credits, and expansion of higher education programs, especially in Camden and Newark, two cities to land on the *Forbes* 2008 list of the nation's best metro areas for business and careers. Financial institutions such as Capital One Financial Corporation, Wachovia Corporation, the Provident Bank, and Columbia Bank are among those lending support to this revitalization.

Educated urban dwellers and the firms that hire them are looking for a 21st-century experience. They want easier commutes, green buildings, low-maintenance resort lifestyles, and cultural experiences in pedestrian-friendly downtowns. The urban renaissance is meeting these needs.

Camden's residential rebirth began in 1998 with the opening of the Victor, a luxury condominium building converted from an abandoned RCA Victor factory overlooking the Delaware River. In 2007 the Victor won its Philadelphia developer, Dranoff Properties, the Best Adaptive

by the *National Geographic Green Guide*. Selected from a field of about 1,300 facilities across the country, the Gabrellian Pavilion at HUMC is one of only four facilities in the Northeast to make the prestigious list.

The commitment to eliminate toxins also extends to contaminated industrial and commercial sites left over from the state's heyday as a manufacturing leader. The newest effort at brownfields remediation was

announced in January 2008, when Jersey City and Honeywell International agreed in principle to a plan that calls for the removal of chromium-tainted soil along the Hackensack River waterfront in anticipation of a multimillion-dollar, mixed-use redevelopment of the property.

REVITALIZED CITIES
River to river and along the shore, New Jersey is undergoing a dramatic urban renaissance, thanks to

Reuse Award from the National Association of Home Builders.

The Victor is part of a larger public-private waterfront redevelopment plan that has included the Adventure Aquarium (formerly called the New Jersey State Aquarium), which reopened in 2005; Campbell's Field, which opened in 2001 as home to Minor League Baseball's Camden Riversharks; the battleship U.S.S. *New Jersey*, which

Opposite page: L-3 Communications Corporation's Predator Mission Aircrew Training System. This page, left: Cryogenic technician searching for specific vial of human cells, Coriell Institute for Medical Research, Camden. This page, right: Raymond Boulevard art deco office building soon to be converted into living space, downtown Newark.

was retrofitted as a floating maritime museum and opened in 2001; and the newly renamed Susquehanna Bank Center (formerly called the Tweeter Center), which opened to musical acts in 1995.

Also in Camden's redevelopment district is one of the state's three Innovation Zones, where public research institutions, medical research facilities, and technology firms are part of an initiative supported by the state's Economic Development Authority (EDA) to facilitate the creation of commercial products. The other two zones are located in Newark and the Greater New Brunswick area.

Camden's Innovation Zone includes the Waterfront Technology Center and the Camden Aerospace Center. The technology center houses the not-for-profit Coriell Institute for

Medical Research, which examines systems biology, cell differentiation, and genetic diseases and maintains a "biobank" of biological material that serves countries throughout the world. L-3 Communications Corporation, a Fortune 500 company that supplies secure systems to the U.S. government, is a tenant in the adjacent aerospace facility.

A comeback is taking place in academia in the city, as well. Rutgers manages a Camden laboratory available to scientists and engineers throughout the state for leading-edge research in nanotechnology, a field brimming with possibilities for such fields as biotechnology, energy, and communications. The National Science Foundation estimates nanotechnology will be responsible for more than $1 trillion in products and services by 2015. And building on existing cooperative arrangements

with the Robert Wood Johnson Medical School and the University of Medicine and Dentistry of New Jersey (UMDNJ), a $222 million expansion of Cooper University Hospital's Health Science Campus, the hospital's first major expansion in three decades, is under way.

Across the state in Newark, revitalization began with plans between Dranoff Properties and the New Jersey Performing Arts Center (NJPAC) for a mixed-income, high-rise apartment house that will be the first built in Newark in the 21st century. Two Center Street, located across the street from NJPAC and next door to the historic Robert Treat Hotel, will offer views of both the Passaic River and Military Park, the colonial training ground in the run-up to the American Revolution.

Across from the park, a celebrated property from Newark's glorious retail past—the long-shuttered Hahne's Department Store—is tagged for residential conversion by Cogswell Realty Group of New York.

Military Park is the anchor of this cultural arts neighborhood, contributing to the attractions that residents and visitors seek in urban settings. In addition to NJPAC and the Treat, the New Jersey Historical Society is located on the park. Neighboring it are the regional office of New Jersey Network, the state's Emmy Award–winning public television station; and the studio of WBGO, the preeminent jazz station that is an

affiliate of National Public Radio. Interspersed among the street-level addresses are several well-reviewed restaurants and nightclubs.

Nearby, nestled in a bend in the Passaic River and within walking distance of the Pennsylvania Train Station (Penn Station), is the Bears & Eagles Riverfront Stadium. Opened in 1999, it pays homage to the city's baseball history: the original Newark Bears were a New York Yankees farm team; the Eagles, a successful Negro League franchise. Today's Bears play in the Atlantic League of Professional Baseball.

Also within walking distance of the train station is Newark's newest sports and entertainment address, the Prudential Center. It hosts the New Jersey Devils, of the National Hockey League; the New Jersey Ironmen, of the Major Indoor Soccer League; and Seton Hall University's men's basketball team. Prudential Financial, the city's leading corporate benefactor, is the naming rights sponsor of the arena, which doubles as an entertainment venue. Rock musician Jon Bon Jovi formally opened the center in 2007.

The university neighborhood where Rutgers, UMDNJ, Essex County College, the New Jersey Institute of Technology (NJIT), and University Heights Science Park are clustered doubles as Newark's Innovation Zone. Research and development partners here also include the Public Service Electric and Gas Company, Verizon, the New Jersey Technology Council, and the New Jersey Commission on Science and Technology, among others.

The 19th-century factory centers of Jersey City and Hoboken are also

undergoing 21st-century makeovers as corporate and residential addresses. In Jersey City, investment bank Goldman Sachs in 2004 opened a glass-sheathed, 42-story, LEED-certified green office tower on the site of the former Colgate-Palmolive soap factory on the Hudson River waterfront. Its neighbors include other financial services firms, such as Charles Schwab & Company and UBS Financial Services. The abandoned art deco complex that served as the Margaret Hague Maternity Hospital (and is listed on the National Register of Historic Places) is being converted into the Beacon, a full-service condominium complex with meticulously restored lobbies and facades. In Hoboken, the Maxwell House coffee factory and Lipton Tea buildings have been converted into luxury condos with spectacular views of Manhattan. They are known, respectively, as Maxwell Place on the Hudson and the Hudson Tea condos and harborside lofts.

With yesteryear's trolley networks reborn as today's light-rail systems, passengers can get to their destinations quickly and easily. New Jersey has three major light-rail tracks. The mile-long Newark Light Rail opened in 2006 to facilitate transit between Penn Station and the university neighborhood. A longer track, also completed in 2006, links Hudson and Bergen counties. The more than 20-mile-long Hudson-Bergen Light Rail line runs from the Bayonne peninsula through Jersey City, Hoboken, Weehawken, West New York (New Jersey), and Union City to North Bergen. At the Journal Square Transportation Center, a multimodal transit hub in Jersey City, residents can transfer to commuter trains inbound for Manhattan or outbound for the suburbs. With the economic and urban revitalization efforts going on in Hudson and Bergen counties as well as in adjacent Passaic County, *Inc.* magazine named this region one of its 2007 boomtowns. The state's third light-rail track, and its largest, connects Trenton and Camden. Known as the

River Line, the 34-mile track opened in 2004.

The new electric light-rail systems are revitalizing New Jersey's sprawling urban corridors. The state initiated a "transit village" program in 1999, beginning with Cranford, Pleasantville, Morristown, and South Orange, that uses the train station as the focal point of the community. Mixed-use development, which must include residential construction, is built around it. Touted as having "walkable downtowns," successful transit villages offer a variety of ethnic restaurants, performance spaces, shopping, and, increasingly, LEED-certified buildings.

It's not just the rails that are undergoing a millennium-worthy upgrade. Mass-transit transfer improvements are visible at Newark Liberty International Airport (EWR), which was renamed by the Port Authority in the wake of September 11th. The latest undertaking, after its perimeter monorail, which connects long-term parking and the airport's three terminals, are new rail links to Penn Station in Newark and to several suburban New Jersey Transit lines, including the North Jersey Coast Line to the shore.

Newark Liberty's convenience for north Jersey, southern New York state, and western Connecticut travelers prompted the Port Authority to expand flights at Stewart International Airport, just over the state line in New York. The move not only eased congestion at Newark Liberty but also at Teterboro Airport, a popular Bergen County reliever airport for the New York/New Jersey metro area.

Other general aviation airports are Essex County in Caldwell (physically located in Fairfield); Morristown Municipal (in nearby Whippany, three miles from downtown); and Trenton-Mercer in Ewing Township, the capital's northern suburb in Mercer County.

SCIENTIFIC RENAISSANCE
According to government statistics, New Jersey is the professional address for more than 410,000 scientists and engineers. In fact, when ranked by the number of scientists and engineers who hold Ph.D.s per 1,000 workers, the state takes seventh place nationally. The 2007 Aelera State Knowledge Economy Index lists New Jersey as the fourth most competitive state in the country. Fifteen of the world's most successful drug companies have major facilities here, and pharmaceuticals remain the state's top industry. In the ongoing effort to find the universal flu shot and cures for HIV/AIDS and a wide range of other diseases, several of these corporations are expanding.

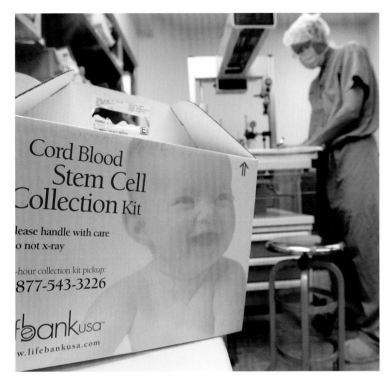

French drug maker Sanofi-Aventis began constructing a new building in 2008 on its sprawling U.S. headquarters campus in Bridgewater. Medical researchers will use the facility to continue their work on central nervous system diseases and cancer and finding new treatments for illnesses such as asthma and Alzheimer's.

Danish drug company Novo Nordisk is expanding for the second time since opening its U.S. headquarters in Plainsboro in 2003. As part of the green movement, the company started building a new, $20 million facility in 2008 that will use recycled and recyclable materials.

Here Novo Nordisk scientists will focus on diabetes research. In 2006 the company built a hemostasis research facility in the state's Greater New Brunswick Innovation Zone with a $3.3 million business incentive grant from the EDA.

Drugs aimed at specific diseases form only a part of New Jersey's medical research industry. In 2002 biopharmaceutical firm Celgene Corporation, based in Summit, acquired LifebankUSA, a Cedar Knolls company that encourages expectant families to bank both placental and umbilical cord stem cells to meet any possible future

medical needs. Celgene's partner is the Saint Barnabas Medical Center, one of the state's more active maternity hospitals, in nearby Livingston.

In a heralded effort to find cures for degenerative and neurological disorders while also laying the groundwork for economic opportunity and job growth, Governor Jon

Corzine committed $270 million for fiscal year 2007 to build and equip stem-cell and biomedical research facilities around the state. In New Brunswick, funds will build the Stem Cell Institute of New Jersey; in Newark, research facilities at the New Jersey Institute of Technology; and in Camden, a biomedical research center operated jointly by

Rutgers, the Robert Wood Johnson Medical School at Camden, the Coriell Institute, and the Cancer Institute of New Jersey. In Belleville funds will go to the Garden State Cancer Center for research; and in Allendale, to the Eli Katz Umbilical Cord Blood Program to aid stem cell research through the collection of cord blood.

The Rutgers Stem Cell Research Center, on the university's New Brunswick campus, is also developing a core facility for human

embryonic stem cell research, which will be aimed at developing therapies for such disorders as neurotrauma. The facility is supported by a grant from the New Jersey Commission on Science and Technology and is undertaken in partnership with Reprogenetics of Livingston, a genetics lab that screens embryos for the assisted-reproduction process.

Beyond the race for cures, various New Jersey medical centers are participating in the nationwide wellness movement. Shore Memorial Hospital in Somers Point holds classes designed to help patients make healthy lifestyle choices, partners with fitness clubs, and broadcasts a weekly television program, "Health Today," in cooperation with the local NBC affiliate. Somerset Medical Center in Somerville and CentraState Medical Center in Freehold promote wellness with a variety of exercise programs; the latter opened a 40,000-square-foot fitness facility in 2007.

Technological innovation in New Jersey also springs from fields other

than preventative medicine and organic chemistry. ECI Technology, now based in Totowa, developed a new chemical monitoring system for the semiconductor industry in 1998; the breakthrough led ECI to capture more than 90 percent of the worldwide market for equipment that regulates the copper-electro-deposition process. In 2004 UV Solutions, based in Newark, began developing environmentally safe and energy-efficient ultraviolet light sources for use in paint and adhesive curing, disinfection, and dermatological treatment.

GOOD LIVING

The quality of life in the Garden State is highly appealing. Prospective homeowners find a wide variety of housing options, from the rolling Hillsborough estates (which neighbor the U.S. Equestrian Team Foundation headquarters in Gladstone) to the elegantly restored Victorian mansions of Moorestown. In 2007 *Money* magazine singled out Moorestown and Hillsborough, along with Montville, River Vale, Berkeley Heights, Readington, Marlboro, and

Sayreville, as the best places to live in New Jersey.

When it comes to public education, the state is known for investing in its students. Technology education is required in every public school's core curriculum, and nearly 85 percent of New Jersey high-school graduates go on to college.

Not surprisingly, many Fortune 500 companies call the state home.

Johnson & Johnson in New Brunswick, Medco Health Solutions in Franklin Lakes, and Prudential Financial in Newark were New Jersey's top three revenue producers on the Fortune 500 list in 2007, placing within the top 100 companies on the list. They were followed by Honeywell in Morristown, Merck in Whitehouse, Wyeth in Madison, the Chubb Corporation in Warren, Public Service Enterprise Group in Newark, Toys "R" Us in Wayne, and American Standard (renamed Trane in late 2007) in Piscataway, as the state's top 10 Fortune 500 companies.

Higher education is keeping up with the evolving business needs of New Jersey's corporations. The Rutgers School of Business–Camden has initiated a four-year undergraduate program in place of its upper-division courses; incoming freshmen and transfer students can now obtain a traditional bachelor's degree in business, making them competitive with undergraduates across the country. The School of Business also offers a new accelerated management program for workers who want to fill the gap as baby boomers begin retiring. At Rutgers Business School–Newark, a new curriculum allows full-time MBA students to acquire deeper knowledge in their concentration area with more electives and fewer required courses.

Stevens Institute of Technology in Hoboken, Kean University in Union, and Centenary College in Hackettstown have taken some of their academic programs to China and Korea, while other colleges and universities have, like Rutgers, expanded their curricula at home. The College of New Jersey in Ewing opened its School of Culture and Society to promote understanding and humanity in those taking leadership roles. Seton Hall

University launched the graduate Clinical Nurse Leader program, a fast track into the profession for students with non-nursing bachelor's degrees. NJIT inaugurated a degree program in engineering management. Georgian Court University in Lakewood established an undergraduate degree in tourism, hospitality, and recreation management. Bergen Community College in Paramus developed its Center for the Study of Intercultural

Understanding in response to the compelling diversity challenges of the 21st century. And a variety of vocational and two-year colleges have culinary curricula to train aspiring chefs for the state's burgeoning restaurant industry.

New Jersey changes seasons four times a year, providing ample opportunities to hike, ski, sail, fish, or simply lounge along the 256 miles of beaches that stretch from the Raritan Bay south along the Atlantic coast to the Delaware Bay.

In this new century, two regions quite opposite in character have emerged as worthy competitors in attracting year-round travelers: Atlantic City, with its venerable casino hotels, and picturesque Sussex County, with its rural resorts.

Leading the charge in revitalizing Atlantic City is the wildly popular Borgata Hotel Casino and Spa, known for its stunning bronzed glass exterior and magnificent lobby embellished with artist Dale Chihuly's glass chandeliers. It

opened in 2003 after five years of market research to determine what overnight casino patrons really wanted. Surveys revealed the desire for convenient underground parking, ultramodern rooms, a full-service spa, gourmet dining, edgy nightlife, and of course, the latest in gambling options. The Borgata is repeating its

success with the Water Club, a 43-story, $400 million hotel opened in June 2008 with a two-story spa, five heated pools, and 18,000 square feet of meeting space.

Two other new additions are dazzling Atlantic City's revitalization scene. Harrah's Resort opened the

elegant, 44-story Waterfront Tower, which completes the resort's lavish expansion; and the Trump Taj Mahal Casino Resort debuted its opulent 39-story Chairman Tower, along with extensive renovations to the rest of the property.

With the Borgata proving that travelers would flock to Atlantic City, even in the dead of winter, if they were given a fresh, 21st-century combination of amenities and entertainment, Harrah's Showboat Casino Hotel on the boardwalk rose to the challenge. In 2007 its hospitality offerings were diversified with the opening of a House of Blues, the international franchise that attracts those who love live music and southern cooking. Not to be outdone, the Tropicana Casino & Resort opened two nongaming venues: Providence, a New York–style nightclub, and the Quarter, a Latin-inspired shopping and dining complex. And on and on goes the competition to revitalize the Queen of Resorts into a year-round destination.

Enhancing Atlantic City's accessibility to international travelers is the Atlantic City International Airport, just 10 miles away in Pomona. It puts out the welcome mat to an average 1.2 million air travelers annually. An ongoing expansion has increased the size of its terminal to accommodate the growing number of passengers, lengthened the runways to handle additional daily flights for both Spirit Airlines and Delta's Comair, and added a six-story parking garage.

The unique blend of great outdoors and luxury getaway experiences that people find in Atlantic City is also available in Sussex County's Skylands region, nestled in the foothills of the picturesque Kittatinny Mountains of northwestern New Jersey. The Crystal Springs Resort, a multifaceted destination in expansive Vernon Township, graces this natural environment. Among the Crystal Springs properties is the Minerals Resort & Spa, which opened in 2004. In addition to its award-winning restaurant and country club, the Minerals Resort is complemented by the Biosphere, an imaginative indoor pool complex. Another section of Crystal Springs houses the Grand Cascades Lodge. Designed in the style of America's great 19th-century wood lodges, it offers stunning views of New Jersey, New York, and Pennsylvania. Guests can avail themselves of six different championship golf courses.

Clearly, New Jersey has relaxation down. It's the reward for meeting the challenges of the new millennium head-on. The ports are expanding direct-rail shipments and upgrading local roads to facilitate faster truck delivery. Businesses and municipalities are pursuing green initiatives. Research continues to generate ideas that eclipse even those hot innovations of the 1980s–90s. And cities that yesterday seemed on the verge of slipping away, today vibrate with daytime commerce and nighttime entertainment. Where else but in the Garden State could all this opportunity exist?

PART TWO

CHAMPIONS OF COMMERCE:

Profiles of Companies and Organizations

PROFILES OF COMPANIES AND ORGANIZATIONS

Consumer Foods, Food Processing, and Supermarkets

Wakefern Food Corporation

This corporation is comprised of 44 member companies who individually own and operate supermarkets under the ShopRite® banner. In addition to serving as the merchandising and distribution arm for more than 200 ShopRite stores located across the north Atlantic, Wakefern operates stores under the PriceRite® banner.

The end of World War II brought with it the end of food rationing and the return home of the American soldier. In the suburbs, a housing boom was under way. And in a small warehouse in Newark, New Jersey, eight independent grocers, with a vision of offering supermarket products at low prices, joined together to form Wakefern Food Corporation.

These innovative grocers were brought together by a sales representative from Del Monte Foods who introduced them to cooperative buying.

They experimented by ordering and splitting a few cases of grocery products. Pleased with the results, they formalized their relationship on December 5, 1946. Each of the eight grocers invested $1,000 and using the first letters of the founding members' initials, Wakefern Food Corporation was born.

CALLING NEW JERSEY HOME

In 1951 the store owners in the cooperative agreed that operating under a single banner would help customers realize that this brand represented great value. The ShopRite® name grew out of the cooperative's commitment to "buy right" so that consumers could "shop right." Their venture succeeded so well that Wakefern grew to become the country's largest retailer-owned (non-farm) cooperative.

Today, Wakefern's 44 members individually own and operate more than 200 ShopRite stores. In 1995 a new banner was added to the Wakefern family with the introduction of PriceRite®. With this addition, Wakefern's commitment to deliver quality and value to its customers now extended to families throughout New Jersey as well as Connecticut, New York, Pennsylvania, Delaware, Massachusetts, and Rhode Island.

As the merchandising and distribution arm of the company, Wakefern operates more than 2.5 million square feet of warehouse space to supply its stores, and retail sales are approaching the $10 billion mark. In 2007, this Elizabeth, New Jersey–based company moved its corporate offices to Keasbey, New Jersey. Along with its ShopRite members, Wakefern is one of New Jersey's largest employers, with an extended family of about 32,000 dedicated associates in the state and 50,000 nationwide.

CHANGING WITH THE TIMES

In the 60 years since Wakefern's founding, this cooperative family has continued to provide Garden State and New York metropolitan-area customers with exceptional services and outstanding value, building trust and loyalty among shoppers, suppliers, and families in its communities.

As customers change and their tastes evolve, Wakefern keeps an eye on the future. Each year ShopRite introduces dozens of new and specialty items, such as its line of imported foods for shoppers who have a taste for cuisines from around the globe. Each week Wakefern/ShopRite proudly serves four million customers, offering them more than 3,000 private-label brand items that range from meat and dairy, general merchandise, and health and beauty aids to organic and all-natural foods, and kosher and ethnic items. In 2004, with the introduction of online shopping, customers could now shop from the comfort of their homes.

Equally important for shoppers' peace of mind, ShopRite's quality assurance teams use their extensive experience to ensure that customers can count on the company's high standards of quality and safety every time.

REACHING OUT

As a longtime supporter of the hunger-fighting community, Wakefern recognized the pervasive problem of hunger that is experienced by so many people right in the neighborhoods served by their stores. And

so, in 1999, Wakefern conceived of and began ShopRite Partners In Caring®, a year-round program dedicated to helping in the fight against hunger. Each year, ShopRite Partners In Caring donates millions of dollars to more than 1,400 local charities that help feed underprivileged families and the elderly. In 2008, giving through this program exceeded $17 million.

Another community effort supported by Wakefern for the past 20 years is the three-day New Jersey Special Olympics Summer Games. Wakefern associate volunteers and their families provide food and other support to more than

2,500 New Jersey residents who are involved in the games.

In addition, ShopRite's Supermarket Careers program educates and trains special-needs students for meaningful careers in the supermarket industry. This groundbreaking program gives students in 20 area schools real-world work experience in supermarket operations.

With its rich history of dedication to communities and a commitment to value, Wakefern Food Corporation—and its ShopRite and PriceRite stores—will continue to succeed in the present and for many years to come.

Far left: This ShopRite® grocery store is located in Lodi, New Jersey.
Above: ShopRite stores offer specialty food products to meet changing consumer tastes.
Left: Through its Partners In Caring® program, ShopRite works to end hunger in its communities.

PROFILES OF COMPANIES AND ORGANIZATIONS
Education

This great public research university drives society's highest ambitions: individual advancement, the discovery of new knowledge, economic development, and social progress. For this institution of higher learning, that vision begins in New Jersey.

Rutgers, The State University of New Jersey, was chartered as Queen's College in 1766, nearly a decade before the start of the American Revolution. In the nation's struggle for independence, Rutgers students, faculty, and alumni were active participants. During the war, classes were suspended on several occasions, according to the college archives, as "all members of the small college community were caught up in the Revolutionary struggle." Above: The Old Queens Building, shown here, was completed in 1823. This was the first structure to be designed for the original college.

Nurturing New Jersey start-up companies. Making domestic ports safe. Building stronger democracies abroad. Understanding Antarctic climate change. With its Jersey roots and global reach, Rutgers, The State University of New Jersey, touches many lives. Rutgers is New Jersey's past, founded before the American Revolution and older than the state itself. Rutgers is New Jersey's future, educating and innovating to keep New Jersey strong. Rutgers is

world class, sharing knowledge and discovery across the globe.

Rutgers is the leading comprehensive public research university in the New York/New Jersey metropolitan area and the only public university in New Jersey in the Association of American Universities (AAU). AAU institutions are North America's leading research universities, recognized for the quality and scope of their research and educational programs. With campuses located in

Camden, Newark, and New Brunswick/ Piscataway, Rutgers excels as a great New Jersey institution and as a unique resource for the region.

EDUCATION AND WORKFORCE DEVELOPMENT

Rutgers prepares men and women to succeed in a complex world. By attending a research university, students work alongside faculty, gaining special insights and often participating as knowledge is discovered. More than 50,000 students enroll at Rutgers each year in 27 schools and colleges offering more than 100 majors and 4,000 courses. Rutgers awards more than 10,000 bachelor's, master's, doctoral, and professional degrees annually.

Rutgers is devoted to workforce preparation and lifelong learning. Each year, Rutgers University Continuous Education enrolls more than 50,000 students who seek to grow professionally and personally. The university's John J. Heldrich Center for Workforce Development raises the effectiveness of the American workplace by strengthening workforce education, job placement, and training programs and policies.

In every field imaginable, Rutgers alumni work and lead. More than 370,000 alumni, including 210,000-plus in New Jersey, contribute to society worldwide. Alumni include Nobel laureate and economist Milton Friedman; actor, singer, and social activist Paul Robeson; former U.S. poet laureate Robert Pinsky; Home Depot cofounder Bernard Marcus; National Basketball Association commissioner David Stern; Saatchi & Saatchi Americas CEO Mary Baglivo; award-winning actor James Gandolfini; and Pulitzer Prize–winning novelist Junot Díaz.

FUELING THE ECONOMY, BRINGING HOPE

Rutgers powers economic growth, making discoveries that solve problems and bring hope. The university has more than 180 specialized research centers, bureaus, and institutes, including world-class centers for the life sciences. The university's W. M. Keck Center for Collaborative Neuroscience is acclaimed for promoting international cooperation among spinal cord researchers. The Center for Molecular and Behavioral Neuroscience produces groundbreaking research on neurological functions and brain disorders.

In biomedicine, Rutgers pioneers new uses for plastics, or polymers. Dental implants, coronary stents, artificial joints, and plastic medicines are all part of the contribution of Rutgers to the revolution in life science biomaterials. The Rutgers University Cell and DNA Repository and the Protein Data Bank are vital resources for scientists around the globe.

RESEARCH AND DEVELOPMENT, BUSINESS RESOURCES

Thomas Edison. Bell Labs. RCA. These communications giants made their marks in New Jersey, and Rutgers carries on this pioneering spirit with award-winning communications research and development (R&D). The university's WINLAB ORBIT radio grid is the world's largest open-access wireless R&D test bed, and sponsors across the globe use it to study new products. Among other industries that use the university's extensive R&D

resources are the agribusiness, chemical, engineering, food, and pharmaceutical sectors. Rutgers is home to New Jersey's only school of pharmacy.

Complementing the powerful Rutgers R&D network are its business resources. The Rutgers Business School–Newark and New Brunswick and Rutgers School of Business–Camden offer a full range of academic programs and research and outreach services. Small Business Development Centers, the Food Innovation Center, and the Rutgers-Camden Technology Campus help strengthen small firms and start-ups.

A LONG HISTORY OF EXCELLENCE

Chartered in 1766 as the nation's eighth institution of higher learning, Rutgers is one of only nine colonial colleges established before the American Revolution. In the more than 240 years that have passed since then, Rutgers has grown

from a small, private liberal arts college to become a land-grant college and one of the nation's largest and most esteemed public research universities. Rutgers provides a rich learning environment, with classes taught by leading scholars in such fields as anthropology, biology, chemistry, economics, English, geology, history, mathematics, philosophy, physics, and psychology.

Such august, learned societies as the National Academy of Sciences and the National Endowment for the Arts recognize the achievements of Rutgers faculty and alumni, among whom are winners of the Nobel and Pulitzer prizes and many other preeminent awards. In 1952 Rutgers alumnus and professor

of microbiology Selman Waksman won the Nobel Prize for his work, conducted with several graduate students, that led to the discovery of the antibiotic streptomycin, the first remedy for tuberculosis.

BEST POLICIES AND PRACTICES

In New Jersey, Rutgers helps to ensure that policies are backed by sound information. Education, law, and transportation are just three of many sectors that rely on Rutgers to prepare professionals and assist in solving problems and improving practices.

Rutgers educates teachers and contributes to curriculum standards for preschool and also kindergarten through 12th grade. The Graduate School of

Above left: Group study is common in the 26 libraries of Rutgers. Above center: The Center for Law and Justice houses the School of Law–Newark, the School of Criminal Justice, and the Division of Global Affairs. Above right: A student works in a biotechnology laboratory. Rutgers students collaborate with each other and with faculty, gaining a solid education in the liberal arts and sciences, preparing for future professions, and conducting research that advances the frontiers of knowledge.

dozens of academic, service, and research facilities and programs. Bringing Rutgers research to the community, the New Jersey Agricultural Experiment Station's Rutgers Cooperative Extension offers programs that focus on the environment, human and community development, health and nutrition, and economic growth and agricultural sustainability. Beyond New Jersey, Rutgers students, faculty, and alumni live, learn, and work in all 50 states and on seven continents.

The university provides additional information about all that it offers on its Web site (www.rutgers.edu). Rutgers and its people are remarkable and resourceful, valued partners in cultivating success.

Above left: Students work in a computer laboratory. Above center: A choral music education class is conducted outdoors. Right: A faculty member guides student research in a science laboratory. Transmitting knowledge to the next generation is the university's most important mission. As technology reinvents the art and science of teaching, Rutgers evolves and transforms, ever mindful that great teaching remains at the core of a great education.

Education offers the state's only Ph.D. program in education.

The School of Law–Newark and the School of Law–Camden prepare students for the law professions and provide vital services to the community through law clinics in such areas as domestic violence, child advocacy, environmental law, and special education law.

The Rutgers Center for Advanced Infrastructure and Transportation and the Alan M. Voorhees Transportation Center devise safety solutions for highways, skyways, and ports; provide training for transit workers in New Jersey

and elsewhere; and create improved road materials.

Worldwide, Rutgers influences policy through such entities as the Center for State Constitutional Studies, which helps shape subnational constitutions in the United States and other countries, and the Division of Global Affairs, which analyzes events that have a global impact.

FINE AND PERFORMING ARTS
The arts at Rutgers enrich and enliven the region's cultural landscape. The university's Mason Gross School of the Arts is known as New Jersey's premier school for the fine and performing arts. Alumni include stars of stage and screen, such as Calista Flockhart,

Kristin Davis, and Avery Brooks. Tony award–winning alumnus Roger Bart has appeared in a string of Broadway hits.

Other arts resources include the Institute of Jazz Studies, located in Newark, an unparalleled trove for all things jazz; the Jane Voorhees Zimmerli Art Museum, one of the finest university art museums in the country; and the Center for the Arts–Camden, with an extensive array of programming.

A PRESENCE WORLDWIDE
The three Rutgers campuses are the university's focal points for learning, research, and service, and beyond these, the university reaches all 21 New Jersey counties through

This organization works to create an optimal environment to achieve excellence in public education in New Jersey. Its goals are to preserve and improve the economic interests, working conditions, and job security of its members while enhancing and enriching the public education system.

The New Jersey Education Association (NJEA) was founded in 1853 by a group of educators with a desire to improve public education and elevate the teaching profession. The primary interest of NJEA in the early years was related to teacher preparation, professional development, and instruction.

Today NJEA represents more than 200,000 public school employees who work in school districts and county colleges throughout the state. The majority of NJEA members are teachers and professionals such as counselors, nurses, and psychologists. About one-quarter are educational support professionals, including school secretaries, paraprofessionals, classroom aides, cafeteria workers, school custodians, maintenance and grounds crews, bus drivers, and school security personnel. The remaining members are retired educators and students enrolled in New Jersey colleges who wish to pursue careers in education.

NJEA continues to serve members' professional and personal needs by providing comprehensive services. Supporting and strengthening public education, offering opportunities for

professional growth, protecting members' rights, and working for improved member recognition and compensation are all part of the NJEA commitment to "great public schools for every child."

Traditionally, careers in education offered low salaries and few fringe benefits. NJEA recognized that in order

to compete with similarly educated professionals, teaching needed to offer competitive salaries and benefits. The NJEA campaign $40K Right Away—launched in 2001—resulted in more than 500 New Jersey school districts offering teachers a starting salary of $40,000 or more. NJEA also worked closely with New Jersey's governor

and legislature to secure its members' pensions and benefits.

WORKING FOR GREAT PUBLIC SCHOOLS

NJEA members are proud of the role they play in making New Jersey's public schools great for every child. New Jersey has been named one of the four smartest states in the nation based on the quality of its public schools, which lead the country in academic achievement according to the U.S. Chamber of Commerce.

New Jersey's students are among the nation's best. According to the National Center for Education Statistics, New Jersey students' reading and math scores rank among the highest in the nation. New Jersey's public high school graduation rate leads the nation. The National Center for Public Policy and Higher Education gives New Jersey a grade of "A" for how well its public schools prepare students for college. The U.S. Chamber of Commerce ranks New Jersey's public schools as the highest in the nation based on how well they prepare students for college and the workforce.

Above right: The members of the New Jersey Education Association (NJEA) strive to make New Jersey's public schools great for every child.

All New Jersey public school students, regardless of zip code, are entitled by the state constitution to a thorough and efficient education. NJEA maintains a strong presence in Trenton to ensure that legislators work in the best interests of children and public education.

New Jersey's urban preschool programs have been rated among the best in the nation by the National Institute for Early Education Research. Mathematics and reading scores in urban schools continue to rise, and New Jersey leads the nation in reducing the achievement gap between urban schools and other schools.

ENSURING HIGH QUALITY TEACHING

NJEA is a national leader in bringing the best training and cutting-edge resources to benefit the children of New Jersey. NJEA works to provide professional development for all school employees— both professional and educational support personnel—as they come together to solve problems and enhance public education in the modern age.

In September 2000, the state passed a mandate requiring New Jersey teachers to acquire a minimum of 100 hours of professional development every five years. NJEA worked with the Department of Education and the Professional Teaching Standards Board to create a framework of goals to meet these new criteria. Every school district in the state has a local professional development committee (LPDC) that works with school administration to ensure its teachers receive top-notch training opportunities.

The NJEA Convention has been a mainstay of the association's history. What began as an annual meeting in 1853 has evolved into the largest professional development conference for educators in the world. Held over the course of two days in November, the convention has a tradition of providing hands-on workshops. The event features more than 300 offerings on topics ranging from forensic counseling to grant writing to Core Curriculum Content Standards, and tens of thousands of New Jersey teachers attend each year.

NJEA is also leading the way in creating a 21st-century approach to professional development. This paradigm shift features a focus on job-embedded

Above left: New Jersey's public schools rank among the top in the nation. In urban areas, NJEA members are working hard to close the achievement gap. As a result, test scores in New Jersey's urban schools have doubled in mathematics and quadrupled in reading. Above right: The NJEA Convention in Atlantic City is the largest professional development conference for educators in the world. Each year this convention attracts more than 50,000 teachers and educational support professionals.

professional development, such as collegial coaching and action research. The professional development portal on the NJEA Web site allows New Jersey teachers and support personnel to receive online training and meet the demand for professional development according to 21st-century standards.

PARTNERING WITH PARENTS

In New Jersey, school staff, families, communities, and policymakers work hand in hand to share responsibility for children's education. NJEA takes pride in working with parents through public schools to strengthen parental involvement. Under the theme Together We Can, NJEA shares information with families and community members to build ever-stronger bonds between home and school.

Family involvement is central to student success. Research demonstrates that when families are involved in their children's education, children achieve higher grades and test scores, have better attendance at school, do more homework, and behave better. Through NJEA's Family Involvement Training (FIT), New Jersey schools reach out to parents so they can learn more about helping their children succeed in school. Through NJEA, schools can provide further information on topics ranging from homework and study skills to discipline and building self-esteem.

NJEA is also active in ensuring that all students receive the support and encouragement they need to succeed. The NJEA program Families and Schools Together (FAST) forms a coalition of education advocates, community groups, and schools in New Jersey's larger cities who come together to strengthen family involvement in their urban districts. The goal of the FAST program is not only to encourage family involvement but also to enhance urban children's academic progress and make parents feel welcome in public schools.

PROMOTING PUBLIC EDUCATION SUCCESS

Since 1994 NJEA has conducted the Pride in Public Education campaign, a statewide effort to share the successes of public education with all New Jerseyans. The Pride campaign helps build strong support for public schools and encourages community involvement.

The Pride campaign includes *Classroom Close-up, NJ*, an Emmy award–winning television program

focusing on innovative projects happening in New Jersey public schools. A 30-minute weekly program, *Classroom Close-up, NJ* features students, teachers, school staff, and communities who create and participate in successful school projects and events. The series is a coproduction of NJEA and NJN Public Television and Radio and airs on the NJN television channel.

PREPARING FOR THE FUTURE

Through NJEA's initiative, New Jersey became a member of the Partnership for 21st-Century Skills—a leading organization focused on including 21st-century skills in public school education programs. The organization brings together education leaders, the business community, and state policymakers to define and support a powerful vision for 21st-century education. The goal of the partnership is to ensure that students emerge from New Jersey's schools with the skills needed to be effective citizens, workers, and leaders, and to better prepare the state for global competition. The partnership encourages schools and educators to advocate for the infusion of technology and higher-order thinking skills in current education programs.

The partnership promotes a global approach to education, with critical thinking, problem-solving, creativity, communication, and collaboration skills. It focuses learning on core academic subjects, but also recognizes the importance of other key skills, including global awareness, financial and civic literacy, and health and wellness. Most importantly, it incorporates technological literacy throughout all content areas.

By promoting a collaborative approach to education—involving education, business, government, and community leaders—the partnership brings many key stakeholders to the table. New Jersey's commitment to the partnership helps ensure strong outcomes for the state's students so that they have the requisite knowledge, communication, technology, and problem-solving skills to live and work effectively in a complex and dynamic world.

Above left: From ensuring that children arrive safely at school to feeding them nutritious lunches to teaching the basics and more, NJEA members serve the children in New Jersey's public schools in a wide variety of valuable ways. Above right: Vice President Barbara Keshishian of NJEA visits with students during a filming of *Classroom Close-up, NJ*. This Emmy award–winning show spotlights New Jersey's public schools.

Founded in 1870, this is one of the leading technological universities in the world dedicated to learning and research. It offers broad-based curricula designed to nurture creative inventiveness and cross-disciplinary communities.

Stevens Institute of Technology is in the forefront of global challenges in engineering, science, complex systems, and technology management. Partnerships and collaborations with business, industry, government, and other universities contribute to the enriched environment at Stevens. In addition, Technogenesis®, the mature model created by Stevens for technology commercialization in academe, involves external partners working with undergraduates and faculty to develop and launch technology enterprises that create broad opportunities and shared value.

The spirit of entrepreneurialism that invigorates all aspects of the education environment at Stevens is a vibrant legacy of the Stevens family, whose members played key leadership roles in both the American War of Independence and the American Industrial Revolution. Their concept of an intensive, broad-based technology education, meant to create highly competitive leaders for American industry, is enshrined at the university that Edwin A. Stevens bequeathed to the nation.

At the dawn of the 21st century, that spirit emboldens young leaders to tackle the next American century of globally based competition.

SHAPING THE FUTURE

From the invisible microcosm of nano-engineering to the burgeoning macrocosm of complex space-based systems, educational offerings at Stevens are among the most forward-looking in the United States.

Moreover, the Stevens location—along the Hudson River, across from the finance and business capital of the world, New York City—as well as its highly selective admissions policy and its healthy student-to-faculty ratio impart a rare agility to the institution, allowing for the swift adoption and perfection of cutting-edge curricula. The innovative Stevens undergraduate programs launched in this century include Biomedical Engineering, Business & Technology Management, and Cyber Security. The university has now instituted an undergraduate minor in Green Engineering, carrying forward the pioneering commitment to environmental quality for which Stevens is renowned.

In 2007 Stevens initiated two new schools at its Hoboken campus—the first, the School of Systems & Enterprises (SSE), followed by the College of Arts & Letters. SSE is the outgrowth of the Stevens Department of Systems Engineering & Engineering Management, which grew with rapid success to become one of the largest such programs in the United States after its formation in 2000. SSE provides exclusive professional courses at home and abroad, serving industry and government agencies in the United States, Europe, South Asia, and the Far East. The school also provides advanced systems engineering education to the United States' National Security Agency (NSA), the Federal Aviation Administration (FAA), and the National Aeronautics and Space Administration (NASA), among other agencies.

The Stevens College of Arts & Letters was founded in recognition of the importance of the arts and humanities in the spectrum of technological studies. Programs in Art, Music & Technology and the History & Philosophy of Science are now permanent features of the university's undergraduate curriculum. Full information about Stevens Institute of Technology is given on the university's main Web site (www.stevens.edu).

PIONEERING GLOBAL EDUCATION

Stevens provides an award-winning online education component, WebCampus.Stevens.edu, which

reaches students around the world with dozens of rigorous graduate courses in science, engineering, and systems and technology management.

Stevens has also been successful in delivering graduate courses in China. These courses are delivered partly online and partly on-site and are presented in collaboration with the Beijing Institute of Technology and the Central University of Finance and Economics. Stevens Institute of Technology International (SITI), which represents the first establishment of a university outside the United States based on the Stevens model, is located in Santo

Domingo, Dominican Republic, and is strongly endorsed by that nation's innovative president.

President Harold J. Raveché of Stevens Institute of Technology has also initiated talks with the South Korean government to establish a university on the Stevens model in the fast-expanding port city of Pyeongtaek, located just southwest of Seoul.

INNOVATING CROSS-DISCIPLINARY COMMUNITIES

Also in 2007, leaders at Stevens propounded a long-range Strategic Positioning Plan that serves as a topographical guide to the "New University of the global-technological era." The establishment of "communities of creative enterprise" across the spectrum of disciplines is the centerpiece of this plan. The continued growth of Stevens as a graduate research institution is also carefully balanced with the

recognition that the undergraduate engineering program is the university's beating heart, which nourishes all the other endeavors.

The Strategic Positioning Plan identifies three major focus areas of education and research for the next century —systems and enterprise management and architecture; security, including for maritime, cyber, information, and communications networks; and multiscale engineering, science, and technology. Cross-disciplinary communities of faculty, students, and external partners are already performing strongly in each of these focus areas.

Going forward, Stevens will continue to execute the bold mission bequeathed by its founder: To prepare extraordinary young leaders to master the challenges of new technologies, new markets, and new ways of thinking and competing in a constantly changing global landscape.

Above left: Shown here are students at work in the Microelectronics Laboratory. Above center: Stevens students report for morning classes at the South Gate of the university's campus. Above right: Students chat in the Lawrence T. Babbio, Jr. Center for Technology Management, with an inspiring backdrop of midtown Manhattan.

Seton Hall University

This Catholic university located on a 58-acre campus in South Orange, New Jersey, is home to about 10,000 students from all 50 states and 67 foreign countries. It prepares future leaders through excellent teaching, inspired spiritual and academic development, and a highly supportive educational experience.

Above, both photos: The 58-acre campus of Seton Hall University is located in the quaint village of South Orange, New Jersey, just 14 miles from Manhattan. The university's eight colleges offer more than 60 major fields of study.

Committed to academic excellence for more than 150 years, Seton Hall University provides students of all religious denominations with a teaching environment that fosters learning through questioning, discovering, and doing that enables them to explore some of the world's greatest books, ideas, and thinkers. Seton Hall students are given an outstanding education that teaches them to be servant leaders in their community and build a solid foundation on which to lead successful and prosperous lives.

Seton Hall offers more than 60 major subjects and concentrations, as well as honors and leadership programs. Undergraduate and graduate courses are offered in a broad range of disciplines. The university includes the College of Arts and Sciences, the College of Education and Human Services, the College of Nursing, the Immaculate Conception Seminary School of Theology, the Stillman School of Business, the Whitehead School of Diplomacy and International Relations, the School of Law, and the School of Graduate Medical Education.

Seton Hall is ranked as one of the top universities in the nation by *U.S.News & World Report* and the Intercollegiate Studies Institute's *Choosing the Right College*. The university is just 14 miles from New York City, the hub of finance, fashion, art, and entertainment. Its location in the New York–New Jersey metropolitan area makes it accessible to thousands of international companies and organizations—many of which visit the school for recruiting.

ENGAGING STUDENTS FROM THE START

Seton Hall offers the resources of a large university with the attention typical of a small college. With a student body of 5,300 undergraduates and 3,300 graduate students, the average class size is 25 and the student-to-faculty ratio is 15 to one, enabling students to obtain the personal attention they need. A student's first two years include exposure to a wide spectrum of ideas and perspectives, including the history and achievements of many cultures, a curriculum that assists many freshmen in choosing their major and minor fields of study.

At Seton Hall, faculty members, administrators, and student leaders provide individual attention and support to help students in making the transition from high school to college. One of the university's top priorities is for new students to feel welcome even before they arrive on campus. The award-winning Freshman Studies Program gives students a direct link to a faculty member who serves as their academic advisor and mentor and to a student peer advisor (PA) who guides them in becoming acclimated.

The university considers that regular connections between students and mentors are important and it facilitates this through its Mobile Computing Program, an online community that provides all incoming full-time freshmen with their own laptop computer before classes begin. Equipped with state-of-the-art technology, students are set to communicate electronically with their mentor or PA, to review courses, and to explore career-assessment activities. This makes freshmen part of the Seton Hall family right from the start.

GUIDED BY FAITH

In 1856, when Bishop James Roosevelt Bayley founded Seton Hall—the first diocesan college in the United States—he envisioned the institution as "a home for the mind, the heart, and the spirit." He named the college after his aunt, Elizabeth Ann Seton, a pioneer in Catholic education who also became the first American-born saint. During the school's early years, the 500 freshmen it enrolled were from 17 states and six foreign countries, establishing a tradition of diversity that remains today.

The university teaches that leadership cannot be defined by a title and salary but is characterized by the way individuals live their lives and the examples they set. Servant leaders must possess the ability to change people's hearts, heal divisions, and build community while displaying virtues of courage, foresight, empathy, and stewardship of the common good. At Seton Hall, student participation in service-learning courses and affiliation with the campus ministry's Division of Volunteer Efforts

(DOVE) results in the contribution of more than 40,000 hours of community service locally and internationally.

To develop students as servant leaders, the university presents a learning community influenced by Catholic ideals and universal values and also requires all students to take classes in ethics. Emphasis is placed on the importance of integrity, compassion, and a commitment to helping others while helping oneself. Experiential situations are created to assist students in developing a moral code of their own to guide their actions and decisions in life.

A VIBRANT COMMUNITY

Seton Hall University has created a campus environment offering a close-knit, inclusive community that is well-rounded and lively. It includes a thriving athletics program with 17 men's and women's NCAA Division I varsity athletic teams that compete in the Big East Conference, as well as intramural sports and recreation programs. In addition the school radio station, WSOU; the Madrigal Choir; Student Government;

Greek fraternities and sororities; and more than 100 other clubs and professional societies give students many opportunities to pursue their interests and participate with fellow students. While Seton Hall is a Catholic institution, its faculty, staff, and students come from a variety of faiths, colors, and nationalities.

The Career Center maintains an eRecruiting system with thousands of employment opportunities, sponsors recruiting events on campus, and offers job-placement services. Professional career-related guidance and services are designed to give students confidence and to assist them in making the right decisions for their future success.

Above left: Scientific research and technology partnerships thrive at Seton Hall's innovative, state-of-the-art Science and Technology Center, which was opened in 2007. Above right: Seton Hall is a close-knit community and yet is known internationally for its resources and programs. Students, faculty, and staff members from around the world bring a kaleidoscope of experiences and perspective, creating a campus that is both unified and diverse.

The College of New Jersey

This selective public institution is acclaimed nationally for its commitment to excellence and its academics, which include more than 50 majors offered to its 5,900 students. Its 289-acre campus is an ideal environment for learning and life, and its 'Knowledge is Power' initiative is a challenging pledge to attain climate neutrality.

Above left: At The College of New Jersey (TCNJ) Georgian-style buildings recall Colonial America. Above right: TCNJ has a full-time undergraduate enrollment of approximately 5,900 students, 95 percent of whom are from the state of New Jersey.

Serving students who are among the best and brightest, The College of New Jersey (TCNJ) is a top competitive college on an idyllic campus in Ewing. With its fine reputation, the college is able to choose outstanding applicants. In 2008 TCNJ received a record number of approximately 9,700 applications for the 1,300 seats available for the freshman class of 2012.

TCNJ offers the rare combination of small classes, talented faculty, and affordable tuition. The college has received many national accolades for quality and value, including listings in *U.S.News & World Report*'s "America's Best Colleges," *Barron's,* The Princeton Review, and *Kiplinger's Personal Finance*. TCNJ is also one of less than 10 percent of colleges and universities nationally to be awarded a Phi Beta Kappa chapter, which denotes an extraordinary academic experience.

TCNJ began as the New Jersey State Normal School. Founded in Trenton in 1855, it was the first teacher-training school in the state and the ninth in the nation. In 1958 it became Trenton State College. In 1996, to reflect its expanded curriculum and growing stature, the school was renamed The College of New Jersey.

A BROAD RANGE OF MAJORS

TCNJ developed into a multipurpose institution by expanding its degree offerings. Today, students major in more than 50 liberal arts and professional programs for bachelor's degrees, along with 35 graduate programs. TCNJ's seven schools are Arts and Communication; Business; Culture and Society; Education; Science; Nursing, Health, and Exercise Science; and Engineering.

Degrees awarded include bachelor of arts, bachelor of science, bachelor of fine arts, bachelor of music, master of arts, master of arts in teaching, master of education, master of science, and educational specialist. Specialized degrees are awarded in nursing and various engineering disciplines.

With in-depth courses, TCNJ fosters knowledge, arts, and wisdom while it prepares students to excel in their chosen fields. The school's public service mandate is to educate the leaders of the state and the nation. For example, its Urban Teacher Academy for high school juniors aims to attract teachers of the future.

In addition, TCNJ has an honors program and many options for study abroad. The college's special attention to freshmen has earned it an enviable retention rate, and its graduation rate is also one of the highest in the nation for an institution of its type.

ELEGANT EWING CAMPUS

In 1928, the college needed space to expand from its site in Trenton and purchased a large tract of land in nearby Ewing. The first wave of construction took place from 1930 to 1936, yielding 10 buildings; the first classes were held at the new campus in 1931. Additional acres were acquired through the years, and with continuing construction, today the college occupies 39 major buildings.

The stately Georgian-style buildings that grace the TCNJ campus evoke a feeling of Colonial America. Students have the benefits of a modern library, more than 20 academic computer laboratories, and laboratories for health, science, and technology programs.

VIBRANT CAMPUS LIFE

At TCNJ, students can choose from a rich variety of athletics, clubs, organizations, and other activities. Fourteen residence halls provide housing for 3,600 students. Full-time freshmen and

sophomores are guaranteed campus housing and occupy most of the spots, and some upperclass students also live on campus, especially in the college's town house complexes.

Brower Student Center is a hub of activity, with a bookstore, games room, lounges, conference rooms, the Rathskeller restaurant, *The Signal* student newspaper, and three cultural centers. The college has theaters and an art gallery, and at the music building is a 300-seat concert hall.

TCNJ has one of the finest NCAA Division III athletic programs in the nation. In addition, there are intramural and club athletics, and other recreational opportunities.

Lions' Stadium hosts football, soccer, field hockey, and lacrosse. Packer Hall features basketball courts, an aquatic center, and strength-training facilities. The campus has indoor and outdoor tennis courts and an all-weather

running track. Fitness facilities also are provided at the Recreation Center.

Recreation at TCNJ also includes 150 clubs and organizations. There are leadership and community service opportunities, professional societies, Greek fraternities and sororities, and performing ensembles. A sampling includes dance, chess, a Habitat for Humanity division, a French club, the Mixed Signals improvisational comedy troupe, the Society of Automotive Engineers, the Swing Dance Club, and the All College Theater (ACT).

'KNOWLEDGE IS POWER'

TCNJ has developed an energy-conservation campaign titled "Knowledge is Power." The campus-wide initiative urges the implementation of simple changes in energy use that can positively affect operating costs and the environment, while also lessening pressure on institutional resources.

Students thrive in the ever-stimulating and challenging environment of The College of New Jersey, which continually strives to fulfill its mission of educating the leaders of tomorrow.

Above left: In addition to housing traditional library collections and services in an atmosphere that is elegant yet friendly and inviting throughout, the TCNJ library provides 24 group study rooms, a café, a late-night study area, and a 105-seat multipurpose auditorium. Above center: Known for its natural beauty, the college's campus is set on 289 tree-lined acres in suburban Ewing Township. Above right: Students at TCNJ can take advantage of the more than 20 academic computer laboratories available on campus.

Designed to fuel the growth of southern New Jersey by providing both educational opportunities and economic development, this highly rated university has evolved from a local state college to a top-tier regional public university.

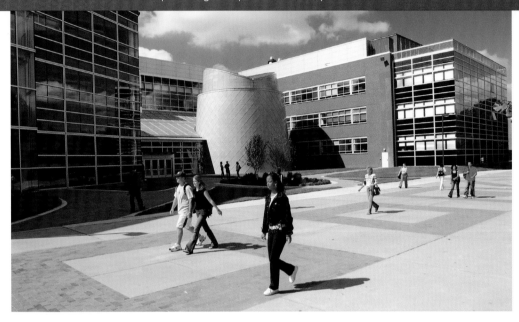

Rowan University is an outstanding comprehensive institution that offers a wide range of educational opportunities for its diverse student body and strives to improve the quality of life for the citizens of its region. With campuses in Glassboro and Camden, Rowan University provides education for more than 10,000 full-time and part-time students from around the country and the world, and employs more than 1,400 people.

The university offers 58 undergraduate majors through seven colleges— Business, Communication, Education, Engineering, Fine & Performing Arts, Liberal Arts & Sciences, and Professional & Continuing Education. Graduate students may choose from seven teacher-certification programs, 38 master's degrees and specializations, 19 graduate certification programs, and a doctoral program in educational leadership.

RESPONDING TO COMMUNITY NEEDS

Since its founding in 1923 as Glassboro Normal School, a school that trained teachers, Rowan University has had a remarkable history. Landmark events— such as serving as host for the 1967 summit conference between President Lyndon Johnson and Soviet Premier Alexei Kosygin, as well as receiving a $100 million gift in 1992 from Henry and Betty Rowan—brought international attention to the university.

At the time, the Rowan gift was the largest donation given to an American public college or university in the history of higher education. Later that year, to honor the donors, the school changed its name from Glassboro State College to Rowan College of New Jersey. The college achieved university status in 1997 and its name was changed to Rowan University.

EDUCATION FOR THE 21ST CENTURY

President Donald J. Farish, Ph.D., J.D., is leading the school into a new era. "This has been a transformational decade for Rowan University," he says. "We have implemented a detailed Campus Master Plan that is creating the campus of the future. The university's vision is to accommodate a greater number of students, establish an increasingly diverse curriculum, and expand the campus in ways that benefit both the students and the communities of southern New Jersey."

Rowan University's 200-acre, tree-lined main campus includes contemporary facilities such as town houses and upgraded student residence halls and apartments. New academic buildings include an education building, a science center with a planetarium, and an engineering building.

To further expand the university's facilities, the West Campus—a 600-acre plot of land located one mile from the main campus—is being developed. The West Campus is the site of the university's South Jersey Technology Park, whose first building is the Samuel H. Jones Innovation Center. The technology park is designed to provide competitively priced, first-class facilities for start-up and established companies to bring innovative technologies to the marketplace.

CAMPUS OF THE FUTURE

Years of careful planning by the Borough of Glassboro and Rowan University have led to the creation of an ambitious redevelopment plan that officials believe will propel both the university and borough forward for decades to come. The borough has started construction on Rowan Boulevard, a new roadway linking the east edge of the campus to the borough's historic downtown.

The plans call for the construction of a 100-bed hotel, an 884-bed student apartment complex, and a Barnes & Noble store that will serve as a coffee-house and bookstore. Spanning the area around these venues will be build-ings with retail shops on the ground floor and above.

Rowan Boulevard is designed to be a hub of retail activity and student housing. Envisioned as the center of a campus village, the boulevard will help the university achieve its goal of providing living quarters for all under-graduate students and to have these facilities placed within walking distance of many necessary services.

A REPUTATION FOR EXCELLENCE

Rowan University is noted for maintain-ing a student-to-faculty ratio of 15 to one and for having classes taught only by professors. Classes are held at the Glassboro and Camden campuses, as well as at community colleges and online via the Internet. The university is also known for its NCAA Division III athletics program, which is one of the most successful in the nation.

Rowan University is proud to have earned and upheld a reputation for excellence since its inception. For the eighth consecutive year, in 2008 Rowan University was ranked in the "First Tier" of the Northern Region by *U.S.News & World Report* in its annual "America's Best Colleges" report on the nation's best colleges and universities.

U.S.News & World Report also ranked Rowan University's College of Engineering 16th nationally among colleges of engineering in 2008; the college's department of chemical engineering ranked second nationally; the department of electrical and computer engineering ranked eighth;

the department of mechanical engi-neering ranked ninth; and the depart-ment of civil engineering ranked 11th.

Rowan University has been recognized by other national organizations that evaluate colleges. *Kiplinger's* named Rowan University one of the "Top 100 Best Values in Public Colleges," and the Princeton Review included Rowan University in the 2007 edition of *The Best Northeastern Colleges* and the guidebook *The Best 366 Colleges*.

Rowan University was selected for the Colleges of Distinction, a Web site and college guide profiling more than 240 of America's best bets in higher education, and was named one of "America's 100 Best College Buys" by Institutional Research & Evaluation, Inc.

Rowan University's commitment to the environment was recognized when the

U.S. Environmental Protection Agency (EPA) named it a "Top Green Power Purchaser" in its athletic conference. It was ranked number 18 among the top 40 "Green Partners."

The College of Business was included in Princeton Review's *Best 282 Business Schools, 2007* and Rowan University's undergraduate program in Entrepreneurship was named one of the "Best Schools for Entrepreneurs" in the nation by *Entrepreneur* magazine.

Rowan University offers an outstand-ing education at an exceptional value. It is able to compete with private colleges and to create opportunities that are not available on most state university campuses.

Additional information is available on Rowan University's Web site at www.rowan.edu.

Above left: Rowan University offers a residential commu-nity with housing that is guaranteed for freshmen and available for all full-time students. Above right: Construction has begun on Rowan Boulevard, a new roadway linking the east edge of campus to down-town. This roadway will be a hub of retail activity and student housing.

A New Jersey institution for over 150 years, this comprehensive metropolitan teaching university offers more than 50 undergraduate and more than 30 graduate degrees. Among its many advantages are excellence in academics, high-tech facilities, a vibrant athletics program, and a commitment to the success of every student.

- Construction of the New Jersey Center for Science, Technology and Mathematics Education, which includes six stories of technology-oriented classrooms, laboratories, and auditorium space.
- Two new undergraduate residence halls that will provide housing for an additional 848 students and include dining, recreational, and study space.
- The renovation of the Wilkins Performing Arts Complex.
- The expansion of the Nancy Thompson Library, which will house the new Institute for Human Rights and provide additional space for the library's holdings, gallery, and meeting space.
- The Nathan Weiss Graduate College, which will be moved to a showcase building in the East Campus complex and include high-tech classrooms and offices and a landmark speech pathology and communications clinic.
- Built in 1772, Liberty Hall Museum was acquired by Kean in 2007. This valuable historic resource now serves as a venue for classes, lectures, and special presentations

Above right: Kean University students study while enjoying a unique environment.

Whatever a student's goal—teaching, medicine, performing arts, or other career—Kean University offers a world-class education and support that can make such dreams come true. Dedicated to preparing students for rewarding careers, lifelong learning, and fulfilling lives, Kean offers a broad range of disciplines, the expertise of a diverse faculty and student population, and a student-centered learning environment and campus community.

Kean is the third-largest public university in New Jersey and the largest producer of teachers in the state. Founded in 1855, Kean moved to Union County in 1958, establishing a permanent home on a campus of more than 150 acres. Granted university status in 1997, Kean offers a world-class education at an affordable price. In addition to its curriculum, Kean offers an outstanding NCAA Division III athletics program with

national rankings in soccer, baseball, and women's basketball.

PREPARING FOR FUTURE GENERATIONS

Kean is transforming its campus into a dynamic community with state-of-the-art facilities designed to support academic excellence and cutting-edge research. The $150 million expansion and construction plan, most of which is projected for completion in 2009, includes:

and is available to every department within the university for creative learning opportunities.

A COMMITMENT TO EXCELLENCE

Kean is a comprehensive institution offering more than 50 undergraduate and more than 30 graduate degree programs to a population of about 14,000 students. The university's four undergraduate colleges are the College of Education, the College of Humanities and Social Sciences, the College of Natural Applied and Health Sciences, and the College of Business and Public Administration.

Excellent educational opportunities are also available at the School of Visual and Performing Arts (SVPA); the New Jersey Center for Science, Technology and Mathematics Education; and the Nathan Weiss Graduate College. Along

with its more than 30 master's and doctorate degree programs, the graduate college offers two professional diplomas, as well as 45 program options ranging from education to accounting to biotechnology and psychology. The university also offers a Doctor of Education (Ed.D.) in Urban Leadership and a Doctor of Psychology (Psy.D.) in School Psychology.

A GATEWAY TO MEDICAL SCHOOL

Undergraduates may pursue a dual bachelor's and master's program in occupational therapy, available through the Nathan Weiss Graduate College. In 2008, Kean was recognized for having one of the best graduate occupational therapy programs in the nation by *U.S.News & World Report*.

For students wishing to pursue a career in medicine, the university also

offers an opportunity through a partnership formed by Kean, Drexel University College of Medicine in Philadelphia, and Saint Peter's University Hospital in New Brunswick. Qualified undergraduates can participate in a 4 + 4 Bachelor of Science/Doctor of Medicine (B.S./M.D.) program at Kean and then transfer to Drexel to attend medical school after graduation.

SUPPORTING THE EDUCATIONAL PROCESS

The Center for Academic Success (CAS) is a cornerstone of Kean's commitment to providing opportunity. This center integrates all advisement, learning support, and career counseling in one building and is the only facility

of its kind in New Jersey. CAS provides a one-stop academic service center for students from the time they enter the university and offers a broad range of resources, assistance, support, and services.

The center's goal is to address the academic and informational needs of Kean students. Its basic offerings include career development and advancement services, college advisement, transfer admissions and evaluation services, a general education and learning assistance program, registration services for new students, orientation services, tutoring support services, and services for students with undecided or undeclared majors.

Above left: Kean's Center for Academic Success (CAS) provides students with a comfortable learning environment. Above right: Students enjoy the excitement of Kean's NCAA Division III athletics program.

Bergen Community College

This community college enrolls students from more than 140 countries into its associate's degree and certificate programs and prepares them for transfer to four-year universities or for immediate entry into a career. Since its inception, the college has offered open admissions, small classes, and affordable tuition.

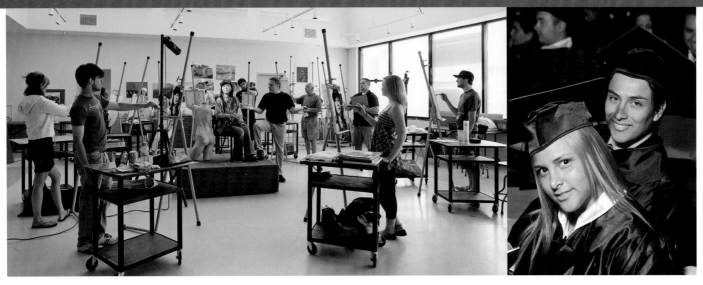

Above left: Bergen Community College's most technologically advanced building, West Hall, enables academic experiences not found anywhere else. Above right: Bergen has graduated more than 33,000 students and prepares them for transfer to four-year universities or for immediate entry into a career.

At the heart of New Jersey's most populous, diverse, and enriching county stands Bergen Community College. With more than 15,000 enrolled students working toward degrees in 76 wide-ranging academic programs on the Paramus and Hackensack campuses and at the Meadowlands site, the point is clear: Bergen is around the corner, but ahead of the curve.

The college's humble beginnings saw the parklike Paramus main campus rise from the land of a county-owned golf course. Its first classes were held in 1965, and its first degree was conferred in 1968. Since opening, the college has graduated over 33,000 students. These graduates have made use of the college's dozens of transfer agreements, which enable a seamless transition to many of the state's and region's finest four-year institutions.

Today, the pastoral Paramus campus houses four major instructional buildings including West Hall, a high-technology facility opened in 2007 and fitted with state-of-the-art equipment in media studios, computer graphics and animation laboratories, and classrooms dedicated to the arts. In addition to West Hall's advanced amenities, other instructional areas house the 300-seat Anna Maria Ciccone Theatre, a newly renovated library, and an observatory with two large reflecting telescopes.

The college's honors and study-abroad programs promote a Bergen student's rich knowledge and sense of identity, while dedicated, specialized professors and lecturers provide Bergen students with everlasting knowledge and mentorship. With 340 full-time faculty who hold master's degrees, doctorates, or both, the college maintains a roster of exceptionally qualified teachers. Bergen's accreditation by the Middle States Association of Colleges and Schools solidifies its standing as one of the top community colleges in the region.

The college supplies real-world experience to make a student successful whatever his or her area of interest. Whether it is the college's simulated operating room, dental hygiene clinic, full-service restaurant, 2,500-square-foot greenhouse, or Child Development Center, students learn their craft in the classroom—and in practice.

As the needs of today's student continue to change—and with time at a premium—the college has adapted to meet those needs through its award-winning technology. The college now offers 350 sections of online and

partially online (hybrid) courses. Armed with smart classrooms and interactive tools, the college will continue to stay ahead of the curve when it comes to technological innovation in academics.

Bergen's diverse clubs, programs, and activities draw thousands of participants, including the college's athletic teams which vie for conference championships each year. In 2007 the women's volleyball team notched its seventh conference and regional title. Even for non-Bergen students, the college remains a cultural center with hundreds of events open to the public, including awareness days, lectures, and forums. The college has hosted events featuring dozens of national, state, and local dignitaries.

Administrators believe students should feel comfortable and secure in their educational environment, and college officials remain intimately concerned with campus health and safety. In 2008, for example, the college's entire main campus became smoke-free; smoking is not permitted anywhere on the college's 167 acres. Meanwhile, acknowledging the importance of campus security, college officials arranged for Bergen County police officers to maintain a permanent, 24-hour presence on Bergen's grounds.

Another exciting development for the college is its expansion into the southern part of the county, which will begin in earnest with the construction of Bergen Community College at the Meadowlands site, scheduled for completion in 2012. The facility, which will

become part of the East Rutherford sports complex and the Xanadu shopping and entertainment complex, will provide workforce training and credit-bearing classes to students residing in southern Bergen County. Emerging public transportation makes Bergen's newest site more accessible and attractive than virtually any other in the region.

In addition to the main campus and Bergen Community College at the Meadowlands, Bergen maintains the Philip J. Ciarco Jr. Learning Center in

Hackensack, which offers educational and counseling services for adults who have not completed a formal high school education or those interested in English as a Second Language and tuition-funded college-level and noncredit courses. Through the Division of Continuing Education, the college offers job-training, career-enhancement, and career-enrichment programs. The division also carries programs in computers, construction, fashion and interior design, insurance and finance, health and fitness, and foreign languages.

"Our college is not just a place where students come to earn degrees," says Bergen Community College president G. Jeremiah Ryan, Ed.D. "Bergen is an institution where students learn the importance of civic engagement, service, and the depth of the world outside the academic walls. We foster well-rounded, involved men and women who become professional leaders. As we continue to spread our reach in Bergen County and regionally, we will bring our vision to more New Jersey residents than ever before."

Above left: Bergen Community College continues to flourish and expand. The institution has set a record enrollment of more than 15,000 students. Top right: The college's 167-acre main campus is located in Paramus. The institution also has campuses in Hackensack and Bergen Community College at the Meadowlands. Above right: Bergen's diverse clubs, programs, and activities draw thousands of participants, including the college's athletic teams which vie for conference championships each year.

This statewide system of teaching hospitals, health care facilities, and centers of excellence is devoted to improving the health and quality of life for New Jersey citizens through patient care, education, research, and community outreach.

The University of Medicine & Dentistry of New Jersey (UMDNJ) is the nation's largest freestanding public health sciences university and the backbone of New Jersey's health sciences system. Dedicated to the pursuit of excellence in education, research, and health care, UMDNJ has campuses in Camden, New Brunswick/Piscataway, Newark, Scotch Plains, and Stratford. University Hospital in Newark is a Level I trauma center, and University Behavioral HealthCare is a statewide mental health and addiction services network.

UMDNJ provides world-class education to practicing and future health care professionals and scientists: physicians, dentists, researchers, nurses, and allied and public health professionals. More than 5,600 students and more than 1,000 interns and residents are educated at eight schools: New Jersey Medical School, Robert Wood Johnson Medical School, School of Osteopathic Medicine, New Jersey Dental School, School of Health Related Professions, School of Nursing, Graduate School of Biomedical Sciences, and the School of Public Health.

UMDNJ is one of the nation's top research universities and serves as an incubator for new medical knowledge, resulting in better health care for everyone. Discoveries made in the school's laboratories are transformed into improved medications, new techniques for diagnosis and treatment, and advanced medical equipment. UMDNJ's mission—to improve the health of New Jersey—means its research programs focus on the state's most urgent health problems. Faculty members are recognized nationally for their research efforts in autism, tuberculosis,

cancer, environmental medicine, neurosciences, heart disease, genetics, and treatment for mental illness.

Determined to practice what it teaches, UMDNJ strives to provide all New Jerseyans with access to a full range of high-quality health care services. This includes state-of-the-art specialized treatment programs offered regionally on a referral basis and primary care and prevention programs for needy residents. Specialized services include treatments for trauma and liver disease, reproductive endocrinology, cancer treatment, neurology, neuro-surgery, and cardiology, as well as comprehensive primary care, dental treatment, and mental health services.

While improving the health of New Jersey's citizens, the University of Medicine & Dentistry of New Jersey also improves the health of the state's economy. With more than 15,000 workers and 5,600 students, the university is one of the state's largest employers and delivers an economic impact of up to $3 billion a year.

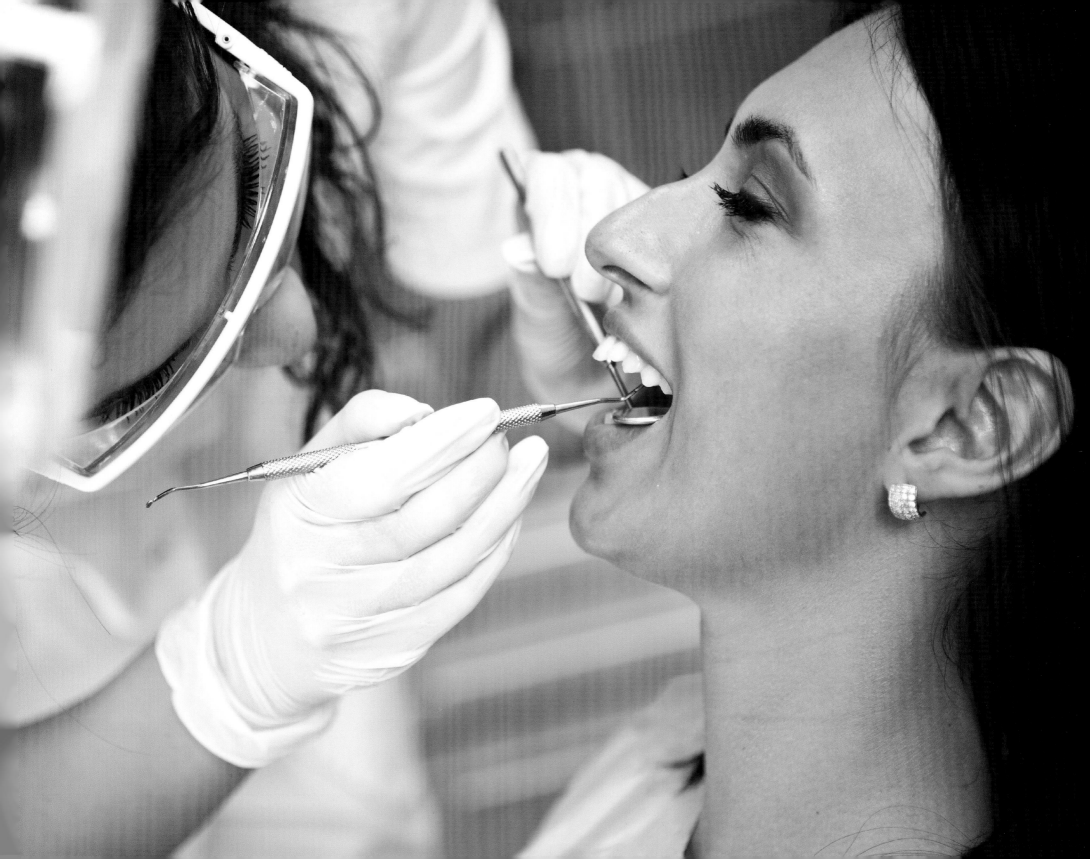

PROFILES OF COMPANIES AND ORGANIZATIONS

Energy

By meeting customers' expectations for exceptional quality and value in an environmentally responsible manner, New Jersey Resources is setting a standard for reliability as a leader in the competitive energy marketplace.

A Fortune 1000 company and a leader in the natural gas industry, New Jersey Resources (NYSE: NJR) provides reliable retail and wholesale energy services to customers in New Jersey and in other states from the Gulf Coast to New England and Canada.

NJR's principal subsidiary, New Jersey Natural Gas (NJNG), keeps homes warm and businesses running for nearly half a million customers in central and northern New Jersey. Other subsidiaries include NJR Energy Services, which provides wholesale energy services and management of natural gas storage assets, and NJR Home Services, which provides heating, air-conditioning, and water heating service, sales, and installations to residential and commercial customers.

At its core, NJR is about people helping people. And with the support of its more than 800 employees, NJR is committed to providing customers with safe, reliable service.

STRENGTH IN COMMUNITY
Well rooted in the neighborhoods it serves, NJR is dedicated to the success of its local communities. Partnerships with organizations that focus on economic growth, education, health, safety, and the environment are forged with a passionate belief that teamwork can make communities stronger.

NJR's community commitment is most evident in its Volunteers Inspiring Service in Our Neighborhoods (VISION) program, through which employees, retirees, and their families generously donate their time to support community projects,

lending a helping hand where it is needed most.

Additionally, NJR's Energy for Education program supports lifelong learning opportunities, especially in urban areas. The Libraries On-Line program provides technology upgrades and improved access to online resources for public libraries. Project Venture, a mentoring program, gives students a firsthand look at the business world while helping them to build skills to prepare for a future career.

This commitment strengthens neighborhoods, empowers children, and helps to enhance the quality of life in these communities and throughout the state.

CONSERVE TO PRESERVE®
Recognizing the nation's ever-increasing demand for energy, NJR took a bold step to help its customers Conserve to Preserve®. The umbrella for NJR's commitment to environmental stewardship, Conserve to Preserve effectively aligns the interests of NJR, its customers, and the state, helping all to achieve their goals.

Above right: New Jersey Resources' (NJR) long-standing tradition of service to the community goes far beyond customers' energy needs, focusing on education, wellness, and the environment.

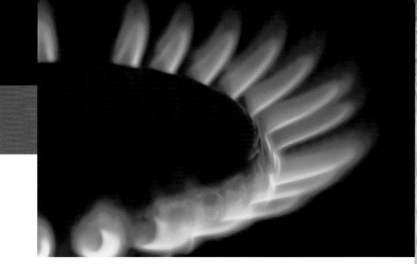

NJR was the first business to support the state's goal to reduce carbon emissions 20 percent by 2020. To help achieve this, NJR became the largest consumer of renewable energy in the state through the New Jersey Board of Public Utilities' CleanPower Choice Program by purchasing 100 percent of its electricity from renewable sources.

To help customers, NJR launched Planting for Our Future, through which customers can offset their own carbon footprint by purchasing trees that are planted in protected forests across the country. Through programs such as Ocean Fun Days, NJNG helps to raise awareness of New Jersey's precious environmental resources.

As a part of its conservation commitment, NJNG provides customers with tools they can use to make smarter

energy choices. E-Tips, a free e-mail service, notifies customers about energy-related rebates and programs. The Conserve to Preserve Dashboard, an online, interactive tool, enables customers to analyze and track their energy use and receive custom-tailored energy-saving tips.

These powerful tools are part of a forward-thinking approach to customer service for which NJNG was recognized with the prestigious J. D. Power and Associates Founder's Award, a discretionary award presented to individuals or organizations that demonstrate exemplary dedication, commitment, and performance in serving customers.

"New Jersey Natural Gas joins a select list of world-class, customer-focused organizations that set the standard for all businesses," said J. D. Power III in presenting the award.

"New Jersey Natural Gas has a companywide focus on customer satisfaction that extends from the boardroom to the field. This commitment to customers extends from billing to a focus on good community citizenship and the environment."

NJR was also recognized by the U.S. Environmental Protection Agency with its Environmental Quality Award for the company's education of the public and for its involvement in environmental action through Conserve to Preserve.

The hallmarks of NJR—safety, reliability, value, and service, combined with

sound business strategies and a talented team of employees—were designed to ensure that it will remain a leader in the competitive energy marketplace. NJR is well positioned to fulfill the expectations of all its stakeholders—customers, employees, investors, business partners, and the community—in an environmentally responsible way for generations to come.

Conserve to
Preserve®

www.njliving.com

Jersey Central Power & Light

Jersey Central Power & Light (JCP&L) powers the prosperity of New Jersey. Customer satisfaction, economic development, workforce development, safety, and community and employee involvement serve as top priorities for the electricity-delivery company.

Its focus includes operational excellence, exceptional customer service, and the safety of employees, customers, and the public.

Above right: Jersey Central Power & Light delivers on its promise to keep the "future bright with safe and reliable power."

RELIABILITY AND SERVICE

JCP&L employees are dedicated to providing customers with safe and reliable electricity service 24 hours a day, seven days a week. In doing so, the company promotes an accident-free workplace, offers comprehensive training programs, and gives employees the tools, information, and processes needed to support a safe working environment. In 2008 employees surpassed a record two million hours worked without a disabling accident.

Exceptional customer service and significant investments in the construction and maintenance of its infrastructure have helped JCP&L to reduce the frequency and duration of power outages and to minimize the impact of major weather-related events on the system. The company's investments include new modular substations, new and upgraded conductors, a new regional dispatching office, and new technology for adaptive relays. JCP&L also has enabled its workforce to be able to respond quickly and efficiently following storms to restore service to customers in a safe and timely manner.

JCP&L forestry experts are qualified and trained in maintaining the company's distribution and transmission systems. They work with state, county, municipal, and company representatives to educate customers about regulations and standards for trimming trees near power lines.

The company's efforts since 2004 have resulted in the average number of customers affected by outages decreasing by 20 percent, the average duration of customer service interruptions decreasing by 30 percent, and the average duration of tree-related outages decreasing by 33 percent.

AN EYE ON THE FUTURE

JCP&L has embarked on a number of programs and partnerships to help ensure a skilled and educated future workforce:

- The company's Power Systems Institute program at Raritan Valley Community College and Brookdale Community College is a two-year Associate of Applied Science degree program in electrical technology. With classroom learning and hands-on training, the program is designed to prepare the next generation of line workers and substation electricians.
- Georgian Court University provides an accredited MBA program for JCP&L employees, offering evening classes at JCP&L facilities. The program is also available via distance learning.
- JCP&L is a patron of the New Jersey State Chamber of Commerce Business Coalition for Educational Excellence, which offers programs designed to help high school students achieve at high levels, become productive citizens, and be well prepared to succeed in the workplace.

POWERING COMMUNITY INVOLVEMENT

JCP&L works hard to make New Jersey a great place in which to live, work, and do business. It supports community involvement, employee leadership in the community, and employee volunteer efforts, including:

- the Neighborhood Revitalization Tax Credit Program, enabling a $200,000 grant to Interfaith Neighbors, Inc. for revitalization in the West Side

neighborhood of Asbury Park,

- The Jersey Shore Partnership to help protect state beaches and promote tourism,
- New Jersey State Safety Council community education programs,
- Liberty Science Center programs for professional development for science teachers,
- the Urban League of Morris County's Community Outreach Programs, and
- Employee Volunteer Power Grants.

JCP&L employees collected the equivalent of 200,000 pounds of food for Harvest for Hunger and raised $300,000 for United Way. Since 2002 JCP&L employees and the FirstEnergy Foundation have contributed more than $6 million to community-based charitable organizations in the state.

GOOD BUSINESS SENSE

JCP&L believes in advancing opportunities to support the vitality of local businesses and neighborhoods and the economic development of the business community. Its activities include finding new sites for corporate relocation and expansion within New Jersey; offering the software program e-Synchronist, a

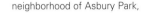

business expansion and retention program that can be used by counties to retain businesses; and creating the Export Now program, which makes export trade opportunities available to JCP&L customers.

Economic development initiatives by JCP&L were recognized during 2007 with the annual Economic Vitality Award from the Somerset Business Partnership; listing among *Site Selection* magazine's Top 10 Economic Development Groups; the Synchronist 2007 Award, bringing national recognition to the Morris County Economic Development Corporation's use of the program; and the Export Now Excellence Award at the Northeastern Economic Developers Association Annual Conference. During 2007 JCP&L participated in 20 economic development projects with state agencies that produced nearly

$308 million in capital investments and created or retained more than 3,280 jobs.

ILLUMINATING NEW JERSEY

JCP&L was incorporated in 1925 when 11 separate utility companies merged. Today JCP&L serves 1.1 million customers in 13 counties across northern and central New Jersey. JCP&L is a subsidiary of Akron, Ohio–based FirstEnergy, the fifth-largest investor-owned electric system in the nation, based on 4.5 million customers served within a 36,100-square-mile area of Ohio, Pennsylvania, and New Jersey. For the future, JCP&L remains committed to making customer service a top priority while helping to make New Jersey a better place to live through environmental protection, economic development, community involvement, and workforce training and education.

Above left and bottom left: Students at the JCP&L training facility in Phillipsburg, New Jersey, receive hands-on experience. In conjunction with colleges in the area, the company's Power Systems Institute serves to prepare a new generation of electrical workers. Above center: The employees of JCP&L are dedicated to providing customers with safe and reliable service 24 hours a day, seven days a week. Above right: Shown here is a dispatcher at one of the JCP&L regional dispatch offices.

The subsidiaries of this energy-services holding company provide safe, efficient natural gas to more than 332,000 residential, commercial, and industrial customers in 112 municipalities in southern New Jersey counties and also offers on-site energy production, commodity marketing, and residential and commercial services.

South Jersey Industries
Where we put all of our energy®

Above: South Jersey Industries subsidiaries serve utility customers and also provide numerous related energy-production services for commercial and industrial customers across the nation.

During changes in the energy environment over the past several years, the businesses of South Jersey Industries (SJI) have been in the forefront of the energy industry— seeking new opportunities to mitigate the impacts of price volatility for customers while also creating shareholder benefits. SJI, an energy-services holding company, is headquartered in Folsom, New Jersey.

SJI's regulated utility, South Jersey Gas (SJG), also based in Folsom, was among the first utilities in the nation to implement an innovative Conservation Incentive Program (CIP). Under the CIP, SJG strongly advocates energy efficiency for its customers. Those who consistently practice conservation and/or install energy-efficient equipment can reduce their utility usage and energy costs.

The CIP restructured SJG's rates so that profits are based on the number of customers served and the way the company controls operating costs, rather than on the amount of natural gas used. This change results in greater earnings stability, in addition to having a positive impact on the environment.

ENERGY SOLUTIONS

South Jersey Energy Solutions (SJES), SJI's energy-services company, develops innovative projects designed to promote energy efficiency, help sustain the environment, mitigate high energy prices, and increase profitability. SJES has three distinct business lines:

- On-site energy production—by Marina Energy—is a key factor in SJES's strategy. Marina Energy specializes in the design, construction, and operation of large-scale energy production facilities across the nation. It is well known for its thermal-energy facility that serves the Borgata Hotel Casino and Spa in Atlantic City, New Jersey, and in 2007 it entered into a 25-year contract to develop, design, own, and operate a district energy system and central energy center for Echelon Place resort in Las Vegas, Nevada. Marina Energy also develops landfill methane gas for electricity generation and cogeneration facilities.

- Commodity marketing—by South Jersey Resources Group—also is an important driver in the success of SJES. South Jersey Resources provides wholesale natural gas trading, sales, storage management, and other related services nationally. Also, South Jersey Energy offers services for the acquisition and transportation of natural gas and electricity for retail customers.

- Residential and commercial services —by South Jersey Energy Service Plus (SJESP)—is SJES's third key business segment. SJESP offers residential and commercial heating, ventilation, and air-conditioning (HVAC) installation and service, service contracts, and appliance repair. SJESP also provides plumbing services and installations of solar-electricity systems.

SJI provides additional information about all of its subsidiaries on its Web site (www.sjindustries.com).

COMMITMENT TO IMPROVING THE QUALITY OF LIFE

While pursuing its business goals, SJI retains a deep-rooted commitment to practicing good corporate citizenship. Adhering to the principle "people first and foremost," SJI is both a partner with the communities it serves and a catalyst for change that positively impacts the quality of life in New Jersey. SJI employees actively support the company's community relations efforts through volunteerism in more than 200 charitable and business organizations.

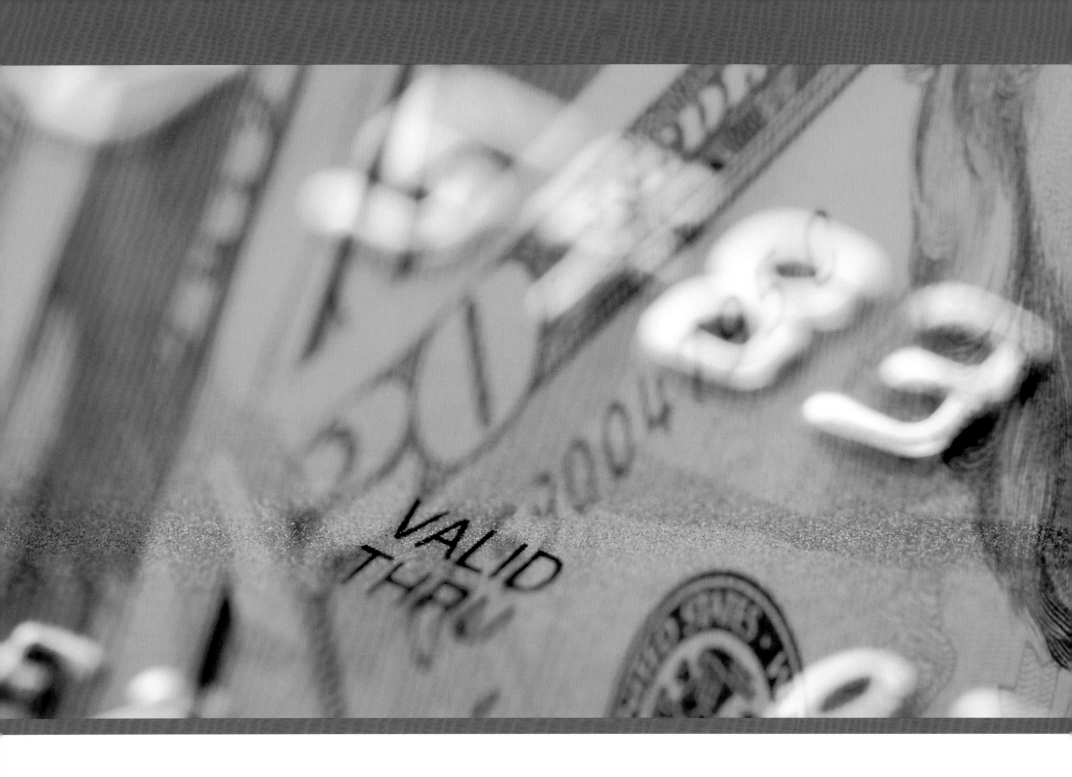

PROFILES OF COMPANIES AND ORGANIZATIONS

Financial and Insurance Services

This broadly diversified financial services company—with operations in the United States, Canada, and the United Kingdom—features more than 740 retail locations throughout New Jersey, New York, Connecticut, Louisiana, and Texas.

Capital One Financial Corporation is a diversified financial services company offering a broad array of credit, savings, and loan products to customers in the United States, Canada, and the United Kingdom. In the state of New Jersey, it established a sizeable and respected banking operation with its acquisition of North Fork Bank in December 2006. Capital One operates 78 branch locations covering New Jersey's northeast corridor. It does business in 10 counties, spanning the area from Bergen County in the north to Ocean County in the south.

CAPITAL ONE'S BANKING EFFORTS IN NEW JERSEY

Capital One, measured on deposits, is the ninth-largest commercial bank in the state. And New Jersey is one of the high-priority markets within the organization. Capital One's unique approach to providing fast, flexible service that is delivered by a team of highly trained local decision makers has been a major differentiating factor for this leading financial institution.

Within Capital One, local banking is considered an important component

Above right: Capital One Financial Corporation has 78 branch locations in New Jersey and conducts business in 10 counties.

of its long-term strategic vision. Relative to the overall lending industry, Capital One's banking franchise stands out as a local-scaled business.

GIVING BACK

At Capital One, the approach to community involvement mirrors the company's approach to business— a relentless focus on innovation, inquisitiveness, and collaboration. Creating opportunities by working

in collaboration with community partners and by sharing skills and expertise to help affect social change, Capital One focuses contributions and investments, business resources, and the service of associates on the goal of helping families build a solid foundation to provide for their children and to ensure future success.

Capital One and its associates have developed a broad range of national

and local partnerships to help provide programs and services to those who are most in need of support. These programs and services include:

- access to quality education;
- community revitalization through investments in affordable housing, workforce development, and economic development activities; and
- financial education programs to

give participants the confidence to make sound financial decisions for their economic future.

Community involvement by associates is the cornerstone of the Capital One philanthropic strategy. Each year, the company's associates volunteer tens of thousands of hours in support of Capital One–sponsored programs.

In 2007 Capital One began to collaborate with one of Newark's most promising nonprofit organizations—Newark Now. This citywide civic leadership organization provides Newark residents with the skills, tools, and support to transform their neighborhoods. Newark Now designs and implements neighborhood and citywide initiatives that increase safety, economic independence, and civic participation.

In addition, Capital One supports Newark Now's year-round Volunteer Income Tax Assistance (VITA) sites. At these sites, tax services have been provided for more than 850 Newarkers, resulting in more than $1 million in tax credit income for Newark citizens. And Newark Now's financial-literacy program reaches hundreds of Newarkers with Capital One's MoneyWi$e curriculum, which was developed in partnership with Consumer Action. Information is provided on the MoneyWi$e Web site (www.money-wise.org).

INVESTING IN NEW JERSEY

Capital One's strategic programs provide both partners and members of the New Jersey community with the resources they need in order to make a positive impact in neighborhoods throughout the region. These efforts include financing the construction and rehabilitation of affordable homes and rental housing for low- and moderate-income residents. Traditionally, Capital One has focused on economically distressed communities in northern New Jersey and provided capital to improve life in those communities whenever possible. Overall, Capital One invests millions in low-income housing tax credits, which results in hundreds of units of affordable housing throughout northern New Jersey.

Capital One's work, however, is not limited to investments in affordable housing. The company also realizes that small businesses are the cornerstones of local communities. In honor of this recognition, Capital One's $econd Look Small Business Referral Program helps small-business loan applicants who are not able to be funded in the traditional manner by referring those entrepreneurs to select, approved nonprofit lenders for a "second look." These alternative lenders are often able to help such aspiring entrepreneurs secure financing as well as provide the technical assistance to expand their businesses.

A cornerstone partner of Capital One's $econd Look program in New Jersey is the Union County Economic Development Corporation (UCEDC). The UCEDC is dedicated to stimulating economic growth and creating an environment for progress. Most of the small businesses funded through Capital One's $econd Look are owned by women, minorities, and immigrants.

Capital One Financial Corporation provides additional information about the company and its activities on its Web site (www.capitalone.com).

THE BEST DAYS OF CAPITAL ONE ARE STILL TO COME

Capital One is the product of innovative, strategic thinking that places a priority on creating real, long-term value for investors, customers, communities, and associates. Capital One remains dedicated to this priority and philosophy in its work and contributions throughout New Jersey and in the additional markets in which the company operates.

Above left: Lynn Pike is Banking President at Capital One.

Prudential Financial, Inc.

For more than 130 years, people have enjoyed financial security by opting to 'Own A Piece of The Rock.' Today, this company provides individual and institutional customers worldwide with a multitude of products and services—from life insurance to mutual funds and flexible retirement and annuity plans—for the 21st century.

Right: Prudential Financial, Inc., shown here from the plaza of its headquarters in Newark, New Jersey, has grown from its founding in 1875 to become one of the largest insurers in the nation.

Prudential Financial, Inc.—distinguished as one of the largest insurers in the nation—offers a comprehensive array of products and services, including life insurance, investment management, and retirement plans. With more than $600 billion in assets under management, Prudential is here to stay, like the Rock of Gibraltar that is its iconic symbol.

A HISTORIC PARTNER IN PROGRESS

John Dryden founded the Prudential Friendly Society in 1875 in Newark, New Jersey. This was the first company in the United States to make life insurance available to the working class, with premiums as low as three cents a week. By 1879 the company's sales expanded into New York and Philadelphia, and America's newly emerging middle class formed an expanded customer base.

In the 20th century, Prudential became a mutual company, owned by its policyholders, and growth continued. Even during the Great Depression, the company was committed to working families. The 1940s saw the expansion of the company's monetary assets. And over the next three decades, eight regional offices opened around the country.

In the 1980s, Prudential became the first major company to offer variable annuities. In 1984 it offered policies that let customers invest their policy cash values. The company continued to grow, including making acquisitions, so that by the beginning of the 1990s, its assets reached more than $100 billion.

MOVING FORWARD

In 2001 Prudential demutualized and became a public company (NYSE: PRU). Since then it has expanded through various transactions such as the acquisition of a large variable annuities company and a large retirement business. Today Prudential provides the opportunity to "Own A Piece of The Rock" through a multitude of products, from life insurance to individual retirement accounts (IRAs), mutual funds, and annuities. With divisions around the world, Prudential helps individual and institutional customers grow and protect their wealth.

Embracing advances in technology, Prudential offers many services online, including access to various accounts. The company provides a number of tools to assist customers in managing assets and avoiding costly mistakes. For example, its online calculators aid in estate planning and help determine life insurance needs, and its tutorials explain annuities, life insurance, and IRAs.

LEADERSHIP COUNTS

As one of the leading companies in the United States, Prudential strives to be one of the best for which to work. In recognition of this accomplishment, for 18 years *Working Mother* magazine has included Prudential in its annual "Working Mother 100 Best Companies" feature and has selected the company for its Hall of Fame for 15-plus years. In addition, from 2004 to 2007 Prudential earned a score of 100 percent on the Human Rights Campaign's Corporate Equality Index.

Prudential was also named by *Fortune* from 2004 to 2006 in the magazine's "50 Best Companies for Minorities"; by *Hispanic Magazine* from 2003 to 2006 in its "Hispanic Corporate 100," identifying companies that provide the most opportunities for Hispanics; and by *LATINA Style* magazine from 2004 to 2007 in "The Top 50 Companies for Latinas to Work for in the U.S.," in which Prudential was named one of the top 12 companies.

From 2003 to 2008 *CAREERS & the disABLED* magazine included Prudential in its "Top 50 Employers." Moreover, from 2003 to 2007 *Essence* magazine honored Prudential in its "25 Great Places to Work" for African-American women. Many other organizations have also honored Prudential for its commitment to diversity and equal opportunity in the workplace. For Prudential employees in the United States and in more than 30 other countries in Latin America, Europe, and Asia, diversity is valued.

A GREEN FOOTPRINT

In addition to being a financial asset locally, nationally, and globally, Prudential has been an architectural asset in Newark since the company's beginning to the present. In 1942 Prudential helped to shape the skyline of the city with its landmark 21-story Prudential Building on Washington Street. Next came Prudential Plaza on Broad Street, with 24 stories, built in 1960.

Fall 2007 marked the opening of the Prudential Center arena, nicknamed "The Rock" and home to the National Hockey League's New Jersey Devils and the Major Indoor Soccer League's New Jersey Ironmen. During the center's inaugural week, rock band Bon Jovi headlined. The city-owned, 18,000-seat sports and entertainment arena, for which Prudential is the naming rights sponsor, is also home to college basketball, concerts, family shows, and a variety of special events.

In the 21st century, Prudential combines architectural leadership with environmental consciousness. A signatory to the Business Roundtable's Climate RESOLVE (Responsible Environmental Steps, Opportunities to Lead by Voluntary Efforts) initiative, Prudential is steadfastly committed to reducing its environmental impact. Since 1998 its programs to decrease energy consumption have cut the company's net greenhouse-gas emissions by 33 percent. Prudential recycles, and

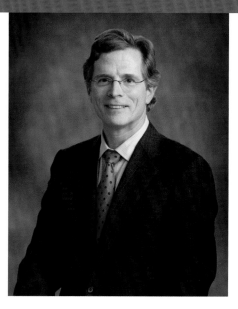

it uses recycled paper products. Its investments in alternative energy, especially wind power, help provide enough clean energy to power 450,000 homes in the United States.

From Prudential's worldwide network of offices to the company's presence in the media and online, people see the Prudential brand. Strong, steady, and rock solid have defined and will continue to define Prudential Financial, Inc. well into the 21st century.

Above: John Strangfeld is chairman and chief executive officer of Prudential Financial, Inc.

CIT Group Inc.

This leading global finance company has redefined capital to succeed in a changing global economy while it helps businesses and industries achieve their goals. With a century of experience, it provides innovative financial solutions designed to drive growth and create opportunities worldwide.

Credit is always in demand. That was the visionary thinking of Henry Ittleson when he founded CIT in St. Louis in 1908. Today, celebrating its centennial, CIT has more than one million customers in 30 industries worldwide. Credit is more in demand than ever.

With global headquarters in New York City and corporate headquarters in Livingston, New Jersey, the company is a leader in middle-market financing, serving companies with annual revenues between $25 million and $1 billion. A Fortune 500 company, CIT is in the S&P 500 Index. It provides financial solutions for more than half of the Fortune 1000 companies.

CAPITAL REDEFINED

The essence of the CIT brand is distilled in a new kind of equation:

financial capital + intellectual capital + relationship capital = infinite possibilities. As CEO Jeffrey M. Peek explains, "We know the middle market and know that our customers expect more than just traditional financing."

CIT has been the U.S. Small Business Administration's top lender for eight consecutive years. In 2007 its small-business lending unit provided more than $882 million in SBA 7(a) loans to 1,601 small businesses. It has been a leader in SBA loans to women and minorities.

In addition to small-business loans, CIT has corporate, trade, transportation, and vendor divisions. It provides asset-based loans as well as acquisition and expansion financing. Services include capital risk management, asset management, debt restructuring, and accounts receivable collection.

FROM STUDEBAKERS TO DREAMLINERS

Through the years, CIT has stayed true to its mission of helping businesses and individuals realize their potential and take advantage of opportunities.

The company helped invent the auto finance industry back in 1916 when it joined with Studebaker to provide financing to buyers at the automaker's 4,000 dealerships. At the time, it was the widest-reaching program of its kind, helping families to buy cars as well as allowing the automaker and its dealers to sell more cars.

Today, CIT Aerospace—a unit of CIT— is one of the world's largest aerospace financing and leasing companies. It owns or finances a fleet of more than 300 aircraft. In 2007 the aerospace unit ordered five of the fuel-efficient, next-generation Boeing 787 Dreamliner aircraft. The unit also has plans to lease six Airbus aircraft to Qatar Airways.

Other CIT units are making similarly impressive arrangements. These include financing for the production of 15 films by Dark Castle Entertainment, funding for a power-generating plant in San Diego, California, and assisting American Medical Systems Holdings in its acquisition of Laserscope.

The CIT Corporate Finance division helps middle-market companies with

lending, leasing, and debt restructuring. CIT Commercial Services provides factoring and credit protection to businesses that sell to retail channels, including international customers. The division has offices in Asia and Germany.

CIT Vendor Finance offers sales-aid financing for manufacturers and distributors, as well as lease financing directly to end users. Serving customers in more than 30 countries, the division has a Pan-European servicing platform and is the largest foreign-owned leasing company in China.

GIVING BACK

CIT works in partnership with many worthy organizations, including the Liberty Science Center in Jersey City, New Jersey, and Habitat for Humanity in Morris and Burlington counties, for which local employees volunteer their

time. CIT employees participate in the annual walk to support the mission of the American Heart Association of Morris and Essex County. In addition, CIT supports Citymeals-on-Wheels, the New York City Ballet, and the Mayor's Fund to Advance New York City. Global partners include The National Ballet of Canada, Community Health Charities, Shanghai Red Cross, Global Impact, and Earth Share.

Volunteerism is strongly encouraged at CIT, especially during Global Employee Volunteer Month, which takes place annually in May. Employees around the world volunteer their time in their local communities on behalf of CIT. In 2008 CIT had seven countries participate, making this program a truly global effort. For its 2008 centennial celebration, CIT is working in partnership with community organizations located in the

company's six international regions, allowing local employees to vote on the charities to be sponsored. Giving back is part of the CIT legacy.

Many years ago, Blanche Ittleson, wife of the company founder, helped start a

New York City–based social services agency that was originally named Big Sisters, and is now the Partnership with Children. In 2008 the agency gave CEO Peek its Ann Vanderbilt Award in recognition of his personal contribution to the organization over the years.

Above left: Among the wide variety of projects underwritten by CIT is film production. The company has served the movie industry since the introduction of the talkies in 1930. In the mid 1990s, CIT invested in Magic Cinemas LLC and is now financing 15 films by Dark Castle Entertainment. Above right: CIT's 300,000-square-foot global headquarters is located at 505 Fifth Avenue in New York City.

Wachovia Corporation

This leading financial services company provides a broad range of retail banking and brokerage, asset management, and corporate and investment banking products and services. It is also committed to creating a diverse and inclusive workplace and helping to protect the environment and build strong communities.

Above: Wachovia Corporation moved its regional headquarters for southern and central New Jersey to East Front Street in Trenton in 2006.

Wachovia Corporation's success and financial strength are based solidly on a century of banking expertise. In September 2001, First Union Corporation, which was founded in 1908 in Charlotte, North Carolina, and the former Wachovia Corporation, founded in 1879 in Winston, North Carolina, merged to form the new Wachovia Corporation. Today, from its corporate headquarters in Charlotte, North Carolina, Wachovia offers a wide range of products and services while striving to be the most trusted and admired financial services company.

Wachovia offers full-service retail and commercial banking in 21 states from Connecticut to Florida, including New Jersey, and west to Texas and California, and full-service retail brokerage nationwide. Other products and services offered nationwide include asset and wealth management; mortgage, student, and home equity lending; automobile dealer finance; credit and check card products; and trust services. Wachovia also offers investment banking products and services globally in selected sectors and financial expertise in treasury services, corporate and investment banking, and international banking for business customers. These products and services are offered through its key subsidiaries—Wachovia Bank, N.A.; Wachovia Mortgage, FSB; Wachovia Securities, LLC; and Wachovia Capital Markets, LLC.

Wachovia is the fourth-largest bank holding company in the United States based on assets, which were $809.9 billion as of first quarter 2008. It is also the third-largest full-service brokerage firm based on the number of financial advisors. Through 3,400 financial centers, 1,500 retail brokerage offices, 5,100 ATMs, toll-free and online banking, and 122,000 employees, Wachovia serves 15 million household and business customers. Committed to providing excellent financial products and services to its clientele, Wachovia is equally dedicated to its employees, the environment, and its communities.

AN ACCLAIMED EMPLOYER

Believing that diversity enhances the company, Wachovia works to create an inclusive workplace, one that values individuals and differences. To this end, its leadership chairs a Corporate Diversity Council that develops and maintains a plan for diversity and then monitors the company's progress.

Wachovia has been recognized as a top employer by numerous publications and organizations, including *Black Enterprise, BusinessWeek, DiversityInc, Essence, Latina Style, Military Spouse, PINK, Training,* and *Working Mother* magazines and by the National Association for the Advancement of Colored People (NAACP), the Human Rights Campaign, and the American Society for Training and Development.

ENVIRONMENTAL STEWARDSHIP

Wachovia is dedicated to protecting the environment locally and globally. It manages its internal operations in an environmentally responsible manner and encourages its clients to do the same, particularly with regard to forest protection and climate change.

Wachovia was a founding member of the Environmental Bankers Association and serves on its board of governors. It is a signatory to the United Nations Environment Programme's Finance Initiative, a partnership between the United Nations Environment Programme and the private financial sector. Within the company, Wachovia has set up an Environmental Stewardship Working Group, which develops environmental initiatives, and an Environmental Affairs group, which manages the company's day-to-day environmental-protection practices.

COMMUNITY INVOLVEMENT

Wachovia strives to improve its communities by improving education and strengthening neighborhoods. Toward achieving these objectives, company

efforts in 2006 included nearly $118 million in donations to charitable organizations and more than 710,000 hours of employee volunteer community services. In that same year, Wachovia contributed more than 121,000 books to classrooms and was named a Founding Corporate Partner by Teach For America. Wachovia also provided training through its financial literacy programs to more than 26,000 families and individuals. Additionally, the company invested or loaned $30 billion for the revitalization of neighborhoods.

As a responsible corporate citizen, Wachovia remains dedicated to serving its clientele with a variety of financial services while providing its employees with an inclusive workplace, responsibly caring for the environment, and building stronger communities.

Wachovia, the second-largest bank in New Jersey, has a long and proud

tradition in the Garden State. Under the leadership of Lucia DiNapoli Gibbons and Susanne Svizeny, regional presidents for northern and southern New Jersey respectively, and with approximately 325 financial centers and more than 6,000 employees, Wachovia provides unmatched customer service and community leadership to the people of the state. With its size and reach, as well as its broad array of products and customized services and solutions, Wachovia is a bank of choice for individuals and businesses alike.

Wachovia sets the standard for customer service, having been recognized for the seventh consecutive year as the number one bank in the country for customer satisfaction by the University of Michigan American Customer Satisfaction Index. Its commitment to best-in-class customer service is matched by its

commitment to the communities it serves. In 2006 Wachovia announced a five-year, $8 billion commitment to the economic and community development of New Jersey, which includes mortgage, consumer, and small-business loans, as well as multifamily housing, community development loans, and capital to low-income and moderate-income communities in the state.

Wachovia's commitment to its New Jersey customers and communities is to marshal its resources to turn dreams into reality by helping to build strong and vibrant communities, improving the quality of life, and making a positive difference where people live and work.

Above left: Wachovia is a strong supporter of its communities. Here, Wachovia executives present a sizeable donation for the Essex County Parks Foundation. Above right: Wachovia presents a Reading First program in cities across the country. Through this program, employee volunteers read books to children in elementary school classrooms and donate the books to classroom libraries over 20 weeks each year.

Columbia Bank

For more than 80 years, this bank has helped its customers live the American Dream of home and business ownership. With a growing network of 43 full-service branches, the bank provides savings, lending, investment, retirement, and wealth-management services to individuals, families, and businesses.

Above: With its hometown in Fair Lawn, Columbia Bank is the largest independent mutual bank headquartered in New Jersey. Also the nation's third-largest mutual financial institution, the bank creates relationships based on experience, financial stability, and quality service.

By today's banking standards, Columbia Bank is a unique entity. By choice, this bank, founded in 1927, serves only New Jersey customers; operates as an independent bank with no external stockholders; serves dual markets, both consumer and commercial; and, as an exemplary community bank, actively supports community-based initiatives within the towns it so proudly serves. Appropriately, this Garden State bank's popular service credo is "Count on Columbia!"

As the third-largest mutual financial institution in the nation and the largest mutual bank headquartered in New Jersey, Columbia features a unique operating structure that provides a distinct competitive advantage over chain and regional banks. Without external shareholders, Columbia does not have the business issues that can face traditional stock companies, and Columbia can more effectively control its future growth and profitability.

A TRUE COMMUNITY BANK

Managing more than $4.4 billion in assets, Columbia has earned a respected reputation as a reliable, professionally managed community bank, providing financial services to more than 100,000 households. Columbia's portfolio of personal banking products and services includes checking and savings accounts, investment services, all types of personal loans, mortgages, retirement programs, and wealth-management services.

When it comes to New Jersey home ownership, Columbia regularly underwrites residential first and second mortgages, with a wide choice of fixed-rate and adjustable-rate terms. Jumbo mortgages, exclusively for larger home loans, are also available. For homeowners, Columbia offers home equity loans, which are equity-based lines of credit that can be used for expenditures such as home remodeling projects, vacations, purchases, and college tuition payments.

While some competitors have been driven out of business by the much-publicized national subprime mortgage crisis, Columbia has actually increased its mortgage portfolio due to its strict underwriting standards, which do not permit such lending practices. As a result, the image of Columbia in the marketplace as an experienced and reliable mortgage lender remains a model for the industry.

At Columbia, convenience and choice are important parts of the bank's day-to-day operation. Today Columbia's customers have the option of banking in person, by drive-up teller, by 24-hour ATM, by telephone, and online around the clock by personal computer. Most branches feature convenient lobby service hours and extended drive-up teller service hours, with selected locations open for limited banking on Sunday. Advanced banking technology also permits customers to perform many routine

transactions electronically, including paying bills without leaving the comfort of home or office.

NEW JERSEY'S BUSINESS BANK

Columbia, also renowned as "The Business Bank of New Jersey," serves a varied client base of commercial customers, including residential and commercial developers, manufacturers, auto dealerships, retailers and wholesalers, nonprofit organizations, and municipalities. In addition, Columbia regularly provides banking services custom-designed for professional specialties, including certified public accountants (CPAs), attorneys, architects, medical providers, and real estate brokers.

Columbia's commercial lending takes place on four specialized levels: Construction Lending, Permanent Commercial Mortgages, Working Capital and Term Financing, and Small Business Lending. Columbia's lending activity is also supported with all of the financial tools necessary to operate and expand a business, including business checking and money market accounts, investment and retirement programs, payroll processing, Online Cash Management, and Online Business Banking with bill-pay options.

A PARTNER IN PROGRESS

In addition to its banking distinctions, Columbia is also distinguished for its strong commitment to community support. This philanthropic support takes many forms, including donations, grants, event sponsorships, program underwriting, and local scholarship awards. In addition, many Columbia executives regularly serve on the boards of local hospitals and charities, chambers of commerce, rotary clubs, and service organizations that promote home ownership, business prosperity, and civic pride.

The bank has also established the Columbia Bank Foundation, which actively seeks civic and charitable grant opportunities that champion affordable housing, community investment, health and human services, and financial literacy. For example, Columbia Bank Foundation grants have provided funding for many statewide Habitat for Humanity affordable-housing projects, the purchase of new emergency vehicles for two local Volunteer Ambulance Corps, and the refurbishing of a fire-damaged shelter for the homeless.

Sustained growth and profitability will certainly remain part of Columbia's future plans. Motivated by its steadfast commitment to quality service, independent ownership, and ongoing community support, and backed by its strong balance sheet and strict underwriting standards, which do not permit subprime lending practices, Columbia Bank will continue to set the pace for the future of both community and business banking throughout the Garden State.

Above left: To help Garden State residents live the American Dream, Columbia Bank provides a variety of home mortgage financing products. This bank is not a subprime lender. Above center: Columbia provides a full range of banking services, including 24-hour drive-up ATMs. Above right: Columbia believes that encouraging neighborhood pride is a catalyst for change. Each year, Columbia's volunteer crews perform community service projects, such as painting the exterior of a senior citizen's home in a lower-income neighborhood.

Delta Dental of New Jersey, Inc.

Delta Dental of New Jersey, Inc. is New Jersey's leading dental benefits carrier, providing or administering coverage to more than one million people through contracts with employers in New Jersey and Connecticut.

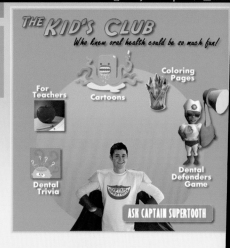

Since 1969 Delta Dental of New Jersey, Inc. has been dedicated to promoting oral health to the greatest number of people by providing accessible dental benefit programs of the highest quality, service, and value. Located in Parsippany, Delta Dental of New Jersey provides group dental benefits to its more than one million members throughout New Jersey and Connecticut, via group contacts. In Connecticut, Delta Dental Insurance Company writes dental coverage on an insured basis. Delta Dental of New Jersey administers self-funded dental benefit programs.

Delta Dental of New Jersey employs more than 300 New Jersey residents and is part of the national Delta Dental system. This national system allows Delta Dental to offer seamless dental benefits administration for groups throughout the country and access to the largest network of credentialed dentists in the nation.

PROVIDING THE RIGHT BENEFITS FOR MEMBERS

Delta Dental of New Jersey offers a full line of fee-for-service, PPO, and HMO programs. Its range of available dental plans makes it easy for companies and groups with more than 10 members to offer dental benefits. Additionally, Delta Dental of New Jersey offers a dental access plan for New Jersey residents who do not have dental insurance. Called Delta Dental Patient Direct, the plan is a dental membership program that offers access to a network of dentists who have agreed to provide dental care at fees no higher than the Delta Dental Patient Direct fee schedule.

CUSTOMER SATISFACTION

Affirming Delta Dental's commitment to good oral health, more than one in five clients have been with Delta Dental of New Jersey for 20 consecutive years— some since as early as 1973. In surveys of benefits managers in New Jersey and Connecticut, nearly 99 percent said they would recommend Delta Dental to other benefits administrators.

CONNECTING THROUGH TECHNOLOGY

The Delta Dental of New Jersey Web site (www.deltadentalnj.com) offers a variety of ways for members and the public to enhance their oral health awareness and care. A click on Oral Health links visitors to a vast amount of information on dental topics, specialties, and terms regarding oral health and wellness. Through the Members section, members can locate a dentist in the area, check their benefits and claims, take a risk-assessment quiz, and print a copy of their identification card. Additionally, the Kid's Club page provides educational information,

ORAL CANCER awareness VIDEO

trivia challenges, and the Dental Defenders game, an interactive mission that allows children to learn proper oral health habits.

COMMUNITY OUTREACH

Through its philanthropic efforts, the company's Delta Dental of New Jersey Foundation brings awareness and resources to organizations and communities throughout New Jersey and Connecticut. In 2008 the foundation granted more than $700,000—its largest annual contribution as of that time—to organizations providing access to care to the underserved and to children, as well as to academic institutions that prepare dentists, dental hygienists, and dental assistants for their professions.

Through various community- and school-based programs, the foundation works to instill good oral health habits for all. To expand upon existing oral health education in New Jersey, the foundation has created "Captain Supertooth," a costumed superhero who teaches children in kindergarten and 1st and 2nd grade about proper oral health habits. Using a giant red toothbrush, Captain Supertooth educates children about brushing, flossing, a balanced diet, and visiting the dentist. This 25-minute program is free of charge.

According to the American Dental Association, instances of tooth decay among children from low- and modest-income households are increasing. In 2007 the foundation developed an opportunity for New Jersey's Abbott school districts to initiate an Oral Health Education Program in their third-grade classes. The goal of the program, by awarding grants annually, is to help develop sustainable oral health education curricula throughout the state.

In an effort to continue oral health education through adulthood and to raise awareness of what people can do to safeguard their own health, the foundation began working in partnership with members of the Oral Cancer Consortium in 2008 for a comprehensive Oral Cancer Awareness Campaign. To educate the public about early detection, Delta Dental created a 60-second public service announcement that can be viewed on the Delta Dental of New Jersey Web site.

DELTA DENTAL VOLUNTEERISM

In addition to the outreach provided by these programs, Delta Dental of New Jersey remains a Premier Sponsor of Special Olympics New Jersey through the annual Delta Dental Classic, a golf outing that has been in existence since 1991 and has raised more than $650,000 to help these athletes. Delta Dental of New Jersey also sponsors the Winter Games Ice Show. The company also encourages community service through its associate volunteer program, allowing employees two paid days off per year for volunteer activities. With more than 40 employees participating—lending their time to organizations such as Habitat for Humanity, Boy Scouts of New Jersey, and Family Services of Morris County—this program allows Delta Dental of New Jersey to continue its enthusiastic commitment to the community.

At Delta Dental of New Jersey, there are many ways to gauge accomplishments—from business performance and customer commitment to ongoing efforts to improve oral health through dental access and education. Delta Dental of New Jersey continues to remain true to its mission—making sure that everyone has the smile they deserve.

Above left: Delta Dental of New Jersey has created a 60-second public service announcement, which can be viewed on the company's Web site, to promote awareness of the importance of oral cancer screenings. Above right: Delta Dental of New Jersey employee volunteers take part in a Dentistry Merit Badge Day held for the Boy Scouts of New Jersey by the Delta Dental Foundation.

As the oldest savings bank in New Jersey, this financial institution has established a long record of reliable and trustworthy service to its customers. Serving northern and central New Jersey, it strives to be a leader in the financial industry.

Headquartered in Jersey City, The Provident Bank serves its customers through 84 branch offices across 10 counties throughout northern and central New Jersey. At the end of 2007, its total deposits were $4.2 billion. It is dedicated to meeting the business and personal banking needs of its clients and providing the products and services needed to manage their financial resources.

A HISTORY OF STRENGTH

Chartered in 1839—one year after Jersey City, its birthplace, was incorporated—Provident is the oldest savings bank in New Jersey. It was opened as The Provident Institution for Savings in Jersey City in 1843 to serve the financial needs of the many immigrants who settled there. As a mutual savings bank, it was organized for the benefit of its depositors, who received most of the bank's earnings as interest on their savings. Its first president—Dudley S. Gregory, who was also Jersey City's first mayor—saw the bank's assets grow from just $250 to $3.5 million during his 31-year tenure.

In 1939, Provident celebrated its 100th anniversary and 86 years of uninterrupted dividends. Surviving multiple panics in the 19th century and the Great Depression in the 20th century proved its reliability and strength. In 1970 it changed its name for the first time since its founding, to The Provident Savings Bank. The bank continued to grow, expanding first beyond Jersey City and then Hudson County during the 1970s.

Provident merged with Bloomfield Savings in 1983, bringing the bank's total assets to more than $1 billion and expanding the bank's services to include the full range of trust services. Shortly after this significant merger, Provident became the first billion-dollar-plus savings bank to join the First Nationwide Network, an organization of independent, locally owned and managed financial institutions, allowing Provident to successfully compete with industry giants. In 1987, Provident moved into its current headquarters, a Jersey City landmark crowned with a 30-foot clock tower.

In 2003, Provident converted from a mutual savings bank to a stock savings bank. This conversion increased the flexibility of the bank as it continued to expand. In 2004 Provident merged with First Savings Bank, and in 2007 it merged with First Morris Bank & Trust.

TRUSTWORTHY LEADERSHIP

Provident Chairman and CEO Paul M. Pantozzi began working for Provident more than 45 years ago as a teller. He was named president in 1989 and CEO in 1993, and in 1998 he was elected chairman. He has guided the bank through many developments and changes, including its transformation into a public company. Pantozzi also serves as chairman and CEO of Provident's holding company, Provident Financial Services, Inc., and as president of the bank's charitable organization, The Provident Bank Foundation.

Pantozzi believes in continuing education for banking professionals and strives to develop and support the financial industry. To this end, he has served on the boards of the

New Jersey League of Community Bankers, America's Community Bankers (ACB), and the ACB's National School Advisory Council.

An active member of his community and of New Jersey, his native state, Pantozzi has also served as a board member for the Hudson County Chamber of Commerce, the Canterbury Health Board, Goodwill Industries of Greater New York and Northern New Jersey, the Salvation Army Advisory Board, and the Saint Ann's Home Board in Jersey City. Additionally, he helped to found the Hudson County affiliate of Habitat for Humanity.

In 2007 the New Jersey Business Hall of Fame (NJBHOF) honored Pantozzi by naming him to its inaugural class of inductees. The NJBHOF recognizes individuals who stand out as role models in business by their quality of leadership, community involvement, and high ethical standards.

GIVING BACK

Provident has established a priority of supporting its communities throughout its long history. In 2003 it created and funded The Provident Bank Foundation to improve the quality of life in the communities it serves, benefiting a wide range of causes including education, the arts, health and wellness, recreation, and

social and civic services. Over five years, the foundation has given more than $11 million to more than 1,500 nonprofit organizations, including the American Cancer Society in Elizabeth; Algonquin Arts, an organization dedicated to providing cultural enrichment; New Jersey City University; and 180 Turning Lives Around, an organization committed to ending domestic violence and sexual

assault. Provident is closely connected to its communities. "Supporting our communities has always been one of The Provident Bank's priorities during our 169-year history," Pantozzi says. The bank remains committed to providing excellent financial products and services that meet the needs of its clients while improving the quality of life in New Jersey.

Above left: Chairman and CEO Paul M. Pantozzi guides Provident.
Above right: In 1987 Provident headquarters moved to 830 Bergen Avenue, a Jersey City historic landmark with a four-sided clock tower atop the building.

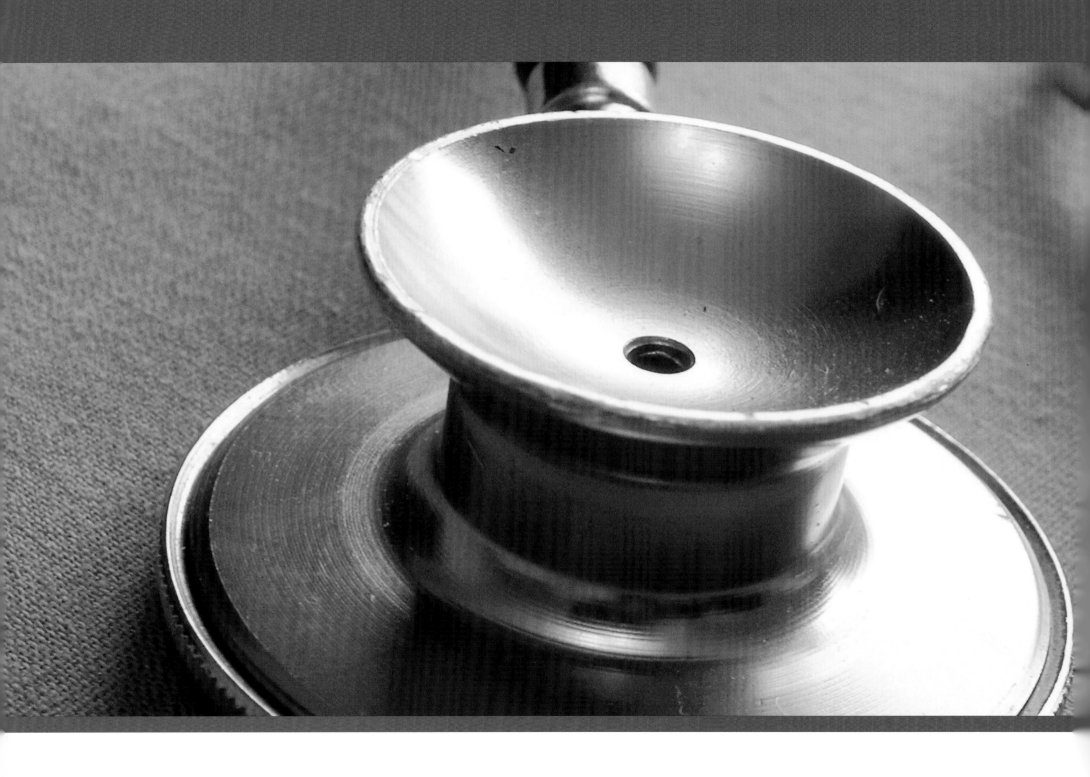

PROFILES OF COMPANIES AND ORGANIZATIONS

Health Care and Medical Services & Facilities

With 75 years of 'Making Healthcare Work,' the company has grown to become New Jersey's leading health care insurer, committed to offering innovative medical, dental, and prescription insurance plans. It provides programs for health care and disease management as well as for preventive care to serve its three million–plus members.

Right: Corporate headquarters for Horizon Blue Cross Blue Shield of New Jersey (Horizon BCBSNJ) is located at Three Penn Plaza East in Newark, New Jersey.

Horizon Blue Cross Blue Shield of New Jersey (Horizon BCBSNJ) has a long and storied history dating back to the year 1932. In that year, Associated Hospitals of Essex County was incorporated as the first multihospital prepaid health plan. It would become one of the first Blue Cross plans in the nation.

Starting from a small office in Newark, the company enrolled 1,000 subscribers in its health plan in its first month of operations and enrolled 5,000 people by year-end 1933. For a $10 annual premium, approximately three cents per day, initial subscribers received 21 days of prepaid hospital coverage.

In 1942 prepayment plans for physician services began, with the incorporation of Blue Shield of New Jersey. The two companies operated separately until 1986 when they merged to become Blue Cross and Blue Shield of New Jersey, Inc. The company changed its name to Horizon Blue Cross Blue Shield of New Jersey in 1998.

From the simple idea of offering people prepaid hospital coverage at a few Essex County hospitals,

Horizon BCBSNJ now offers its members access to a network of 68 hospitals and access to over 27,000 physicians across the state. The company offers health and dental insurance as well as Medicare for individuals and for employers from small to large. Through its fully owned affiliate Horizon NJ Health, the company also serves more than 316,000 publicly insured Medicaid members in all 21 New Jersey counties.

Today Horizon BCBSNJ is the oldest and largest health insurer in New Jersey, serving more than 3.5 million members. It is one of 39 independent companies and licensees of the Blue Cross Blue Shield Association (BCBSA). Through BCBSA, Horizon BCBSNJ members also have access to more than 600,000 physicians and over 6,000 hospitals nationwide.

Horizon BCBSNJ's history echoes the history of health insurance. As the initiator of one of the first Blue Cross plans, the company is a trusted name in health care insurance. Whether being among the first health insurers in the state to offer Medicare or

creating the first health maintenance organization (HMO) in 1973, Horizon BCBSNJ has always been in the forefront of change in health care.

In 2007 Horizon BCBSNJ marked its 75th anniversary. Ever since its inception, the company and its employees have been a part of the fabric of New Jersey.

The company has a long history of supporting charitable organizations and communities throughout the state. In January 2004, Horizon BCBSNJ formalized its charitable giving by creating The Horizon Foundation for New Jersey. Its mission is to promote health, well-being, and quality of life for all New Jersey residents.

As of 2007 The Horizon Foundation for New Jersey had already granted more than $11 million in support of more than 300 charitable organizations across New Jersey. In December 2006 it announced its largest grant award, a multiyear $5 million initiative to support health centers across New Jersey. These health centers provide primary health care to thousands of uninsured and underserved populations.

Horizon BCBSNJ continues to play a leading role in providing innovative products and services to meet the needs of employers and individuals throughout New Jersey. The company is focused on improving the health care experience for everyone it serves.

Today, Horizon BCBSNJ is also working with employers and individuals to keep health care affordable. The company considers that since health insurance premiums are just a reflection of the underlying cost of health care, the best way to hold the line on rising health care costs is to keep people healthy. It is developing a number of products and services to stem health care costs.

Horizon BCBSNJ has paid for 90 percent of the cost of state-of-the-art technology at a number of its network hospitals in order to reduce the rates of hospital-acquired infections. Participating hospitals have seen average infection rates reduced by 11 percent. It is a program that is keeping hospital patients safer and reducing hospital costs.

Another patient safety issue for which Horizon BCBSNJ is a national leader is in promoting electronic-prescribing technology. The company has purchased the hardware and software for physicians' offices to help them electronically prescribe medications, in order to reduce errors and the costs associated with adverse drug interactions.

Horizon BCBSNJ offers a number of Health and Wellness programs designed to proactively educate members who have chronic illnesses, in order to help them obtain the most appropriate care to improve their quality of life. For members who are healthy, other programs are available to help them remain healthy through exercise and diet.

In 2007 Horizon BCBSNJ launched My Health Manager, a powerful Internet-based tool developed with health-information services provider WebMD to help members take control of their own health care. Horizon BCBSNJ members use a health-assessment test to determine how their health is aligned with people of their own age. They also can receive trusted information about symptoms, diseases, and medications. My Health Manager allows members to create a personal health record and provides a single repository of health information that is safe, secure, and private.

Horizon BCBSNJ believes that the future of health care lies in empowering individuals to take better control of their health. For 75 years the company has been a trusted leader in health care. It will continue to focus on its mission, "Making Healthcare Work," by developing innovative ways to help the people of New Jersey obtain access to quality health care.

Above left: The longtime building of Horizon BCBSNJ overlooking Washington Park figures prominently in the Newark skyline, shown here in 2002. Above right: Horizon BCBSNJ is the official health care sponsor of the New Jersey Performing Arts Center (NJPAC) in Newark, which was opened in 1997. Shown here during construction of the complex is, at left, Lawrence P. Goldman, president of NJPAC, and William J. Marino, president and CEO of Horizon BCBSNJ.

Committed to excellence in overall quality, safety, and patient satisfaction, this integrated health care delivery system is a recognized leader nationally and regionally and offers a wide range of programs that represent the most advanced treatment and technology.

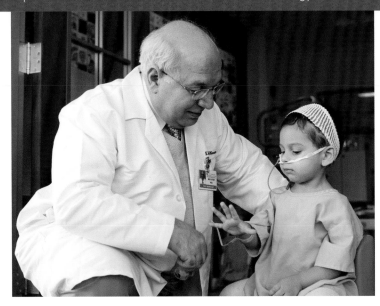

Right: E. Hani Mansour, M.D., is medical director of the Burn Center at Saint Barnabas Medical Center in Livingston, one of Saint Barnabas Health Care System's many affiliates. Dr. Mansour is shown here with a young patient who is one of nearly 30,000 patients treated at the Burn Center since 1977.

The Saint Barnabas Health Care System (SBHCS) is the largest integrated health care delivery system in New Jersey and one of the largest in the country. With six acute care hospitals, eight nursing and rehabilitation centers, an assisted-living residence, ambulatory care facilities, geriatric centers, a free-standing inpatient psychiatric hospital, a statewide behavioral health network, and home care and hospice programs, SBHCS, headquartered in West Orange, New Jersey, has offered patients a complete continuum of health care since 1996.

SBHCS hospitals have been recognized by some of the leading national sources of health care information. In 2007 three hospitals were named among the 100 Top Hospitals Performance Improvement Leaders by Thomson, and Solucient recognized the outstanding outcomes in adult cardiac care at the Saint Barnabas Heart Center at Newark Beth Israel Medical Center, naming it to its 2006 list of the nation's 100 top hospitals for cardiovascular performance and in the top 20 nationally for teaching hospitals with cardiovascular residencies. All SBHCS hospitals have received multiple HealthGrades awards in the areas of clinical excellence, patient safety, and specialty care excellence.

SBHCS provides treatment and services for more than two million patients each year: 225,000 inpatients and same-day surgery patients, 450,000 emergency department patients, and over 1.5 million outpatients annually. More than 200,000 children receive treatment and 17,500 babies enter the world at a Saint Barnabas System hospital every year. Delivering these services are 20,000 employees and 4,750 physicians, making the Saint Barnabas System the second-largest private employer in the state with one-fourth of New Jersey's practicing physicians. Throughout the system, dedicated physicians, nurses, and other health professionals are committed to providing the highest quality of patient care and health education, with strong attention to patient satisfaction, all delivered cost-effectively to the community and the region.

Graduate Medical Education programs are sponsored by the three teaching hospitals for 443 residents and fellows. The system hosts medical students from the University of Medicine & Dentistry of New Jersey–New Jersey Medical School in Newark and Drexel University College of Medicine in Philadelphia, Pennsylvania; SBHCS is also a major clinical campus for New York College of Osteopathic Medicine and is affiliated with the St. George's University School of Medicine in Grenada.

The Saint Barnabas Health Care System Research Institute was developed in 2006 to unite and expand the breadth of research and scholarly endeavors across the system. The Research Institute also focuses on public health issues in the communities served by SBHCS.

SBHCS includes Clara Maass Medical Center in Belleville, Community Medical Center in Toms River, Kimball Medical Center in Lakewood, Monmouth Medical Center in Long Branch, Newark Beth Israel Medical Center in Newark, Saint Barnabas

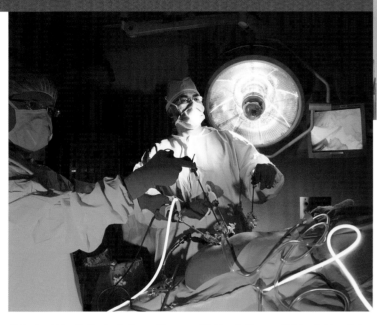

Behavioral Health Center in Toms River, and Saint Barnabas Medical Center in Livingston.

SBHCS also includes the Saint Barnabas Outpatient Centers with the Ambulatory Care Center in Livingston and the Saint Barnabas Breast and Women's Imaging Center in Bedminster; the Cranmer Ambulatory Surgery Center at Monmouth Medical Center; Clara Maass Medical Center, West Hudson Division in Kearny; Children's Hospital of New Jersey at Newark Beth Israel Medical Center; the Children's Hospital at Monmouth Medical Center; the Women's and Children's Specialty Center in Lakewood; Saint Barnabas Nursing and Rehabilitation Centers; and Saint Barnabas Hospice and Palliative Care Center.

SBHCS provides full information on its Web site (www.saintbarnabas.com).

Among SBHCS's nationally recognized services and facilities are:

- New Jersey's only certified burn-treatment facility
- world-class cardiac surgery services for adults and pediatrics
- heart transplant program ranked in the top 10 by volume in the United States
- one of the nation's finest and most comprehensive cardiovascular programs
- New Jersey's only lung transplant program
- six certified chest pain centers
- three Joint Commission–accredited Primary Stroke Centers; one state-accredited Comprehensive Stroke Center; and three state-accredited Primary Stroke Centers
- the most comprehensive robotic surgery service in the region, including cardiothoracic surgery, general surgery, adult and pediatric urology, gynecology, and gynecologic oncology
- two kidney transplant centers, which are among the most active of 240 programs in the United States
- a renowned neurology and neurosurgery program
- a widely recognized reproductive medicine and science program
- nationally recognized geriatric services
- comprehensive cancer services providing patients with state-of-the-art technology and cutting-edge treatment options through participation in clinical research trials
- three Valerie Fund Children's Centers for Cancer and Blood Disorders
- renowned women's and children's services, with three highest level neonatal intensive care units
- New Jersey's only neonatal ECMO program for life support.

Above right: Craig R. Saunders, M.D., is chairman of Cardiothoracic Surgery for the Saint Barnabas Health Care System. Left: Frank Borao, M.D., is the surgical director of the Center for Minimally Invasive Surgery at Monmouth Medical Center in Long Branch, an affiliate of the Saint Barnabas Health Care System.

Raritan Bay Medical Center

This nonprofit medical center provides the residents of central New Jersey with excellence in service and high quality, compassionate health care, including medical and surgical, maternity, pediatric, general, and critical care as well as emergency, interventional cardiology, and physical rehabilitation services.

Above left: One of the two campuses of Raritan Bay Medical Center (RBMC) is located in Perth Amboy, New Jersey. Above right: A surgical procedure is performed in an operating room at RBMC's Perth Amboy campus.

Raritan Bay Medical Center (RBMC) is a leading acute care community hospital with campuses in Perth Amboy and Old Bridge that has provided state-of-the-art, compassionate health care to the community for more than 100 years. In the process, RBMC has achieved significant professional recognition in the areas of patient safety and satisfaction, clinical outcomes, efficiency, and administrative excellence.

RBMC is licensed for a total of 501 beds, with 388 beds at the Perth Amboy facility and 113 beds at the Old Bridge

facility. The hospital provides medical and surgical, maternity, pediatric, general, and critical care as well as emergency, interventional cardiology, physical rehabilitation, and adult behavioral health services. As part of its mission to offer excellent service and quality health care, RBMC provides a clinically diverse medical staff, advanced medical technologies, ongoing development of new services, continuing education for physicians and staff, and a level of nursing care that has earned the American Nurses Credentialing Center's Magnet Award for Nursing Excellence.

RBMC is a major clinical affiliate of the University of Medicine & Dentistry of New Jersey–Robert Wood Johnson Medical School, through which it offers residency programs in obstetrics, gynecology, pediatrics, and internal medicine. RBMC is also an affiliate of

the Cancer Institute of New Jersey, enabling patients to participate in the most advanced treatment protocols and gain access to ongoing research and cancer treatment. RBMC's Old Bridge campus is home to a positron emission tomography (PET) and computed

tomography (CT) scanner, an important diagnostic tool in cancer treatment. In addition, the hospital offers certificate, master's, and Ph.D. programs in Medical Humanities in collaboration with Drew University in Madison, New Jersey.

RBMC also works in partnership with state medical organizations and universities, which has led to improvements in health care for New Jersey residents. For example, in the area of intensive care RBMC is collaborating with the New Jersey Hospital Association to outline procedures to be used by every hospital in the state to enhance patient safety, decrease the occurrence of pressure ulcers, and reduce the risk of hospital-acquired infection.

In 2006 a grant from the New Jersey Department of Health and Senior

Services positioned RBMC to receive state-certification as a primary stroke center—an important area of expertise for the region. RBMC was chosen for its optimum triage and treatment of stroke patients using the most advanced emergency protocols for stroke patients.

CareOne, a long-term, acute-care hospital, is located at the Perth Amboy campus. CareOne treats patients with complex medical needs requiring extended treatment. Acutely ill patients are treated through an interdisciplinary approach that includes board-certified physicians, specialty nurses, social services, respiratory and physical therapists, and registered dieticians.

The Center for Sleep Medicine at RBMC offers the most advanced technology measuring multiple parameters

during sleep: heart activity, brain-wave activity, breathing, eye and leg movements, muscle tone, and blood oxygen levels. Once sleep disorders are diagnosed, a variety of treatments is available for patients.

RBMC's Central Jersey Wound Care Center treats patients who have hard-to-heal chronic wounds through holistic treatments that best fit their needs, integrating the most advanced wound care techniques, products, and services, including specialized care such as the use of hyperbaric oxygen therapy.

The Pulmonary Rehabilitation Program at RBMC is dedicated to improving breathing capacity, endurance, and overall quality of life for patients with chronic pulmonary disease, chronic bronchitis, emphysema, pulmonary fibrosis, and

those recovering from chest surgery. The treatments make it easier for patients to perform everyday tasks without experiencing shortness of breath.

RBMC's Physical Therapy and Rehabilitation department is committed to promoting independence and the highest possible level of functioning for patients. Its list of therapies includes acupuncture; cold laser therapy, a noninvasive treatment for a variety of pains, stiffness, and muscle spasms; and video urodynamics, a procedure that diagnoses incontinence ailments.

The 2,000 doctors, nurses, and staff at RBMC work as a team to deliver high quality health care that meets the changing needs of the communities they serve, with a commitment to "Advancing care every day."

Above left: Shown here is RBMC's Old Bridge campus.

Virtua Health

Southern New Jersey's largest health care provider is transforming the way health care is delivered with its plans for a 125-acre health care campus of the future, expanding its role in delivering surgical, cardiovascular, women's, pediatric, cancer, orthopaedic, neuroscience, and wellness care.

Above: Virtua Health's digital health care campus in Voorhees Township, to be completed in 2011, features a hospital with 376 private rooms, a Women's and Children's Pavilion, an Adult Medical and Surgical Pavilion, and a comprehensive regional ambulatory center.

Virtua Health is planning a 125-acre health care campus of the future. "Virtua's new health care complex incorporates the most advanced digital technologies and can accommodate technologies not yet developed," says Richard P. Miller, president and CEO of Virtua Health. "Most importantly, the design provides an environment that promotes healing, patient comfort, and family space."

TRANSFORMING HEALTH CARE FOR GENERATIONS TO COME

Adjacent to the hospital will be a comprehensive regional ambulatory center that will include an ambulatory surgery center, a pediatric specialty center, a cancer center, diagnostic and treatment services, and physician offices. The hospital is scheduled for completion in 2011.

Additional ambulatory centers are planned for Washington Township, in Gloucester County, and for Moorestown, in Burlington County. Each will include physician offices, fitness centers, and outpatient services custom-tailored to suit the needs of each community.

Innovative plans are also underway for the development of Virtua's existing facilities in Berlin, Marlton, and Mount Holly. These include the adoption of the most advanced clinical and information technologies and the addition of services. All aspects of Virtua's plans are aimed at achieving Virtua's mission: To provide an outstanding patient experience.

HONORED FOR EXCELLENCE

Virtua has distinguished itself within the health care and business communities as an early adopter of clinical and digital technologies; for its Six Sigma, Change Management, and Lean applications in health care; and for its innovative partnerships with organizations such as GE Healthcare and a host of educational institutions.

Virtua has been honored twice with the New Jersey Governor's Award for Clinical Excellence and recognized with the Leadership Award for Outstanding Achievement by Voluntary Hospitals of America. Virtua has been twice honored as the number-one Best Place to Work by the *Philadelphia Business Journal* and is a multiyear recipient of the Consumer Choice Award by National Research Corporation. It has earned special Joint Commission accreditations for its joint replacement and spine programs, part of the Virtua Musculoskeletal Institute, and for its stroke program.

Virtua Health is a multihospital health care system, headquartered in Marlton, New Jersey, known for its world-class programs of excellence in oncology, cardiovascular disease, orthopaedics, women's health, pediatrics, surgery, neuroscience, and wellness. A nonprofit organization, Virtua employs more than 7,400 clinical and administrative personnel, and 1,800 physicians serve as medical staff members.

In addition to Virtua's four hospitals, an outpatient center located in Camden provides round-the-clock emergency care, primary care, and specialty care. A wide range of other services and facilities, including rehabilitation and long-term care, home care, and physical therapy, and a fitness and wellness center, serves Burlington, Camden, Gloucester, and surrounding counties.

VIRTUA HEALTH FAST FACTS

- Virtua Health has more inpatient visits, more emergency room visits, and more same-day surgeries than any other hospital system in southern New Jersey
- Over 56,000 admissions annually
- Delivers 7,600 babies per year
- Treats more than 184,000 emergency cases each year
- 1,800 highly trained physicians
- Specialists in high-risk obstetrics with Level III neonatal intensive care
- Regional Perinatal Center
- Two full-service digital cardiac catheterization laboratories for diagnostic catheterizations and emergency angioplasties
- Advanced cancer treatment program

for the prevention, diagnosis, and treatment of disease, including medical, surgical, and radiation oncology specialists; preventative, diagnostic, clinical, surgical, and radiation treatments; and technologies and clinical trials for all types of cancer
- Participation in clinical research with two institutional review boards
- Among the most technologically advanced surgical suites in the region
- Thousands of minimally invasive surgical procedures performed annually
- International teaching center for minimally invasive knee surgery
- Southern New Jersey's largest mobile intensive care program and the Southstar Air Medical Program

Virtua Health provides full information on its health care services and its activities on its Web site (www.virtua.org).

APPLYING THE SMARTEST NEW TECHNOLOGIES

Virtua is dedicated to adopting the most advanced technologies in order to bring the highest quality of care to its patients. For example, Virtua Marlton's advanced digital surgical suites enable surgeons to perform intricate, minimally invasive procedures with voice-activated surgical equipment, high-definition digital imaging, and two-way video linkage that enables them to consult with

pathologists or other experts in another building or around the world.

A national shortage of neurologists has been solved at Virtua by the adoption of teleneurology at all Virtua emergency departments, revolutionizing stroke care with a two-way, interactive, high-definition audio-video communication system that connects the patient and emergency room physician with an emergency neurologist 24 hours a day for faster stroke diagnosis and treatment.

Other applications include handheld personal digital assistants that give

nurses and physicians instant access to laboratory results, diagnostic reports, medication lists, and other essential patient data; a picture-archiving and communication system that stores digital radiology images and allows

physicians secure access to images from anywhere with Internet access; and a fully digital, wireless system that transmits and stores a patient's electro-cardiogram data for immediate retrieval anytime, anywhere, via the Internet.

Above left: Patients can stay connected to the outside world by using GetWellNetwork, an interactive online service designed to inform, educate, and entertain.

This Catholic teaching hospital is a full-service health care facility that serves the people who live and work in eastern and central Union County, New Jersey. The physicians and staff at Trinitas Hospital offer state-of-the-art medicine that is complemented with compassion and competence.

Trinitas Hospital was established in 2000 with the consolidation of two hospitals in Elizabeth, New Jersey— St. Elizabeth Hospital and Elizabeth General Medical Center. Trinitas Hospital has two campuses with a total of 531 beds, including a 120-bed long-term care facility. The hospital treats more than 17,000 inpatients annually, 50,000 emergency patients, and several hundred thousand outpatients.

THE HISTORY OF TRINITAS HOSPITAL

The roots of Trinitas Hospital reach back to the turn of the 20th century. In 1877 four Elizabeth-area physicians pooled their resources to fill the demand for a health care facility. The physicians opened a two-room surgical clinic that led to the establishment of Elizabeth General Hospital and Dispensary two years later on May 9, 1879.

On May 30, 1905, the Sisters of Charity of Saint Elizabeth opened the 25-patient St. Elizabeth Hospital. Over the course of the next 20 years, the hospital was expanded both structurally and departmentally. The new building was fireproof and included several wards, patient rooms, and

Above right: Trinitas Hospital's newly modernized main campus is located at 225 Williamson Street in Elizabeth, New Jersey.

three surgical suites. There were also new X-ray and fluoroscopic departments and a new patient clinic, and the bed count stood at 276 beds and bassinets.

TRINITAS HOSPITAL TODAY

Much has changed since the early days, but two things have remained the same—the hospital is still supported by the Sisters of Charity of

Saint Elizabeth (in partnership with the Elizabethtown Healthcare Foundation), and the same compassionate care that was shown to patients in the early part of the century is offered to patients today. In fact, Trinitas Hospital has six core values that it maintains in its daily operations and in its interactions with patients—compassion, community, reverence for life, responsible stewardship, charity, and courage.

CENTERS OF EXCELLENCE

Providing leading-edge medicine and compassionate care, Trinitas Hospital offers numerous Centers of Excellence. These centers offer skilled services in the following specialties:

- The Behavioral Health and Psychiatry department offers comprehensive inpatient and outpatient psychiatric care for

seniors, adults, adolescents, and children.

- The Bloodless Medicine and Surgery center meets specialized patient needs with the option of therapy without blood transfusions.
- The Comprehensive Cancer Center was opened in 2005 and offers the Trilogy linear accelerator, which can treat cancer anywhere in the body, targeting tumors more precisely and more effectively with fewer treatment sessions. The hospital has also opened an inpatient 23-room cancer care unit, with specialized staff and equipment.
- The Cardiology center has provided emergency angioplasty for many years, and it now offers patients the option of elective angioplasty.
- The Diabetes Management center offers a high quality educational program to help people learn how to control and manage diabetes.
- The Maternal and Child Health center is a modern facility featuring care for mothers, newborns, and children.

The 20-bed mother-and-baby post-partum unit features private rooms as well as state-of-the-art labor, delivery, and recovery (LDR) rooms. The center also offers a Level II Intermediate Care Nursery and a 24-hour, in-house neonatologist, obstetrician, and midwife. The 11-bed pediatric unit has centralized monitoring and an in-house physician for the unit 24 hours a day.

- Renal Services is home to the Regional End Stage Program for Eastern Union County, which treats patients with kidney failure. This program has been honored for having some of the best clinical outcomes among all hospital dialysis centers in the Premier network of more than 1,600 hospitals—a leading national health care alliance.
- The sixth-largest nursing school in the nation, the Trinitas School of Nursing offers a Diploma in Nursing along with an Associate in Science degree from its affiliate Union County College. The Cooperative

Nursing Program, established in 1891, provides education and training for nurses, and its students achieve some of the highest success rates among the state's graduates on the National Council Licensing Examination for registered nurses.

- Senior Services provides a full complement of services and includes the Acute Care for the Elderly Nursing Unit and the Brother Bonaventure Extended Care & Rehab Center.
- The Sleep Disorders Center conducts studies to assess physical symptoms that are unrelated to stress and that may prevent restful sleep.
- The Women's Services center pro-vides advanced diagnostic services, including digital mammography, breast biopsy, bone density screening, and ultrasound.

- The Center for Wound Healing & Hyperbaric Medicine offers treatment by specially trained physicians for chronic and difficult-to-heal wounds.

Trinitas Hospital gives additional information about its services on its Web site (www.TrinitasHospital.org).

RECOGNITION FOR TRINITAS HOSPITAL

For its dedication and excellence, Trinitas Hospital was recognized by *NJBIZ* maga-zine for three consecutive years—2006, 2007, and 2008—as a "Best Place to Work." In 2007 AARP distinguished Trinitas Hospital as one of the "Best Employers for Workers Over 50."

Drawing on the successes of its past and present and looking to the innova-tions of the future, Trinitas Hospital will continue to provide high quality care to the people of the communities it serves.

Above left: U.S. Senator Frank R. Lautenberg assisted in the dedication of Trinitas Hospital's new Oncology Patient Care Unit. This facility features 23 private patient rooms that are designed for optimal patient comfort and safety, and its services complement the full range of outpatient services that are available at the Comprehensive Cancer Center at Trinitas Hospital. Above right: Vipin Garg, M.D., FAASM, FCCP, medical director of the Sleep Disorders Center at Trinitas Hospital, reviews a sleep study with Registered Polysomnographer Sandra Land. This center is accredited by the American Academy of Sleep Medicine.

For more than 100 years, this technologically advanced, 478-bed teaching hospital has served central New Jersey. It is dedicated to providing a wide range of lifelong health care for the community, from sophisticated care of premature babies to specialized geriatric medicine.

Saint Peter's University Hospital was founded in 1907 as Saint Peter's General Hospital with 25 beds and was incorporated the following year. Over its more than 100-year history, the hospital has continued to expand its facilities to increase the amount of services it offers and to improve patient flow and accessibility.

In 1929 Saint Peter's moved to its location on Easton Avenue in New Brunswick, expanding to 125 beds. In 1959 the hospital added three wings and in 1976, a five-story tower. It completed a $63 million construction project and the Women and Children's Pavilion in 1991, and in 1999 the Center for Ambulatory Resources (CARES) building was added and the emergency department expanded. Since then, additions include the Telemetry Unit and a second cardiac catheterization laboratory in 2006, as well as new adult oncology and maternity units in 2008.

As a result of these expansions, Saint Peter's, a member of the Saint Peter's Healthcare System, has 478 licensed beds and 77 licensed bassinets at its nearly 14-acre, technologically advanced campus. More than 900 physicians and dentists have privileges at the hospital, which is sponsored by the Roman Catholic Diocese of Metuchen. Saint Peter's employs 2,800 health care and support personnel and offers a wide range of services to its patients, which annually number more than 30,000 inpatients and 200,000 outpatients. The hospital's service area includes 21 municipalities in Middlesex and Somerset counties.

SOPHISTICATED CARE AND SERVICES

Saint Peter's services cover a broad spectrum of care delivered to both inpatients and outpatients. These services include maternity, newborn, and pediatric care; adult and pediatric oncology; adult and geriatric care; cardiac catheterization; ambulatory care; bariatric surgery; wound care; and community and outreach services.

A state-designated children's hospital and a regional perinatal center, Saint Peter's delivered 6,174 babies in 2007. It is renowned for its maternity and newborn services—especially for problem or high-risk pregnancies. Its Neonatal Intensive Care Unit (NICU) was the first in central New Jersey.

The Children's Hospital at Saint Peter's is affiliated with Children's Hospital of Philadelphia (CHOP), named the best pediatric hospital in the country by *U.S.News & World Report* in 2008. Saint Peter's delivers comprehensive pediatric health and surgical services through its Children's Hospital, which includes the CHOP Cardiac Center, its Level III NICU, Pediatric Intensive Care Unit, the Craniofacial and Neurosurgical Center, the Institute for Genetic Medicine, the Pediatric Emergency Department, the Pediatric Neuroscience Institute, and a regional child protection center.

Saint Peter's oncology department uses the most advanced technology, medications, and surgical procedures to treat both adults and children. A cofounder of The Cancer Institute of New Jersey (CINJ)—the only National Cancer Institute (NCI)–designated cancer center in the state—Saint Peter's is a CINJ Clinical Research Affiliate. Saint Peter's cancer program is accredited as a Teaching Hospital Comprehensive Program by the American College of Surgeons' Commission on Cancer. Only 25 percent of the nation's cancer programs are accredited by the commission.

A TEACHING HOSPITAL

A major teaching institution, Saint Peter's is dedicated to providing quality medical education and has been accredited by the Accreditation Council for Graduate Medical Education (ACGME) to sponsor its own residency programs, which include internal medicine, obstetrics and gynecology, and pediatrics. Saint Peter's is an academic affiliate of Drexel University College of Medicine (the largest private medical school in the country) and the University of Medicine & Dentistry of New Jersey.

PRAISEWORTHY CARE

Saint Peter's has received numerous awards and recognitions, indicating the hospital's high quality of care and services. It is fully accredited by The Joint Commission, a nonprofit organization that recognizes high quality health care organizations.

The hospital was the 10th in the nation to be certified as a Magnet hospital for nursing excellence by the American Nurses Credentialing Center, and it has received the Magnet Award for Nursing Excellence for three consecutive four-year terms. In 2006

the American Association of Critical Care Nurses granted Saint Peter's the Beacon Award for Critical-Care Excellence, placing the hospital among only 56 hospitals in the country that have received this accolade. Saint Peter's received the American Board of Nursing Specialties Award for Nursing Certification Advocacy for promoting specialty nursing certification in 2005. The hospital believes that specialty nursing certification improves the quality of patient care. Additionally, the American Diabetes Association recognizes Saint Peter's diabetes education programs. The Division of Mental

Health Services has granted "Deemed Status" to the For KEEPS (Kids Embraced and Empowered through Psychological Services) program at The Children's Hospital at Saint Peter's.

In 2008 Saint Peter's University Hospital celebrated its 100th anniversary of caring for its community. Throughout its long history, Saint Peter's has provided state-of-the-art care to patients through a wide array of specialty services, advanced technology, and academic and clinical affiliations, and it remains dedicated to meeting the health care needs of central New Jersey.

Above: Saint Peter's University Hospital is a 478-bed acute care teaching hospital located on Easton Avenue in New Brunswick.

Hackensack University Medical Center

The largest provider of inpatient and outpatient services in New Jersey, this university medical center is committed to quality medicine and outstanding patient care, with a modern campus that offers the most advanced medical technologies and procedures available.

Right: Hackensack University Medical Center (HUMC)—a guiding light in health care—is nationally recognized for its excellent inpatient and outpatient care; renowned physicians; Magnet Award–winning registered nurses; disease-focused Centers of Excellence; on-site basic, translational, and clinical research; state-of-the-art technologies; innovative programs unique to the hospital industry; and more.

Far right: One example of medical and service excellence is The Joseph M. Sanzari Children's Hospital at Hackensack University Medical Center. This one-stop children's hospital provides a comprehensive, integrated continuum of care in a nurturing environment.

Hackensack University Medical Center (HUMC) has grown and changed in response to the needs of its patients since 1888, when it opened with 12 beds and had the honor of being Bergen County's first hospital. Today this 775-bed, not-for-profit, tertiary-care teaching and research hospital serves as the hub of health care for northern New Jersey and the New York metropolitan area.

HUMC has been ranked in five specialties—geriatric care, gynecology, heart care and heart surgery, neurology and neurosurgery, and orthopedics—in *U.S.News & World Report*'s 2008 "America's Best Hospitals" guide. HUMC is the only New Jersey acute-care hospital to receive rankings in five specialties. Authoritative and influential, the 2008 "America's Best Hospitals" ranks 170 medical centers nationwide in 16 specialties, with full data available online for another 1,500 that are unranked. In addition, the Honor Roll singles out the "best of the best."

Bergen County's largest employer, HUMC has a workforce of more than 7,200 employees, including 1,400 physicians and dentists representing every medical specialty. One of New Jersey's most comprehensive and progressive medical centers, the hospital has been named one of America's 50 Best Hospitals by HealthGrades®, a well-known, independent ranking company. This distinction—earned by only 1 percent of America's hospitals—means HUMC has a 27 percent lower mortality rate than all other U.S. hospitals. HUMC is the only health care facility in New Jersey, New York, and New England to be named one of America's 50 Best Hospitals for two years in a row.

For four consecutive years, HUMC was named a "Hospital of Choice" by the American Alliance of Healthcare Providers (AAHCP), which recognizes organizations that meet their standards of being a physician-friendly institution with high levels of customer satisfaction. HUMC is also proud to be in its 12th year as a Magnet Hospital. In 1995 it became the first hospital in the country to receive the Magnet Award for Nursing Excellence from the American Nurses Credentialing Center, an honor it continues to hold today.

Hackensack University Medical Center has achieved recognition as one of the nation's health care leaders through a steadfast commitment to quality and by delivering the highest level of care to its patients. All of the hospital's medical professionals work as a team and are committed to providing an exceptional patient experience through quality patient-centered care, education, research, and community outreach.

Hackensack University Medical Center campus

PROFILES OF COMPANIES AND ORGANIZATIONS

Information Technology, Telecommunications, and Media

This company brings together a leading portfolio of services, delivery expertise, and continual innovation to instantly connect people to what matters, everywhere they live and work. In New Jersey, it conducts advanced research, manages a vast global network, and showcases new communications and entertainment solutions.

CONNECT PEOPLE EVERYWHERE THEY LIVE AND WORK BETTER THAN ANYONE ELSE

Above: At its Corporate Briefing Center (CBC), located in Bedminster, AT&T showcases its strategic direction and technology advances in action for key client leaders from around the world. Each year some 2,200 visitors are able to experience dynamic, interactive demonstrations of new communications solutions.

AT&T is a premier communications holding company with more than 300,000 employees worldwide and a network that connects more than one billion devices around the globe. AT&T's operating companies are focused on meeting diverse requirements that arise from a common customer need—to share information and ideas when, how, and wherever they want.

As the marketplace reaches into every corner of the globe, so does the ability to connect, collaborate, and transact business internationally. AT&T provides a single source for local, national, and global communications services, offering multinational corporations, government agencies, and service providers the networking solutions and integration expertise needed to successfully conduct business anywhere.

Recognized as the leading worldwide provider of Internet protocol (IP)–based communications services to businesses, AT&T offers predictable, consistent, and secure global connectivity to 160 countries; proven expertise integrating and managing networked information technologies; and deep experience managing enterprise applications and delivering content over distributed global environments. AT&T serves business customers of all sizes with an extensive portfolio of communications solutions. From local to global, mobile to IP, and voice to video, AT&T serves millions of business enterprise customers on six continents, including all of the Fortune 1000. Customers have great flexibility to choose expertly delivered solutions to meet their requirements, from basic networking and infrastructure to advanced collaboration tools and managed applications.

Today's mobile society demands persistent connections between people, information, and content. AT&T provides innovative ways to enable an untethered lifestyle, so that people can connect through conversation, instant messaging, and even video. From almost anywhere, AT&T enables customers to remotely plug into office applications or unplug from reality. Customers increasingly use innovations in both wireless speeds and device interfaces to tune in to music and movies, or tune out the world as they join the conversation on their favorite social networking sites. AT&T serves more than 70 million U.S. customers via the most widely available wireless technology in the world—Global System for Mobile (GSM)

communications. AT&T's third-generation (3G) high-speed wireless broadband services will cover, by the end of 2008, 350 metropolitan areas. AT&T also creates innovative device partnerships—such as its services for the Apple iPhone—to offer richer experiences for customers.

Serving people at home, AT&T provides traditional long-distance and modern IP telephony on a national basis. Within AT&T's 22-state local-network service area, AT&T provides a complete array of all-distance telephony service and call-management features, as well as high-speed broadband services, including digital television. AT&T's three-screen integration strategy is to deliver its services across the mobile device, the PC, and the TV.

AT&T IN NEW JERSEY
AT&T's drive to connect people with their world plays out across the globe every day. Locally, AT&T takes an active role within the New Jersey community, as it has ever since the telephone was invented in 1876. Among AT&T's many facilities in New Jersey today are AT&T Laboratories, the AT&T Global Network Operations Center, and the AT&T Corporate Briefing Center.

AT&T Laboratories—which evolved from Bell Telephone Laboratories, established in 1925—has long attracted some of the world's greatest scientists, engineers, and developers. With locations in Florham Park and Middletown, New Jersey, AT&T researchers continually seek progressive, innovative solutions to instantly connect people around the world. The members of this brain trust are successors to a heritage that produced seven Nobel Prizes and launched entirely new industries. AT&T has made groundbreaking advances in technologies such as voice recognition, network management, security, wireless systems, and information visualization.

AT&T's Global Network Operations Center (GNOC) vigilantly monitors the company's global network to maintain reliability and provide security. At this 198,000-square-foot center, located in Bedminster, personnel monitor and manage traffic flow over the vast network 24 hours a day, seven days a week. Advanced technologies at GNOC allow AT&T to predict and make early identification of many viruses and network attacks, enabling the company to take action to prevent them from reaching customers.

The AT&T Corporate Briefing Center (CBC), also located in Bedminster, is a showcase where the company demonstrates its latest innovations and their impact. At the CBC, AT&T offers interactive displays of its strategic direction and technology for key client decision makers from around the world. The center, which has undergone a multimillion-dollar transformation, provides a contemporary, dynamic experience to some 2,200 business leaders each year. The CBC offers guests real-time, hands-on control of technologies—for example, high-definition video-conferencing—to demonstrate the powerful ways in which advanced networking and collaboration services can help to build a competitive advantage.

AT&T has a talented workforce in New Jersey of more than 10,000 employees, making the company a vibrant part of the state. Along with its mission to serve customers' communications needs, AT&T is making significant investments in the community by addressing local needs. AT&T's generous contributions to the communities where its employees live and work included $1.3 million in AT&T Foundation grants in 2006. Overall, AT&T plans to continue leading the way in connecting people in New Jersey to their world.

Above left: To maintain reliability and provide security, AT&T vigilantly monitors its network from the AT&T Global Network Operations Center (GNOC), which is located in Bedminster. With operations 24 hours a day, seven days a week, the staff at this 198,000-square-foot center monitors and manages communications traffic flow over the worldwide AT&T network.

PROFILES OF COMPANIES AND ORGANIZATIONS

Infrastructure, Development, Construction, and Real Estate Services

NAI James E. Hanson

This leading independent, full-service brokerage and property management firm provides clients with strategic solutions and value-added services including office, industrial, and retail brokerage; investment and land sales; property management; government services; and financing expertise.

Professional real estate services, including full-service brokerage and property management, have been the focus of NAI James E. Hanson (NAI Hanson) for more than 50 years. Founded by James E. Hanson in 1955 and now in its third generation of Hanson at the helm, the company has worked diligently to develop the lasting relationships, professional personnel, resources, and innovative technologies needed to give its clients the best service possible. Through its partnership with NAI Global, NAI Hanson offers its services across the country and around the globe.

Headquartered in Hackensack with a second office in Parsippany, the company's services include site search and selection, property disposition, advisory services, property management, asset management, investment, property valuations, and corporate services. Other services, often needed to complete a project, are expertly coordinated through the staff and partner relationships: appraisal, finance, auction, construction management, space planning, and residential relocation.

Dedicated to excellence, NAI Hanson is staffed by knowledgeable and experienced professionals—from the administrative staff to senior associates—working together to find the best solutions and management for each assignment. Among the company's senior associates are eight individuals who are Society of Industrial and Office Realtors (SIORs) and four who are Certified Commercial Investment Members (CCIMs)—both SIOR and CCIM are prestigious designations within the commercial real estate industry—and three associates have master's degrees in real estate from New York University.

CORPORATE SERVICES GROUP

The Corporate Services Group of NAI Hanson is dedicated to providing corporations throughout America with comprehensive real estate services that exceed their expectations. The company's philosophy for delivering outstanding corporate services is to represent the interests of clients as if they were the company's own and to use the most technologically advanced systems to streamline operations.

Among the company's highly satisfied clients are BP Amoco, Regulus Group, Airborne Express, United Water, Graybar

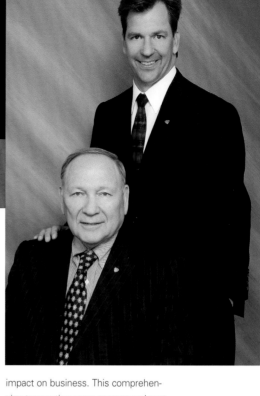

Electric Company, Hackensack University Medical Center, City of Jersey City, and The Hampshire Companies.

PROPERTY MANAGEMENT

Property management has been an integral part of NAI Hanson's business from the beginning, with the goal being to achieve and maintain the highest value for the client's portfolio. As property owners themselves, the company's principals ensure that property management is carried out to reflect pride of ownership as well as profitability. Services include lease administration, project management, property and facilities management, property accounting, and lease and facility audits.

The duties performed by the property management staff include physical maintenance; tenant installation; the collection of rents and the payment of expenses; the implementation of a tenant retention program; the preparation of annual budgets and monthly cash flow statements; the coordination of property tax appeals; and the coordination with the client's accountant for tax return preparation.

To effectively execute these services, NAI Hanson maintains close working relationships with real estate marketing professionals, attorneys, appraisers, accountants, and subcontractors.

THE POWER OF NAI GLOBAL

Since 1981, NAI Hanson has been strengthened and supported by its partnership in NAI Global, a network of independent commercial real estate firms headquartered in Princeton, New Jersey. With staff members positioned around the world, NAI Global provides technology, marketing, and corporate services support through its network of 8,000 real estate professionals in 375 real estate offices.

NAI Global keeps its members on the leading edge of the industry, enhancing their services with state-of-the-art marketing programs; providing REALTrac, a Web-based tool for managing real estate; overseeing ongoing regional and international meetings; and developing specialty marketing councils where sales professionals are trained in the latest techniques, products, and services available to the commercial real estate industry.

A family-owned business, NAI Hanson has fostered a corporate culture based on integrity and treating people fairly. The company invests in its people, focuses on their individual talents, and develops their entrepreneurial skills. Because the staff members function as a team and are loyal, they thrive within the culture and build long-term careers with the company. Since becoming president of NAI Hanson and promoting this atmosphere, William C. Hanson, SIOR, has tripled the company's number of sales associates and increased business by five times.

NAI Hanson offers its clients REALTrac, a proprietary Web-based program that provides them with round-the-clock access to the status of their properties. NAI's technology tools include E-Offerings, a function that allows NAI members to electronically market their listings; standardized assignment templates to track messages; timelines, calendar items, folders, and documents; and other features.

William C. Hanson extols the benefits of REALTrac: "It has made a significant

impact on business. This comprehensive transaction management and portfolio management system allows our professionals to streamline their work process and more effectively service their clients' needs."

Hanson continues, "Our business philosophy is to not get complacent but instead to look to improve all the time. We want to be better, not just bigger. The NAI platform is an important part of what we do every day. It allows us to service our clients' needs on a global basis, working with the finest independent firms worldwide. We have always been more than a local independent real estate firm: our company has done business in more than 30 states and across North America, South America, and Europe."

Above: Peter O. Hanson, chairman, seated, and William C. Hanson, president, are father and son and the second and third generations of Hansons managing operations at NAI Hanson.

Reflecting the positive and cooperative attitude of this attractive county, this agency provides comprehensive assistance for enterprises located in or contemplating relocation to its region. It offers economic information; assists with location, business retention, and development; handles planning; and assists municipalities.

Right: An example of the types of projects supported by the Burlington County Department of Economic Development and Regional Planning is 100 Century Corporate Center, located at 100 Century Parkway in Mount Laurel, New Jersey. Owned and managed by Needleman Management Co., Inc., this business center features techno-logical advancements and attractive appointments.

Widely recognized as one of the nation's most progressive counties, Burlington County, the largest county in New Jersey, is experiencing unheralded growth and prosperity. In fact, in 2006 *Inc.* magazine ranked the Burlington County region as the 10th hottest nationally for business.

MODERN-DAY BURLINGTON COUNTY

Just a short distance from Philadelphia and extending the entire width of the Garden State from the Delaware River to the Atlantic Ocean, Burlington County is home to a sophisticated and diverse business community with more than 7,500 individual businesses in its nearly 820-square-mile area. Among the corporations that are headquartered within its boundaries—taking advantage of Burlington County's strategic location in the heart of the Boston–New York–Philadelphia–Washington corridor—are such nationally recognized firms as Lockheed Martin, Burlington Coat Factory, Canon Business Solutions, and NFL Films. Other well-known companies with major facilities within its jurisdiction include Colgate-Palmolive, Frito-Lay, IKEA, Ocean Spray Cranberries, Mother's Kitchen, Viking Yacht, and Panasonic.

In addition to its business assets, Burlington County has always been a leading agricultural county. Cranberries are at the heart of a formidable industry in the county, where the world's largest blueberries were developed and are grown. Burlington County is the second-largest blueberry- and third-largest cranberry-producing county in the United States. More acres are devoted to farming in Burlington County than in any other county in the state. Burlington County also has a comprehensive land preservation program to ensure that its agricultural industry remains protected.

What Burlington County offers all these businesses and industries is accessi-bility, proximity to market, dependable utilities, available land, and a highly skilled and trained workforce. Equally important is the fact that the county's 40 local municipalities maintain a posi-tive and cooperative attitude toward business and industry. Moreover, the county's proactive Department of Economic Development and Regional Planning staff is readily available and eager to provide objective, comprehen-sive, and confidential assistance for busi-ness and industry in the county and those contemplating relocating to it.

A VOICE FOR BURLINGTON COUNTY

Based in the county seat of Mount Holly, the Burlington County Department of Economic Development and Regional Planning is the point man in attracting enterprise to the area, providing demo-graphic and economic information to businesses, industry, and the public; offering location assistance to businesses and industry; coordinating economic development programs among government agencies; assisting in business retention efforts; and serving as an ombudsperson to improve and

enhance economic development. The department's planning functions include handling regional and county planning efforts and providing planning assistance to local businesses, industries, and the county's municipalities.

Burlington County's diverse and robust economy—with 50,000 new jobs and 2,600 new businesses in just the 10 years from 1997 to 2006—provides its more than 450,000 residents with not only a wealth of employment opportunities but also a high quality of life, complete with affordable housing, a low crime rate, abundant education opportunities, and numerous attractions such as the Burlington County Prison Museum

and Historic Court House, which are National Historic Landmarks; eight county-operated parks; and 10 historic Quaker meeting houses. As a result of its healthy economy and array of recreational and historical amenities, *Outside* magazine named Burlington County one of the 100 most livable counties in the United States.

HISTORIC BURLINGTON COUNTY

In addition to its enviable economic record, Burlington County also can rightfully lay claim to being one of the more important counties in the nation's history. Having been formed in 1694 when America was still a British colony, the county played a key role in the formation

of the country. Its location between Philadelphia and New York caused it to be involved in several important milestones in the Revolutionary War. It was in Burlington County where diversionary activities took place during the Battle of Trenton. The county also served as the gateway to the Revolutionary War's Battle of Monmouth.

Burlington County also played a significant role in the abolitionist movement prior to and during the Civil War. No fewer than 16 African-American historical sites, many of which are directly related to the Underground Railroad movement of the 19th century, are located in Burlington County, which has led to its recognition by many historians as the "Cradle of Emancipation."

The county also has been fertile ground for the advancement of women's talents. Some of the women who called

Burlington County home and had a major impact on American society were Clara Barton, the famed American nurse and first president of the American Red Cross; philanthropist Mary Irick Drexel; American suffragist leader Alice Paul; and the first recognized United States–born sculptor, Patience Wright. James Fenimore Cooper, the 18th-century writer widely considered to be the first true American novelist, also was a product of Burlington County.

On all fronts, but especially in terms of economic development, Burlington County could be defined in one word—progressive. It is no secret that the county's economic vibrancy, its broad range of amenities, its rich history, and its can-do spirit truly make it one of New Jersey's gems as well as one of the gems of the nation's entire Northeast region.

Far left: Among the historical attractions of Burlington County's extensive park system is the Smithville Mansion, which is located in Historic Smithville Park, in Eastampton, New Jersey. Smithville Mansion is the former home of model-village visionary Hezekiah B. Smith and Agnes Smith. Above right: The county's more than 111,000 acres of farmland, which includes cranberry bogs and blueberry fields, annually produce more than $72 million worth of crops, livestock, and ornamental products. And Burlington County is among the largest of all U.S. counties in cranberry and blueberry production. Shown here, cranberries are harvested in the Chatsworth bogs.

Annually performing from $70 million to $80 million in construction work, this longtime leader handles a variety of large-scale projects such as roads and bridges, reclamation centers and landfills, railroads, airports, and pipelines—'Building New Jersey the American Way' by providing quality work reliably completed on time.

Above: The completed projects of George Harms Construction Co., Inc. (GHCCI) include the Route 35 Victory Bridge for the New Jersey Department of Transportation (NJDOT). A $115 million project, this was the first segmental precast concrete bridge to be built in New Jersey.

For some 50 years George Harms Construction Co., Inc. (GHCCI) has maintained a consistent record of success in the high-risk and ever-competitive construction industry. The cornerstones of GHCCI's accomplishments have been its work ethic and its commitment to rewarding employees—especially those who take initiative and use their imagination to solve problems.

From pipe work to bridges, airports to railroads, marine work to large environmental projects, every type of large-scale construction falls within GHCCI's technical and financial expertise. Projects completed by the company include highways, bridges, landfills, airport runways, railroads and railroad electrification, dams, pipelines, buildings, electrical transmission pole lines, toll plazas, and pump stations.

As a heavy highway contractor for both public and private owners, GHCCI's clients include New Jersey Transit, the New Jersey Turnpike Authority, the New Jersey Department of Transportation (NJDOT), the Port Authority of New York and New Jersey, the Army Corps of Engineers, Amtrak, the United States Navy, various county and municipal governments, and the Princeton Forrestal Corporation.

RUNNING A TIGHT SHIP

The more complex and difficult a construction project, the more likely that GHCCI will be involved. The company has even earned a reputation for "solving problems before they happen." GHCCI is closely managed and most upper-management staff members have more than 20 years of service and experience with the firm.

GHCCI manages all of its own construction projects and performs most work without subcontracting. When needed, the company does subcontract, complying with all minority and small-business program goals and requirements.

GHCCI considers its 250 to 275 employees to be the company's greatest asset. Employee development training is continually provided in the areas of safety, management, construction methods, and personal development. With a 100 percent union workforce, the company maintains a steady, consistent group of loyal employees.

USING THE RIGHT EQUIPMENT

GHCCI maintains a fleet of late-model construction equipment that includes some of the world's largest, most technically advanced equipment. Through operating entirely with its own equipment, GHCCI has the expertise and ability to perform the most challenging types of construction work faster and more efficiently than most.

The company also is a technology leader in taking advantage of computer hardware and software systems. GHCCI has updated and linked its main office and all construction sites via computer-networking systems. All project management, cost accounting, estimating, design, and financial functions incorporate the most advanced software tools.

BUILDING NEW JERSEY

GHCCI was founded in 1960 by company owner and CEO George Harms, who purchased a used loader backhoe at the age of 16. After that, he completed some small construction jobs, establishing himself as a young contender who would go on to develop the determination and integrity that would set his company apart from the competition.

GHCCI's successful work on water and sewer projects throughout New Jersey eventually led to transportation-related projects. The company's first project for the NJDOT was the reconstruction of

Route 1 in Trenton. At that point Harms decided to fine-tune the organization in ways that enabled it to meet the challenges of working for state agencies. Subsequently, GHCCI was awarded contracts for many large-scale projects, including the Route 195 and Route 295 Interchange and Route 295 in Hamilton Township, the Route 1 and Route 130 Interchange in North Brunswick, the Route 35 Victory Bridge replacement in Sayreville and Perth Amboy, and other road and bridge construction for the NJDOT. In addition, GHCCI was awarded contracts for major projects for local municipalities, counties, and other state and federal agencies.

Today GHCCI continues as a leader in the construction industry through the successful diversification of its construction sectors. It has evolved with the industry to offer services that today's projects demand, such as design-build and fast-track projects.

SERVING AS A ROLE MODEL

GHCCI has received numerous industry awards in recognition of the company's excellence in concrete construction, engineering technology of construction, asphalt construction, and outstanding achievement. GHCCI also has been rated twice in *Engineering News-Record*'s list of the top 400 construction firms in the United States.

George Harms has made a number of significant contributions to the industry through his service. He has served for years on the Board of Directors of the Utility & Transportation Contractors Association (UTCA) of New Jersey, including serving a term

as UTCA's president, and as a board member and national vice president of the National Utility Contractors Association (NUCA), to name just a few. Harms was also honored as Monmouth University's Distinguished Business Leader of 2008. In addition, several GHCCI representatives serve on various committees of these and other industry organizations, including the American Road & Transportation Builders Association (ARTBA).

The company also supports many scholarship programs, including UTCA's William Feather Memorial Scholarship; the Construction Industry Advancement Program of New Jersey (CIAP)'s Edward O. Davis Memorial Student Summer Employment Scholarship Program; ARTBA's Transportation Development Foundation (TDF) Highway Worker Memorial Scholarship Program; and the Equipment Managers Council of America (EMCA)'s Edward Pawluk Sr. Memorial Scholarship.

Left: Another GHCCI project involved the construction of four bridges to create a grade-separated interchange to replace the Route 1 and Route 130 traffic circle in North Brunswick. Due to heavy traffic and hazardous conditions at the existing circle, the NJDOT identified this work as a fast-track project of high importance. GHCCI completed the project successfully, as well as ahead of schedule.

Right: The GHCCI project for the Route 52 causeway bridges, which link the island of Ocean City (background) with Somers Point on the mainland, replaces the deteriorating low-level bridges with twin higher-level fixed spans. The $141 million project for the NJDOT, scheduled for completion in 2009, is part of a $400 million project to replace all links between the mainland and the island.

Camden County, New Jersey

With world-class corporations and enterprising start-up firms, an advantageous assortment of top-rated educational institutions, easy access to international airports and the Port of Philadelphia, and an abundance of arts and recreation, this county offers opportunity and an enriched quality of life.

Right: One of the best-connected regions in the United States, Camden County, New Jersey, is just a few hours from Washington, D.C., New York City, and Boston, and the county's major ports and airports put foreign markets within easy reach. Top right: Scientists at the Coriell Institute for Medical Research lead the way in groundbreaking studies for the advancement of genome-informed medicine. The institute maintains the world's largest biobanking facility, which serves the scientific community.

Named as one of the "Top 10 Boomtowns" by *Inc.* magazine, Camden County, New Jersey, strategically located on the Delaware River across from downtown Philadelphia, is more than a great place in which to live, work, and raise a family. It is also a major center for national commerce, innovative research, and transportation logistics.

CUTTING-EDGE INDUSTRIES

Health sciences are especially strong in Camden County, with more than $750 million in new health care and research construction for nationally recognized health care leaders, including Cooper University Hospital, the Cooper Cancer Institute, Virtua Health, the Lourdes Health System, and the University of Medicine & Dentistry of New Jersey.

Additionally, Camden County enterprises lead the way in biotechnology—with industry pioneers such as the Coriell Institute for Medical Research, a leading biomedical researcher in genome information and resources and maintainer of the New Jersey Stem Cell Resource. The Waterfront Technology Center at Camden, home to established businesses, is

an incubator for high-technology and life sciences start-up companies, and serves as a gateway to New Jersey's technology corridor. Nearby Rutgers, The State University of New Jersey and Camden County College provide additional research and train candidates for a skilled workforce.

STRATEGICALLY LOCATED

Camden County sits in the middle of the booming East Coast corridor, one

of the best-connected regions in the United States. In fact, more than 40 percent of the U.S. market—with a combined regional gross domestic product of $4.6 trillion—is less than a day's drive away. Minutes from Philadelphia and only a few hours from Washington, D.C., New York City, and Boston, Camden County's central location and highly developed infra-structure offer easy access to points around the region and across the

nation. Major port operations on the Delaware River and two nearby international airports also put foreign markets within easy reach.

BIG ON BUSINESS

Fortune 500 companies have a long history with the county as well. The Campbell Soup Company, founded in Camden in 1869, continues to expand and enhance its world headquarters and is also developing a 110-acre office

park surrounding its campus. L-3 Communications, the sixth-largest defense contractor in the United States, has added factory and research facilities at its L-3 Communications Systems-East site in Camden—the same landmark location once occupied by RCA Victor. Camden County is also the home base for Lockheed Martin Advanced Technology Laboratories, an advanced-computing and applied research and development facility for Lockheed Martin and some of the world's largest aerospace and defense contractors.

One of Lockheed Martin's neighbors includes TD Bank, owned by TD Bank Financial Group of Canada. Subaru of America, a marketing division of Fuji Heavy Industries of Japan, also chose Camden County as its headquarters and as a gateway into the U.S. market.

TALENTED WORKFORCE

Well-educated. Well-trained. A wealth of talent and diversity. Camden County's highly skilled workforce and labor pool provide an economic advantage for a broad range of businesses. More than 14,000 scientists, engineers, technicians, and trade workers help drive innovation in biotechnology, pharmaceuticals, and foreign trade, as well as manufacturing, transportation, and logistics.

Much of this success can be credited to the exceptional education system in Camden County—including nationally recognized elementary and high schools, a top-ranked college, university, and medical school. With one of the highest investment-per-student ratios in the country, all Camden County public schools require technology education as part of their core curriculum. Nearly all high school graduates continue their education, with 85 percent enrolling in colleges or universities.

Camden County provides more information for businesses and residents on its Web site (camdencounty.com).

AN ENRICHED QUALITY OF LIFE

Quality of life in Camden County is enhanced with diverse cultural, arts, and entertainment opportunities. From symphony concerts and summer music festivals to nearby galleries, museums, theaters, and historical monuments, life is rich in Camden County. Residents can enjoy parks, marinas, a boathouse, tennis courts, a golf academy, and open-air entertainment all summer long. For avid golfers, Camden County has 10 private and public golf courses within its borders, including the world-renowned Pine Valley. Sports fans root for their favorite local teams, from Minor League Baseball to professional football, basketball, hockey, and more. The county is home to one of the top-rated rowing courses in the world, hosting national events every year. People who consider shopping their favorite "sport" have a wide choice of shopping malls, boutiques, and bargain-friendly outlets. The world-famous Jersey shore, with 127 miles of white sandy beaches, is also just a short drive from Camden County. Welcoming people who are looking for a place to live or a place in which to grow a business, Camden County's slogan is "Making It Better, Together."

Top left: Minor League Baseball is one of the many recreational, cultural, and community events that make Camden County a great place to work, live, and raise a family.
Top right: Located just across the Delaware River from downtown Philadelphia, Camden County celebrates its strategic site and historical significance as part of the nation's birthplace.
Bottom right: The exceptional educational resources in Camden County include nationally recognized schools, colleges, universities, and medical schools.

Jersey City Economic Development Corporation

This premier economic development agency initiates programs to stimulate industrial and commercial growth and community development in Jersey City. It spurs renewal in urban complexes, historic sites, streetscapes, and infrastructure; assists relocating businesses; and promotes the city's advantages, vigor, and opportunities.

Right: Jersey City's waterfront location offers premier views on both the east side and the west side as well as important transportation links. In addition, Jersey City features a thriving business community, welcoming neighborhoods, many cultural and artistic venues, numerous recreational opportunities, and more. The Jersey City Economic Development Corporation is honored to serve as a significant contributor to the success that Jersey City has achieved and continues to achieve.

Welcoming visitors, new residents, and businesses, Jersey City is New Jersey's fastest growing city and one of its most diverse. With many amenities and resources, Jersey City is the perfect place to live, work, and do business. And the Jersey City Economic Development Corporation (JCEDC) is a driving force behind the success that the city has achieved and continually gains.

Part of the reason for Jersey City's amazing urban renaissance is its vital transportation links. The city has four ferry terminals and four stations of the PATH (Port Authority Trans-Hudson) rapid-transit system, which provide easy, affordable access to New York City, the cultural and financial capital of the world. There is also the Hudson-Bergen Light Rail system, which connects Jersey City to other parts of Hudson County and the region. For many people, however, once they make Jersey City their home, they do not want to leave.

In Jersey City there is a multitude of cultural and artistic venues, as well as fine dining establishments representing a variety of cuisines. The city is also home to dozens of Fortune 500 corporations and other international firms, and many financial offices are located in Jersey City, which is often referred to as "Wall Street West."

Jersey City is an economic engine driving the state's economy, helping to spur an upsurge in employment for the state. The city offers attractive incentives for businesses large and small, including lower operating costs, reduced taxes, and convenient public transportation options. Furthermore, the Urban Enterprise Zone Program in Jersey City has 592 participating businesses, which can offer certain goods and services with a sales tax of 3.5 percent—half of the standard New Jersey sales tax rate. Businesses can take advantage of employee tax credits and some reduced unemployment insurance costs and may be exempt from taxes on certain goods and services.

Jersey City is a national leader in urban redevelopment, and is also home to the state's four tallest buildings. Jersey City offers marinas, golf courses, bicycle paths, and numerous other outdoor venues for recreational activities, along with the most-visited state park in New Jersey, Liberty State Park. The city boasts waterfront views on both the east side and the west side, and its residents enjoy premier vistas.

JCEDC projects include redeveloped urban complexes, blocks, and streetscapes; historic site restoration; Special Improvement Districts; and the establishment of security measures. It assists in real estate marketing projects, business relocation and funding, industrial growth, job creation, and infrastructure renewal, and promotes the advantages of Jersey City for residents and businesses alike.

With all that Jersey City has to offer, it is clear why Jersey City is considered to be a premier New Jersey destination.

Jersey City waterfront

PROFILES OF COMPANIES AND ORGANIZATIONS

Legal Services

Gibbons P.C.

A Newark institution since the 1920s, this law firm has expanded into some of the region's key markets—and unveiled its spacious, high-tech headquarters in downtown Newark—underscoring a smart, client-driven growth strategy that positions the firm to meet and exceed its clients' expectations in the 21st century and beyond.

Above: Gibbons P.C. makes its mark on the Newark skyline with its logo in lights at the top of One Gateway Center, the building that houses the firm's 100,000-square-foot headquarters, brand-new in 2007.

Gibbons P.C. offers legal services within each of its nine broad practice areas: business and commercial litigation, corporate, criminal defense, employment, financial restructuring and creditors' rights, government affairs, intellectual property, products liability, and real property and environmental. The firm focuses its efforts on handling major matters for middle-

market companies and middle-market matters for major companies, notably in New Jersey but also in New York, Pennsylvania, and Delaware.

A GROWTH STRATEGY FOR THE 21ST CENTURY

Gibbons has also harnessed modern technology to take its client service into advanced realms in response to

clients' evolving needs. For example, as courts increasingly contend with the issue of electronically stored information (ESI) and impose complex related regulations, Gibbons formed the E-Discovery Task Force, an interdisciplinary group of attorneys and information technology professionals helping companies prevent and solve document-retention and e-discovery problems. Similarly, Gibbons created an interdisciplinary working group to address client exposures and interests resulting from turbulence in the credit market.

Gibbons has more than 40 lawyers in New York, and it has now expanded its Philadelphia office with the addition of 25 attorneys from a prominent Philadelphia civil-litigation boutique and six intellectual-property attorneys from an international firm. The firm also opened an office in Wilmington, Delaware. Based on initial client demand in more than 40 pending matters, the Wilmington office was launched with a focus on litigation, products liability, financial restructuring, and creditors' rights. Like the firm's New York and Philadelphia offices,

the Wilmington office will ultimately provide the firm's full complement of services.

Today Gibbons has 220 attorneys in five offices. In 2007 it was named among the Am Law 200, a prestigious list of the nation's leading law firms, published annually by the *American Lawyer*. Gibbons also made an impressive showing in *Chambers USA 2007: America's Leading Lawyers for Business, the Client's Guide*, with seven practice areas and eight individual attorneys ranked in the top tiers. *Chambers* provides preeminent annual ratings of the nation's leading lawyers and firms.

Gibbons was also recognized for its well-defined and well-executed business strategy in 2007 when Ernst & Young named Gibbons Chairman and Managing Director Patrick C. Dunican Jr. as an Entrepreneur of the Year in the Professional Services category. These awards honor outstanding entrepreneurs in more than 125 cities and 40 countries who are building and leading dynamic and growing businesses. Dunican was also a

top five finalist for the *NJBIZ* journal's Executive of the Year Award, and Gibbons was a top five finalist for an *NJBIZ* Business of the Year Award. These awards honor an elite group of businesses and business leaders for their contributions to the New Jersey business community.

NEW HEADQUARTERS FOR THE 21ST CENTURY

Gibbons' 100,000-square-foot headquarters at One Gateway Center in Newark, brand-new in 2007, addresses client needs and preferences in its custom-designed six floors. Its innovative layout and technological advances include ample conference and meeting rooms outfitted with the most up-to-date videoconferencing and audiovisual capabilities, a moot courtroom, a lounge area for relaxing, and other features. The leading-edge technology implemented by Gibbons throughout its offices, particularly in its headquarters, increases connectivity, mobility, accessibility, and collaboration capabilities, and enables the firm to deliver legal services efficiently and at a lower cost to clients.

The firm also enhanced its commitment to Newark and its prominent role in the city by adding its logo in lights to the top of One Gateway Center.

A WORKPLACE AND A WORKFORCE FOR THE 21ST CENTURY

Gibbons believes that none of its tremendous achievements would have been possible had it not been able to attract, motivate, and retain the highest level of talent among attorneys, professionals, and support staff. The firm managed to do just that with the promotion of a collegial—many say familial—work environment; open internal communications and senior-level accessibility; an emphasis on mentoring, professional development, and career mobility at the attorney, administration, and staff levels; firm-wide celebrations and team-building programs throughout the year; and a generous, innovative benefits package called "The Gibbons Experience," which adds to the firm's long list of traditional benefits and numerous unique perks. Gibbons has, as a result, been acknowledged to be simply one of the best places to work—in New Jersey, in Pennsylvania, for minorities, and for women—according to various sources, including *NJBIZ*, *Philadelphia Business Journal*, *Central Penn Business Journal*, *MultiCultural Law* magazine, and *Working Mother* magazine.

Above left: Among the firm's demonstrations of its commitment to Newark and to training future attorneys is a $1 million endowment made by Gibbons to Seton Hall University School of Law to establish the Gibbons Institute of Law, Science & Technology. Representatives of the institute, university, and firm include, from left, Gibbons Institute of Law, Science & Technology Director R. Erik Lillquist; Seton Hall University School of Law Dean Patrick E. Hobbs, professor of law; Gibbons P.C. Chairman and Managing Director Patrick C. Dunican Jr.; Gibbons P.C. Intellectual Property Department Chair David E. De Lorenzi; and Seton Hall University President Monsignor Robert Sheeran. Above right: The firm's Moot Courtroom allows attorneys and witnesses to prepare for trial and young attorneys to develop their litigation skills.

PROFILES OF COMPANIES AND ORGANIZATIONS

Manufacturing

BASF Corporation

With North American headquarters in New Jersey, the world's leading chemical company creates high-value products and intelligent systems solutions—in chemicals, plastics, performance products, agricultural and nutrition products, and oil and gas—for virtually every industry, with a commitment to sustaining the environment.

To further strengthen its portfolio, BASF made several strategic acquisitions in 2006. With the acquisition of Engelhard, a pioneer in the area of exhaust catalysts, BASF has become a world-leading supplier of catalysts. Acquiring Degussa's construction chemicals business enabled BASF to become a global leader in this growing market, and the acquisition of Johnson Polymer helped BASF to become a world leader in the production and sale of water-based resins.

MAKING PRODUCTS BETTER

Another factor contributing to BASF's leading global position is its approach to product innovation. More than 8,300 employees worldwide perform research for BASF, resulting in ongoing product advancement and intelligent system solutions. In addition, BASF has some 1,400 collaborative partnerships around the globe with leading universities, research institutes, start-up companies, and industrial enterprises, and BASF invests almost $2 billion globally in research and development.

BASF's products are used to make many everyday items better. Coatings are more vivid, weatherproof, and environmentally friendly. Engines can burn cleaner fuel, and BASF plastics make cars more fuel-efficient by reducing vehicle weight. BASF's products are contained in paper, packaging, construction materials, adhesives, textiles, leather, hygiene articles, detergents, sun care products, skin moisturizers, and cosmetics. BASF is a major supplier of agricultural products and fine chemicals to the farming, food processing, pharmaceuticals, and animal and human nutrition industries. BASF's products help to protect malnourished children worldwide from debilitating and deadly diseases.

Above left: For more than 140 years, BASF SE has been a standard bearer for innovative solutions that benefit its customers.
Above right: BASF's Catalysts division is headquartered in Iselin, New Jersey, where it operates a Global Research and Development Center.

Founded in 1865 as Badische Anilin & Soda Fabrik, BASF SE has grown to become the world's leading chemical company. Based in Ludwigshafen, Germany, with 95,000 employees around the globe, the company posted sales of $79.4 billion in 2007.

BASF Corporation, the North American operation of BASF SE, is headquartered in Florham Park, New Jersey.

A STRONG, GROWING PORTFOLIO

BASF operates six primary business segments: chemicals, plastics, performance products, agricultural solutions, functional solutions, and oil and gas. The company supplies a variety of industries, including construction, automotive, energy, and packaging, with a variety of customer-specific, innovative products; intelligent solutions; and tailored services.

COMMITMENT TO SUSTAINABILITY

BASF's focus on environmental sustainability is reflected in its global manufacturing operations. Six of the company's largest sites contribute to protecting the environment by making use of by-products from one manufacturing plant as raw materials at another plant. Within a site, production plants are connected by an intricate network of pipes, an environmentally friendly means of transport. For example, excess heat can be converted to steam and transported to where it is needed. By combining such conservation of resources with efficient use of energy, waste and greenhouse-gas emissions are reduced. In addition, BASF's products, technologies, and system solutions—insulation materials for buildings, plastics that make vehicles lighter, and additives

that improve fuel consumption—help customers worldwide reduce carbon dioxide emissions and protect the environment.

As a steward for society, BASF takes responsibility for making a positive contribution. In order to make its sites more attractive for employees and neighbors, the company is involved in numerous environmental, welfare, social, educational, scientific, athletic, artistic, and cultural projects worldwide.

AWARDS AND ACCOLADES

BASF receives ongoing recognition awards in its many areas of operation:

- *Fortune* magazine named BASF one of America's Most Admired Companies in Chemicals in 2007.

- BASF Catalysts was awarded Hyundai Motor Company's highest business honor, the Quality 5 Star Certification, in 2007.
- BASF's Cellasto microcellular polyurethanes (MCU) business received an Excellent Award for Quality from Toyota Motor Manufacturing North America in 2005.
- Through the years, BASF has won 13 American Chemistry Council Energy Efficiency Awards.
- BASF's Near-Zero Energy Home in Paterson, New Jersey—part of the company's Better Home, Better Planet Initiative—has received numerous awards, including the New Jersey 2006 Governor's Award for Environmental Excellence.
- A research team at BASF Catalysts received a Society of Automotive

Engineers Environmental Excellence in Transportation (E2T) award in 2007 for innovation in reducing the environmental impact of vehicles.
- BASF was included among the Global 100 Most Sustainable Corporations in the World, as compiled by Innovest, for both 2006 and 2007.

An ongoing commitment to innovative solutions has been the hallmark of BASF for more than 140 years. Its diverse portfolio of high quality products has positioned the company at the forefront of its industry. It will continue to supply businesses with customer-specific, tailored goods and services while enhancing energy efficiency across the world and reducing its own environmental footprint.

Above left: BASF's Agricultural Solutions segment is a major supplier of crop protection products to the farming industry. Above right: Among the tailor-made advances formulated by the BASF Performance Products business segment are improved surfactants that have broad applications for water treatment.

PROFILES OF COMPANIES AND ORGANIZATIONS

Pharmaceuticals, Biotechnology, and Medical Devices

Bristol-Myers Squibb

This company's commitment to patients with serious disease, its focus on finding innovative medicines that combat those diseases, and its dedication to extending and enhancing human life set it apart from other pharmaceutical companies.

Bristol-Myers Squibb medicines help millions of patients in their fight against serious diseases such as cancer, heart disease, diabetes, chronic hepatitis B, HIV/AIDS, rheumatoid arthritis, and psychiatric disorders. And the company's philanthropic programs have given new hope to some of the world's most vulnerable citizens.

Bristol-Myers Squibb is in the midst of redefining its pharmaceuticals business as a new kind of enterprise, one that combines the best qualities of a major pharmaceutical company with the best qualities of a cutting-edge biotechnology company. As such, Bristol-Myers Squibb is transforming itself into a next-generation BioPharma company.

This transformation is already beginning to show results. Since 2002 the company has brought nine new products to market for the treatment of psychiatric disorders, cancer, HIV, and other serious diseases. Two of these medicines are biologic products. In the fight against serious disease, biologics—or protein-derived therapies—are playing an increasingly prominent role.

Other biologic compounds, as well as scores of investigational medicines, are advancing through the pharmaceutical development pipeline. Bristol-Myers Squibb is recognized as having one of the most productive and promising pipelines in the industry.

Biologics have been an important component of the company's growth strategy and a cornerstone of the pharmaceutical business's continued transformation into a next-generation BioPharma company. In 2007 the company significantly boosted its presence in biologics by breaking ground for a large-scale biologics manufacturing facility and with the announced acquisition of a biotechnology company, Adnexus Therapeutics.

Bristol-Myers Squibb's health care business also meets significant

needs of people worldwide. Mead Johnson Nutritionals, known for its Enfamil® line of infant formula, is a world leader in providing infant and child nutrition.

Over the years, Bristol-Myers Squibb and its scientists have received numerous distinguished awards, including the National Medal of Technology, the Lasker Award for Medical Research, and the Prix Galien Award. The company has been hailed year after year as one of the

best companies for working mothers and is an acknowledged industry leader in environment, health, and safety management.

Bristol-Myers Squibb has had a major business and research presence in New Jersey since 1905. Today, thousands of dedicated employees work at five major facilities in central New Jersey, including sites in Hopewell, Nassau Park, New Brunswick, Plainsboro, and Princeton.

PREVAILING OVER HEALTH DISPARITIES WORLDWIDE

In early 2007 the Bristol-Myers Squibb Foundation announced that it was embarking on a new initiative: to help strengthen community-based health care worker capacity and integrate medical care and community-based supportive services. The aim is to mobilize communities to fight serious diseases and improve health outcomes.

The foundation is targeting four specific diseases and regions: hepatitis in Asia,

serious mental illness in the United States, cancer in central and Eastern Europe, and HIV/AIDS in Africa.

Although this initiative is just beginning, the cornerstone has already been laid by the work done in Africa through the Bristol-Myers Squibb SECURE THE FUTURE® program, focusing on women and children affected by HIV/AIDS. "Our focus on children in projects like the Pediatric AIDS Corps and the Children's Clinical Centers of Excellence has helped us better understand how to build bridges to better health," says foundation president John Damonti. "And our work with community-based treatment support sites has given us a new appreciation of the role that communities can play in improving health outcomes."

During 2006 the first contingent of 50 North American pediatricians and family practitioners arrived at their posts in Africa as part of the Pediatric AIDS Corps. These doctors are treating HIV-positive children and their families at the Children's Clinical Centers of Excellence developed by Bristol-Myers Squibb and

Above left, both photos: Scientists at Bristol-Myers Squibb's state-of-the-art research laboratories in Hopewell test novel treatments for serious diseases.

Baylor College of Medicine, as well as working in rural hospitals and clinics. Over the next five years, physicians of the Pediatric AIDS Corps are expected to treat up to 100,000 HIV-infected children and train thousands of local health care workers.

A RESPONSIBLE
CORPORATE CITIZEN

Bristol-Myers Squibb is widely recognized for excellence in providing some of the world's most important medicines and health care products. At the same time, the company is also an acknowledged industry leader in environment, health, and safety management. As the company accelerates discovering, developing, and providing new medicines, it also remains committed to promoting employee health and safety, reducing energy and water use, and making processes more environmentally friendly. The company is making progress on its sustainability 2010 goals, which are among the broadest in the industry.

Some of Bristol-Myers Squibb's recent recognitions are as follows:

- The company was included in the Dow Jones Sustainability North America Index, which is composed of top companies in terms of economic, environmental, and social criteria.
- Covalence, a private Swiss firm that measures the reputation of multinational enterprises, ranked Bristol-Myers Squibb as among the most ethical companies in the world. This ranking is based on 45 criteria, such as contribution to human development, labor standards, waste management, product social utility, and human rights.

- Ceres, a coalition of investor, environment, and public interest organizations, ranked Bristol-Myers Squibb second overall in North America for Sustainability Reporting.

COMPANY CULTURE

Bristol-Myers Squibb is building its future growth and leadership by renewing and strengthening its corporate culture. Through the company mission of extending and enhancing human life, and through the company's core behaviors, there is a common standard of conduct that is understood by every employee.

The company is committed to recruiting, retaining, and developing top talent with a diversity of background and experience. Bristol-Myers Squibb offers an array of career development and advancement opportunities, and a performance management system that rewards behaviors as well as results.

The company is equally committed to its diversity and work-life integration efforts. Examples include the company's state-of-the-art child development centers at many of its U.S. facilities, including Princeton, Plainsboro, and Hopewell; resources for assisting aging family members; employee affinity groups for diverse constituencies, including African American, Asian, Hispanic, female, and gay, lesbian, bisexual, and transgender employees; and the company's ongoing work to broaden workplace flexibility.

As a result of these and other innovative employee programs, Bristol-Myers Squibb is widely regarded as an employer of choice year after year. In recognition of its exemplary employee programs, Bristol-Myers Squibb received the following accolades and awards:

CEO: James M. Cornelius

Company headquarters:
345 Park Avenue,
New York, NY 10154-0037

Global net sales:
$19.3 billion in 2007

Total R&D investment:
$3.28 billion in 2007

Major New Jersey facility locations:
- Hopewell
- Nassau Park
- New Brunswick
- Plainsboro
- Princeton

Additional information about Bristol-Myers Squibb can be found on the company's Web site at www.bms.com.

- *Science* magazine ranked Bristol-Myers Squibb as a Top 20 Employer Worldwide in biotechnology, pharmaceutical, and related industries in 2007.
- Bristol-Myers Squibb was ranked by *The Scientist* magazine as among the best places to work for life-science researchers.

- The National Association of Female Executives named Bristol-Myers Squibb as one of the Top Companies for Executive Women.
- *Working Mother* magazine listed Bristol-Myers Squibb as one of the Top 100 Companies for Working Mothers.

- Bristol-Myers Squibb scored 100 percent on the Human Rights Campaign Corporate Equality Index, recognition of the company's commitment to equality.
- DiversityBusiness.com, the nation's leading multicultural business-to-business online portal, rated Bristol-Myers Squibb as among America's Top Organizations for Multicultural Business Opportunities.

What sets Bristol-Myers Squibb apart? It is a focus on finding innovative medicines, getting them to patients faster and more efficiently, and helping patients to prevail against disease.

Above left, both photos: Bristol-Myers Squibb's groundbreaking SECURE THE FUTURE® program focuses on women and children affected by HIV/AIDS in southern Africa.

189

Novartis Group Companies

A world leader in health care products, including pharmaceuticals, generics, and over-the-counter medications, this innovative company believes that success arises from the dedication of its associates. It is committed to operating with respect for economic, social, and cultural rights and for the environment.

Novartis values human life. From the company's long tradition of social responsibility and its patient assistance programs that help those facing financial hardship to a variety of employee volunteer programs, Novartis's corporate culture reflects a commitment to the health and well-being of others. Novartis associates realize and respect the impact of their work on society, the environment, and the health and safety of customers and fellow employees.

The Novartis Group Companies operating in New Jersey are U.S. affiliates of Basel, Switzerland–based Novartis AG, a world leader in offering medicines to protect health, cure disease, and improve well-being. Novartis AG has approximately 101,000 associates around the world and operations in 140 countries.

NOVARTIS PHARMACEUTICALS CORPORATION

Novartis Pharmaceuticals Corporation (NPC) is headquartered on a 200-acre campus in East Hanover, New Jersey. This pharmaceutical division of Novartis Group Companies is recognized worldwide for providing innovative prescription drugs to treat a broad range of disease areas. The company's business is focused on three key areas: cardiovascular and metabolism, specialty medicines, and oncology. NPC is a leader in the cardiovascular area, with medicines like Diovan®, Exforge®, and Tekturna® to treat high blood pressure and Lescol® to help lower cholesterol.

The specialty medicines area includes treatments for neuroscience disorders, respiratory disease, bone and hormone therapy, ophthalmology, urology, infectious disease, transplantation, and immunology. NPC's medicines in the neuroscience area include the Exelon® Patch for Alzheimer's disease; Stalevo® and Comtan® for Parkinson's disease; Focalin®, Focalin XR®, and Ritalin LA® for Attention Deficit Hyperactivity Disorder (ADHD); Trileptal® and Tegretol® for epilepsy; and Clozaril® for schizophrenia. Medicines in the respiratory area include Xolair® for allergic asthma. Reclast® is a new once-a-year treatment for postmenopausal osteoporosis. Ophthalmics medications include Visudyne® for macular degeneration. Enablex® is used in urology for overactive bladder. Novartis researchers were the first to overcome the problem of organ rejection in transplant procedures when they began using cyclosporine, an immunosuppressive drug. For more than 20 years since then, Novartis has been a leader in this area, with medications such as Neoral®, Sandimmune®, and Myfortic®.

Novartis is also a leader in oncology and hematology medications, with Gleevec® and Tasigna® for chronic myeloid leukemia, Femara® for breast cancer, Zometa® for bone metastasis, Exjade® for chronic iron overload, and Sandostatin® for acromegaly.

NOVARTIS CONSUMER HEALTH

Novartis Consumer Health (NCH) has a demonstrated history of success

in turning prescription medicines into over-the-counter (OTC) products. Among its most popular and successful OTC products are Lamisil AT®, an athlete's foot treatment; Benefiber®, a fiber supplement; and Triaminic®, a children's cough and cold medicine. An OTC leader, NCH has more than 50 years of experience in creating innovative self-medication treatments that are recommended by doctors and trusted by consumers.

The company's primary OTC product categories are cough and cold preparations, allergy formulas, gastrointestinal liquids and tablets, dermatological treatments, smoking cessation products, and pain relievers. Well-known NCH products include such household names as Excedrin®, Ex-Lax®, and Theraflu®. NCH employs more than 4,700 associates in 50 countries, with global headquarters in Parsippany, New Jersey, and manufacturing facilities in Lincoln, Nebraska; Humacao, Puerto Rico; and Nyon, Switzerland.

SANDOZ: HIGH QUALITY GENERICS

One of the largest manufacturers of generic drugs in the United States,

Sandoz Inc. in Princeton, New Jersey, has U.S. manufacturing facilities in Colorado and North Carolina. The company's generic products, which are available to 90 percent of the world's population, include anti-infectives, anti-arthritics, cardiovasculars, gastrointestinals, and psychotherapeutics.

The principal focus at Sandoz is on the development, production, and marketing of medicines that are no longer protected by patents; pharmaceutical and biotechnological active substances

(ingredients); and difficult-to-make generics such as transdermal patches, inhalers, and biopharmaceutical medicines. Experience over decades in these areas, combined with the stability of being part of the Novartis family, makes Sandoz a leader in the generics industry. The company offers patients exceptional cost savings, enhanced by dedicated customer service and reliable delivery.

Novartis AG was created in 1996 from the merger of Ciba-Geigy and Sandoz Laboratories, both long-standing Swiss

companies. Ciba-Geigy was formed in 1970 by the merger of J. R. Geigy, which was founded as a chemical, dye, and drug company in 1758 in Basel, and Ciba, a chemicals company that was also founded in Basel, in 1859. With a history that spans more than 250 years, Novartis remains committed to discovering, developing, and marketing high quality products, bringing outstanding value and performance to shareholders, and rewarding associates whose ideas and hard work make the company a global success story.

Above: Novartis produces some of the most familiar and trusted over-the-counter medications in the world, including cold and flu remedies, pain-relieving compounds, antacid tablets, antifungal powders, and soothing ointments.

Stryker Orthopaedics

Based in Mahwah, New Jersey, Stryker Orthopaedics is the largest division of Stryker Corporation, one of the world's leading medical technology companies with the most broadly based range of products in orthopaedics and a significant presence in other medical specialty areas.

Above: At the Mahwah, New Jersey, campus of the Stryker Orthopaedics division of Stryker Corporation is the Homer Stryker Center and the division's headquarters. Employing 1,400 people, the complex includes Research and Design, Manufacturing, Marketing, Finance, Information Technology, Healthcare Innovations, Sales Support, and other key departments.

Stryker, headquartered in Kalamazoo, Michigan, was founded by orthopaedic surgeon Homer H. Stryker, M.D., in 1941. Today the company operates 21 manufacturing and distribution divisions that employ approximately 16,000 people around the world. Stryker products include implants used in joint replacement, trauma, craniomaxillofacial, and spinal surgeries; biologics; surgical, neurologic, and interventional pain equipment; ear, nose, and throat equipment; endoscopic, surgical navigation, communications, and digital imaging systems; and patient handling and emergency medical equipment.

LIFESTYLE RECOVERY THROUGH QUALITY PRODUCTS AND SERVICES

Stryker works with respected medical professionals to help patients lead more active and satisfying lives. Orthopaedics products are used for the preservation, reconstruction, replacement, and repair of bones and joints. In fact:

- Stryker has become a worldwide market leader in hip implants by meeting both physician and patient needs for innovative products that facilitate daily activities;
- Stryker's total knee replacement systems are uniquely designed to suit varying anatomies and medical conditions;
- Stryker Joint Preservation products play a big role in sports medicine and provide patients with unparalleled treatment options for early indications of osteoarthritis;
- Stryker is a leader in the $1.7 billion worldwide trauma market, making products for fractures of the long bones, arm, hip, pelvis, hand, foot, and ankle; and
- Stryker is also a leader in the $400 million craniomaxillofacial implant market, with micro-implants designed for the skull and face that often allow people to breathe more freely, smile more, and go out in public with confidence for the first time.

At Stryker, quality is the first priority in the manufacturing and sale of its medical devices. Stryker works in partnership with the U.S. Food and Drug Administration (FDA) and other industry organizations to ensure the

quality and safety of every product that Stryker brings to market.

BUSINESS ACCOLADES

As a leader in the $29 billion worldwide orthopaedic sector, Stryker is recognized by *Forbes* among "America's 500 Top Companies" and by *BusinessWeek* among the 50 best performers in the S&P 500 Index. Stryker sales have grown from $43 million in 1980 to $6.0 billion in 2007, representing compounded annual growth of 21 percent over that time period. In addition, Stryker is one of only 14 companies that have achieved 28 consecutive quarters of double-digit sales growth worldwide. Stryker (NYSE: SYK) also delivered 25 percent compounded annual net earnings growth during the same period.

Stryker was included on The Motley Fool's list of "245 Incredible Companies" for having the best stock performance over the preceding decade. According to this report, from January 1998 through December 2007, 245 stocks on U.S. exchanges could have greater than 20 percent annualized returns for investors over the preceding 10 years, and Stryker was one of them.

Stryker has been recognized by *Fortune* as number two among the "Most Admired Companies" in the medical and other precision equipment sector and number one in its industry for financial soundness and long-term investment.

WORLD-CLASS OPERATIONS

Stryker Orthopaedics' world-class headquarters, located in Mahwah, New Jersey, houses Research and Design, Manufacturing, Marketing, Finance, Information Technology, Healthcare Innovations, Sales Support, and other key business departments. Approximately 1,400 employees work on-site, close to half of whom are directly involved in manufacturing, packaging, and distribution. All of these employees help to ensure the quality of Stryker products and services.

At the Homer Stryker Center, located on the Mahwah campus, internationally recognized clinical and scientific surgery faculty members use state-of-the-art training facilities to provide individually tailored learning programs for surgeons, residents, and other health care professionals.

Overall, Stryker Orthopaedics employs more than 3,700 people worldwide, including those at international operations in Ireland, France, Switzerland, and Germany.

Stryker Orthopaedics provides additional information about the company on its Web site (www.stryker.com).

CORPORATE CITIZENSHIP

Stryker enjoys partnerships with many civic, charitable, and educational organizations that create growth, diversity, and strength in the communities where Stryker's employees live and work.

The company is especially proud of its affiliation with some of the leading charitable and education institutions in New Jersey and around the nation. These include the Girl Scouts of the United States of America, Boy Scouts of America, United Way, YWCA of Bergen County, Bergen Community College Foundation, Ramapo College Foundation, Toys for Tots, Reach Out and Read–New Jersey, Speaking of Women's Health, The Women's Fund, and the Center for Food Action.

Stryker is a driving force behind the Manufacturing Technology associate degree (A.A.S.) program at Bergen Community College. The company provides leadership, financial, and practical learning assistance to the college's Technology Center in support of students interested in pursuing manufacturing careers. The curriculum covers basic machining, methods of manufacturing, and a team approach to problem solving and is designed to help keep U.S. manufacturing competitive both locally and worldwide. Stryker also provides funding for education, including both employee degrees and Stryker Foundation scholarships for indigent students.

Top left: Stryker Orthopaedics employs approximately 1,400 people at its Mahwah headquarters. Top right: The use of robotics in its manufacturing has enabled Stryker to make significant advances in the production of its high-precision components. Above: Stryker focuses on procedural and product innovations to provide replacement hip, knee, and shoulder implants that will stand the test of time.

Johnson & Johnson

This family of companies provides research-based and technology-driven products in the consumer, pharmaceutical, and medical devices and diagnostics fields. The corporation's companies are spread across North America, Latin America, Europe, Asia-Pacific, and Africa.

Above: The worldwide headquarters of Johnson & Johnson is located in New Brunswick, New Jersey, where the company was founded in 1886.

Since its invention of the first ready-to-use surgical dressing in the mid 1880s, Johnson & Johnson has become the world's most comprehensive and broadly based manufacturer of health care products, with more than 250 operating companies employing approximately 119,000 men and women in 57 countries.

Johnson & Johnson has achieved 75 consecutive years of sales increases and 24 consecutive years of adjusted earnings increases. The company credits much of its long-term success to its operating model: a commitment to being broadly based in human health care; a decentralized management approach, which allows for proximity to customers and fosters a competitive and entrepreneurial drive; a focus on managing for the long term, which allows the company to concentrate on shaping the future rather than reacting to change; and a foundation of shared values embodied in the company's document titled "Our Credo," a one-page outline of the company's responsibilities to customers, employees, the community, and shareholders.

In 2007 Johnson & Johnson reported worldwide sales of $61.1 billion. With the successful integration of Pfizer Consumer Healthcare, the company solidified its position as the world's premier consumer health care company. In pharmaceuticals, Johnson & Johnson holds a strong competitive position across seven therapeutic areas and continues to advance its pipeline. With a number of recent approvals in the medical devices and diagnostics segment, the company has maintained its position as the largest medical technology business with the capacity to treat some of the world's most pervasive conditions.

Decades of giving, inspired by the Credo, have made the company a pioneer in corporate philanthropy. Johnson & Johnson supports community-based programs worldwide to suit local needs around three strategic pillars: saving and improving lives, building health care capacity, and preventing diseases.

The company's management philosophy, anchored in the value system embodied in the Credo, has driven a track record of success over the long term. Johnson & Johnson remains committed to patients and to customers all around the world, confident in its ability to continually deliver innovative medicines, technologies, and products.

and Company)

BD, headquartered in Franklin Lakes, New Jersey, is focused on improving drug delivery, enhancing the quality and speed of diagnosing infectious diseases and cancers, and advancing the research, discovery, and production of new drugs and vaccines.

BD has three business segments—BD Medical, BD Diagnostics, and BD Biosciences—with facilities in 184 locations in nearly 50 countries. Its total revenue in fiscal 2007 was $6.4 billion.

A Fortune 500 company whose purpose is "Helping all people live healthy lives," BD innovates for impact. The company executes focused strategies targeting specific opportunities to improve human health care. Over its 111-year history, BD has been most successful when it identifies under-appreciated or emerging health care needs, develops and applies technology to solve these problems, uses its manufacturing expertise to make high quality products available and afford-able to people around the world, and surrounds those products with outstanding service and support.

Above left: In 1906 BD founders Maxwell W. Becton and Fairleigh S. Dickinson Sr. purchased a tract of land in the Meadowlands of New Jersey and built their company's headquarters in East Rutherford. Above right: By 1986 BD had grown significantly and relocated its global headquarters to a newly constructed campus in Franklin Lakes. The complex has garnered design awards for its beauty and functionality.

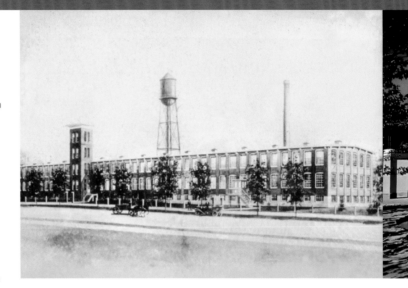

Examples include BD's developing the first syringe designed for insulin injection in 1924 and pioneering the development of safety-engineered devices designed to protect health care workers. BD also invests in products and technologies designed to meet the needs of developing countries, emphasizing affordability.

BD is committed to volunteerism, community, safety, and the environ-ment. It purposefully concentrates its community outreach efforts

in areas where it can effect the greatest change. These efforts tie directly into BD's business goals as well—reducing the spread of infection, advancing global health, enhancing therapy, and improving disease management.

Examples of these activities include advocating international immunization, promoting health care worker safety, raising awareness of pandemic dis-eases, and providing disaster relief. BD also is supporting the development

of an AIDS vaccine, working to reduce the impact of HIV/AIDS and tuberculosis in developing countries, and fighting the spread of disease.

BD provides additional information on its Web site (www.bd.com).

By giving time, talent, and resources as it strives to reduce the burden of disease and raise health standards, BD and its dedicated associates are saving and improving lives around the world.

Hoffmann-La Roche Inc.

This pharmaceutical company has a legacy of innovation and a heritage of saving lives. With its more than 5,000 U.S. employees, the company remains true to its mission: to improve patient care by discovering, developing, manufacturing, and marketing novel, high quality, and cost-effective health care products and services.

Above left: Headquartered in Nutley since 1929, Hoffmann-La Roche Inc. (Roche) is a leading New Jersey employer. Above right: At Roche laboratories, researchers pursue breakthroughs in producing innovative medicines for a wide range of diseases.

Hoffmann-La Roche Inc., headquartered in Nutley, New Jersey, is the U.S. prescription drug unit of the Roche Group, a global health care company that has been in business for more than 100 years. Hoffmann-La Roche (Roche) businesses include pharmaceuticals and diagnostics, and the company operates in more than 65 countries, employing approximately 79,000 people. The company is a leading innovator of medicines and services that make a difference in the lives of hundreds of millions of people. Many of its drugs are now the number one prescribed medicines in their therapeutic areas, because historically Roche has been a global pioneer in the introduction of innovative new therapies.

From its beginnings in a small Swiss laboratory in 1896, Roche has been committed to fulfilling unmet medical needs. And this tradition continues in today's more challenging and dynamic times. Each week, breakthroughs in research bring the company closer to unlocking the underlying causes of disease and the mysteries of arthritis, cancer, diabetes, and other devastating health conditions. Excitement, inspiration, and promise are pervasive feelings in Roche's research laboratories and in its alliances with other leading biotechnical companies. Roche launched the world's first oral chemotherapy pill, the first protease inhibitor for fighting HIV/AIDS, the world's first oral pill effective against all common strains of the influenza virus, and the first monthly oral and quarterly injection product for the treatment and prevention of osteoporosis in postmenopausal women.

Roche was also a pioneer in other important areas. It was one of the first pharmaceutical companies to introduce a formal Indigent Patient Program, in 1963, making drugs available to patients unable to afford treatment. Long an employer of choice, in 1945 Roche was among the first companies to provide a medical insurance plan to offer parental leave decades before it was mandated by law (in the 1970s) and to establish one of the first on-site corporate day-care facilities in the nation, in 1977.

Roche provides additional information about the company and its products, services, and activities on its Web site (www.rocheusa.com).

Looking optimistically toward the future, Hoffmann-La Roche Inc. invests more than $6 billion per year in research and development and has seven pharmaceutical research centers located on three continents. The company's extensive drug pipeline could result in promising new products being made available to health care providers and their patients for a wide range of diseases for many years to come.

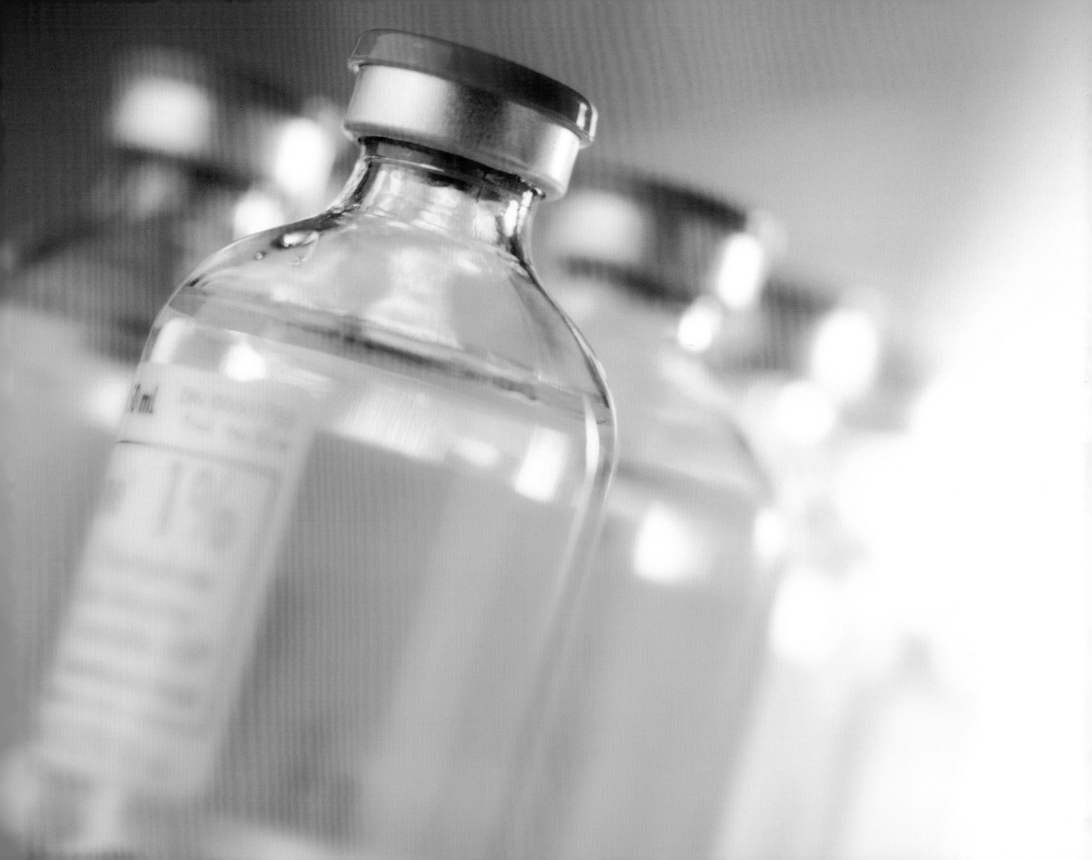

PROFILES OF COMPANIES AND ORGANIZATIONS

Professional and Business Services

WithumSmith+Brown

WithumSmith+Brown believes its people make the difference in its service. This belief is what makes it a high caliber firm, enables it to be recognized and distinguished from independent organizations, and sets it apart from other companies of its kind.

One of the accounti Northea

Accoun
Tax Ser
SOX Com
& Cor

WS+B
WithumSmith+Brown
Certified Public Accountants and Consultants

Above:
WithumSmith+Brown
partners, from left,
Dave Springsteen,
Rebecca Machinga, and
Tom Suarez discuss
the firm's leadership
training initiative.

A large mid-Atlantic regional accounting and consulting firm, WithumSmith+Brown (WS+B) brings clients the benefits of a larger organization without sacrificing the level of attention and personal service that people expect from a smaller firm. The firm continues to embrace a commitment to excellence and integrity, enabling it to consistently provide the very best to its employees, its clients, and the community.

WS+B is ranked among the top 35 accounting firms in the United States by *Public Accounting Report* and *INSIDE Public Accounting* and among the top 10 firms in New Jersey by *NJBIZ* magazine. *INSIDE Public Accounting* rated WS+B "Best of the Best," a distinction granted annually to 25 accounting firms in the United States based on a variety of financial, client service, and management criteria. WS+B has received this recognition for nine consecutive years.

Additionally, for four consecutive years, WS+B has earned a position in the "Best Places to Work in New Jersey" list, placing third in the large-company category for 2007 and 2008 while positioned as the top accounting firm on the 2008 list. The program is administered by the Best Companies Group through a survey conducted in partnership with *NJBIZ*. WS+B was ranked among the top 40 U.S. firms in the 2006, 2007, and 2008 editions of the *Vault Guide to the Top Accounting Firms*. The guide is published by Vault Inc., a media company focused on careers. Moreover, the firm's past six professional peer reviews were completed without a letter of comment, a distinction accomplished by only four out of 10 accounting firms in the nation.

Based in Princeton, the firm has additional offices in Cherry Hill, Morristown, New Brunswick, Red Bank, Somerville, and Toms River, New Jersey; New York City, New York; Philadelphia and Newtown, Pennsylvania; Silver Spring, Maryland; Basalt, Colorado; and West Palm Beach, Florida.

WS+B is home to some of the best and brightest professionals in the field, many of whom have special knowledge in key industry areas, including bankruptcy, construction, government, health care, insurance, international tax, litigation support, not-for-profit, and mortgage services. The firm's Corporate Governance division, WithumSmith+Brown Global Assurance, provides expert counsel and project support for Section 404 Sarbanes-Oxley ("SOX") compliance and other internal audit and risk assurance–related services to all types of organizations. And through its affiliation with HLB International, a worldwide organization of accounting professionals and business advisors in over 100 countries, WS+B is able to provide special business services to help international companies succeed in the global market.

WS+B's long-term vision encompasses becoming the most prominent firm in the New York–Philadelphia corridor, while continuing to provide clients with the superior service they have come to expect. The firm recognizes that the fulfillment of these objectives is only possible through the dedication and hard work of its people, and it will continue to provide an atmosphere that encourages employees to reach their full potential.

PROFILES OF COMPANIES AND ORGANIZATIONS

Spectator Sports

New Jersey

With roaring crowds and outstanding athletes, this university's teams provide thrills for sports fans across New Jersey—and beyond. Excitement fills the air at sellout events at Rutgers Stadium, the Louis Brown Athletic Center, and other stellar venues.

Rutgers, The State University of New Jersey, offers a broad variety of sports programs. Above left: Brian Leonard evades a tackle in a football game at Rutgers Stadium. Above center: Matee Ajavon brings the basketball down the court at Rutgers' Louis Brown Athletic Center. Right: The crowd takes in a baseball game—and a stunning sunset—at Campbell's Field in Camden.

On November 6, 1869, about 100 spectators gathered on a field in New Brunswick to watch two teams doff their hats and coats for a game later described as full of "headlong running, wild shouting, and frantic kicking." Although today's fans might not recognize the game, this was football—the first game of intercollegiate football, in fact—with Rutgers besting Princeton 6–4 in the historic matchup.

The tradition of trailblazing at Rutgers, The State University of New Jersey, continued with football great and class valedictorian Paul Robeson, who was one of the first African-Americans named a college football All-American (in both 1917 and 1918).

Today the Rutgers Scarlet Knights keep the excitement alive as they compete against other NCAA Division I teams, with the thrills reaching fever pitch at Final Four basketball games and football bowl games. When there is a home football game, people hear the cheering crowds upon approaching Rutgers Stadium in Piscataway, where the fans turn the stands into a virtual sea of red.

Thousands flock to the Louis Brown Athletic Center, also in Piscataway, to watch men's and women's basketball squads engage in rousing, inspirational contests. The university provides additional information on its Scarlet Knights Web site (www.scarletknights.com).

Fans often see history in the making, as leading Rutgers athletes have made it to the Olympic Games, Major League Baseball, the NBA, the NFL, and the WNBA. The Scarlet Knights deliver unforgettable moments—the legendary undefeated season and

Final Four appearance by the 1975–76 men's basketball team; the 2006 football team's stunning 28–25 victory over Louisville, led by Scarlet Knights coach Greg Schiano; and the 800th career win by women's basketball coach C. Vivian Stringer in 2008.

Fans also flock to Rutgers events to cheer student athletes competing in soccer, softball, and other sports. Spectacular urban skylines provide the backdrops for baseball games at Campbell's Field in Camden and Bears & Eagles Riverfront Stadium in Newark. No matter the sport, Rutgers teams offer thrills aplenty.

Rutgers women's basketball coach C. Vivian Stringer

PROFILES OF COMPANIES AND ORGANIZATIONS

Tourism, Entertainment, and Hospitality

Center for Golf History

The United States Golf Association Museum is the world's premier center for the appreciation and study of golf. Multimedia exhibitions, a research center, and vast historical collections chronicle and interpret the game's noteworthy history.

The United States Golf Association (USGA) Museum, located since 1972 in Far Hills, New Jersey, is home to the world's premier collection of golf artifacts and memorabilia. Founded in 1936, the USGA Museum is also one of the nation's oldest museums devoted solely to sports.

In the years since the creation of the museum, the collections have grown to comprise more than 42,000 artifacts, a library of more than 20,000 volumes, more than half a million photographic images, and several thousand hours of historic film, video, and audio recordings. Together these collections document the history and evolution of golf in the United States, as well as the role the USGA has played as the game's governing authority since the association was established in 1894.

The museum's original building was completed in 1919 and designed by noted American architect John Russell Pope, who also designed, in Washington, D.C., the National Archives Building, the National Gallery of Art, and the Thomas Jefferson Memorial.

An extensive, three-year renovation completed in 2008 has created an expanded, state-of-the-art museum. Today, the venue includes the Arnold Palmer Center for Golf History, which provides nearly 16,000 square feet of additional space for the museum, with more than 5,000 square feet of new exhibition galleries, a research center, and technologically advanced storage rooms. The museum's signature architectural feature is a clerestory-lighted rotunda called the Hall of Champions, which houses all 13 of the USGA's original national championship trophies. The names of every USGA champion are recorded on the walls of the hall.

The USGA Museum's permanent exhibitions highlight key moments in the history of American golf, with a particular focus on USGA champions and championships. The stories of Francis Ouimet, Bob Jones, Babe Didrikson Zaharias, Patty Berg, Arnold Palmer, Jack Nicklaus, Tiger Woods, and many other legendary figures of the game are told. The galleries also house more than 2,000 artifacts from the museum's collection, with displays including multimedia presentations and interactive kiosks. Visitors to the USGA Museum can see some of the most celebrated artifacts in the history of the game, including golf clubs, golf balls, clothing, and other equipment used by the game's greatest players in some of their most memorable victories.

For avid golfers, scholars of the game's history, casual sports fans, or simply those interested in the history of American culture, the United States Golf Association Museum and Arnold Palmer Center for Golf History aim to provide an experience that is both educational and entertaining.

Doubletree Somerset Hotel & Executive Meeting Center

A member of the International Association of Conference Centers (IACC), this unique hotel in Somerset, New Jersey, blends the service and luxury of a first-class hotel with the facilities and amenities of a modern conference center.

Above left: The Doubletree Somerset Hotel & Executive Meeting Center is a leading source of luxurious accommodations and comprehensive amenities—for business and for leisure travelers. Above right: In the evening, the sophisticated lobby of the Doubletree Somerset is both dazzling and inviting.

Ideally suited to host informal gatherings, black-tie events, and high-technology business conferences, the facilities at the Doubletree Somerset Hotel & Executive Meeting Center are exceptional—31,364 square feet of meeting and banquet space, including a 10,080-square-foot grand ballroom and a 3,480-square-foot social ballroom; 62,000 square feet of exhibit and meeting space connected to the hotel (at the Garden State Convention Center);

as well as banquet seating for parties comprising from 50 to 1,000 people.

Located in one of the nation's busiest corporate communities, the non-smoking Doubletree Somerset also offers 14 meeting rooms equipped with high-speed Internet access and state-of-the-art technology. Additional business services include video conferencing, updated audiovisual equipment, a centrally located concierge, and an

e-business center. All types of events are handled with the highest level of professionalism and outstanding service.

Guests visiting the area on leisure trips will be equally pleased with all the Doubletree Somerset has to offer, including 364 oversized, comfortably appointed guest rooms, six deluxe suites, and a Presidential suite, all set among 16 beautifully landscaped acres. The hotel is minutes from a wide assortment of first-class shopping, dining, and nightlife choices and just an hour's drive from the New Jersey shore, Philadelphia, and Manhattan.

The Doubletree Somerset features its own full-service restaurant, the Tuscany Grill, which specializes in hearty American breakfast dishes and northern Italian dinner cuisine. For a full menu of soups, salads, sandwiches, and pizza, the Doubletree features TK's Lounge—a casual dining and cocktail lounge.

As a leading source of luxurious accommodations, the Doubletree Somerset Hotel & Executive Meeting Center provides an outstanding balance of business and pleasure and a sophisticated place to celebrate some of life's most important events.

Cherbo Publishing Group

Cherbo Publishing Group's business-focused, art book–quality publications, which celebrate the vital spirit of enterprise, are custom books that are used as high-impact economic development tools to enhance reputations, increase profits, and provide global exposure for businesses and organizations.

ABOUT CPG PUBLICATIONS

CPG has created books for some of America's leading organizations, including the U.S. Chamber of Commerce, Empire State Development, California Sesquicentennial Foundation, Chicago O'Hare International Airport, and the Indiana Manufacturers Association. Participants have included Blue Cross Blue Shield, DuPont, Toyota, Northrop Grumman, and Xerox.

CPG series range from history books to economic development/relocation books and from business reports to publications of special interest. The economic development series spotlights the outstanding economic and quality-of-life advantages of fast-growing cities, counties, regions, or states. The annual business reports provide an economic snapshot of individual cities, regions, or states. The commemorative series marks milestones for corporations, organizations, and professional and trade associations.

To find out how CPG can help you celebrate a special occasion, or for information on how to showcase your company or organization, contact Jack Cherbo at 818-783-0040, extension 26, or visit www.cherbopub.com.

Both pages, all: Cherbo Publishing Group produces custom books for historical, professional, and government organizations. These fine publications promote the economic development of America's cities, regions, and states by chronicling their history—the people, enterprises, industries, and organizations that have made them great.

Jack Cherbo, Cherbo Publishing Group president and CEO, has been breaking new ground in the sponsored publishing business for more than 40 years.

"Previously, the cost of creating a handsome book for business developments or commemorative occasions fell directly on the sponsoring organization," Cherbo says. "My company pioneered an entirely new concept—funding these books through the sale of corporate profiles."

Cherbo honed his leading edge in Chicago, where he owned a top advertising agency before moving into publishing. Armed with a degree in business administration from Northwestern University, a mind that never stopped, and a keen sense of humor, Cherbo set out to succeed—and continues to do just that.

Cherbo Publishing Group (CPG), formerly a wholly owned subsidiary of

Jostens, Inc., a Fortune 500 company, has been a privately held corporation since 1993. CPG is North America's leading publisher of quality custom books for commercial, civic, historical, and trade associations. Publications range from hardcover state, regional, and commemorative books to softcover state and regional business reports. The company is headquartered in Encino, California, and operates regional offices in Philadelphia, Minneapolis, and Houston.

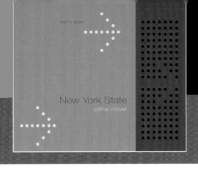
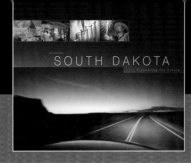

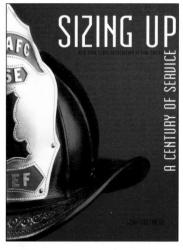

Select CPG Publications

VISIONS OF OPPORTUNITY
City, Regional, and State Series

ALABAMA *The Progress, The Promise*

AMERICA & THE SPIRIT
OF ENTERPRISE
Century of Progress, Future of Promise

AURORA, ILLINOIS *A City Second to None*

CALIFORNIA *Golden Past, Shining Future*

CHATTANOOGA *The Renaissance of a City*

CINCINNATI *Bridges to the Future*

CONNECTICUT *Chartered for Progress*

DELAWARE *Incorporating Vision in Industry*

FORT WORTH *Where the Best Begins*

GREATER PHOENIX *Expanding Horizons*

JACKSONVILLE *Where the Future Leads*

LEHIGH VALLEY *Crossroads of Commerce*

MICHIGAN *America's Pacesetter*

MILWAUKEE *Midwestern Metropolis*

MISSOURI *Gateway to Enterprise*

NASHVILLE *Amplified*

NEW YORK STATE *Prime Mover*

NORTH CAROLINA *The State of Minds*

OKLAHOMA *The Center of It All*

PITTSBURGH *Smart City*

SOUTH DAKOTA *Pioneering the Future*

TOLEDO *Access. Opportunity. Edge.*

UTAH *Life Elevated*

WEST VIRGINIA *Reaching New Heights*

LEGACY
Commemorative Series

ALBERTA AT 100 *Celebrating the Legacy*

BUILD IT & THE CROWDS WILL COME
Seventy-Five Years of Public Assembly

CELEBRATE SAINT PAUL
150 Years of History

DAYTON *On the Wings of Progress*

THE EXHIBITION INDUSTRY
The Power of Commerce

IDAHO *The Heroic Journey*

MINNEAPOLIS *Currents of Change*

NEW YORK STATE ASSOCIATION
OF FIRE CHIEFS
Sizing Up a Century of Service

ROCHESTER, MINNESOTA
Transforming the World: Rochester at 150

VIRGINIA
Catalyst of Commerce for Four Centuries

VISIONS TAKING SHAPE
*Celebrating 50 Years of the Precast/
Prestressed Concrete Industry*

ANNUAL BUSINESS REPORTS
MINNESOTA REPORT *2007*

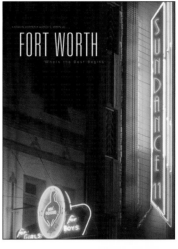
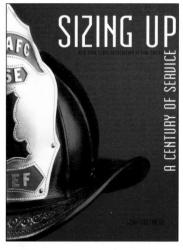
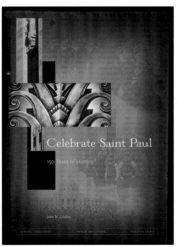
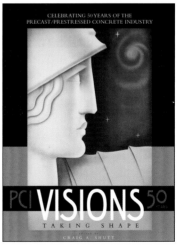
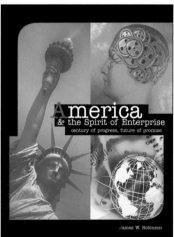

SELECTED BIBLIOGRAPHY

American Chemical Society. "The Trials of Streptomycin." National Historic Chemical Landmarks. http://acswebcontent.acs.org/landmarks/antibiotics/trials.html.

Anderson, Elaine. *The Central Railroad of New Jersey's First 100 Years: A Historical Survey.* Easton, PA: Center for Canal History and Technology, 1984.

Anderson, Steve. Regional Bridges of Southeastern Pennsylvania: Delaware River Bridges, Delaware River–Turnpike Toll Bridge. PhillyRoads.com. http://www.phillyroads.com/crossings/delaware-toll/.

ASME. *The Great Falls Raceway and Power System: National Historic Mechanical and Civil Engineering Landmark Dedication Program.* May 20, 1977. http://files.asme.org/ASMEORG/Communities/History/Landmarks/5561.pdf.

Associated Press. "Atlantic City Airport Experiences a Boom in Passenger Traffic." *New York Times,* Jan. 2, 1983.

Bagli, Charles V. "Goldman Sachs Gets Deal for 2nd Jersey City Tower." *New York Times*, July 19, 2007.

Bastian, Lisa A. "Innovation Zones: New Jersey's Newest Technology Neighborhoods." *Area Development,* Dec./Jan. 2008. http://www.areadevelopment.com/siteSelection/dec07/innovationZones.shtml (accessed April 3, 2008).

Bauers, Sandy. "Three Propose Wind Farms off Jersey Shore." *Philadelphia Inquirer,* March 5, 2008. http://www.philly.com/inquirer/local/nj/20080305_Three_propose_wind_farms_off_Jersey_Shore.html (accessed March 5, 2008).

Ben-Ali, Russell. "Jersey City and Honeywell Craft Plan for Bayfront Cleanup." *Newark Star-Ledger,* Jan. 6, 2008.

Bill, Alfred Hoyt. *New Jersey and the Revolutionary War. The New Jersey Historical Series,* vol. 11. Princeton: D. Van Nostrand Company, 1964.

Blesch, Carl. "News: Nanotechnology Facility Receives State Grant." *Rutgers Focus.* Rutgers, the State University of New Jersey, May 30, 2006. http://ur.rutgers.edu/focus/article/Nanotechnology%20facility%20receives%20state%20grant/1855/.

Brennan, John. "Nets, Xanadu Unite in Marketing Effort." *The Record NorthJersey.com,* May 22, 2008. http://www.northjersey.com/business/news/19166089.html.

Collins, Glenn. "Our Medicine Chest." *New York Times,* March 29, 1998. http://query.nytimes.com/gst/fullpage.html?res=9D00EEDB163BF93AA15750C0A96E958260&sec=&spon=&pagewanted=all.

Colorants Industry History. "Tremley Point Industrial History." http://www.colorantshistory.org/TremleyHistory.html.

Contributors, nycsubway.org. "Around New York: New Jersey Transit, Atlantic City, Atlantic City Line." www.nycsubway.org/us/njtransit/njtac.html.

CECOM LCMC Historical Office. *A Concise History of the U.S. Army CECOM Life Cycle Management Command and Fort Monmouth New Jersey.* http://www.monmouth.army.mil/historian/pub.php.

CNNMoney.com. "Best Places to Live, New Jersey: Top 100." http://money.cnn.com/magazines/moneymag/bplive/2007/states/NJ.html.

Conniff, James C. G., and Richard Conniff. *The Energy People: A History of PSE&G.* Newark: Public Service Electric and Gas Company, 1978.

"Cranberries in New Jersey." *Pinelands Guide.* Burlington County Library System. http://www.burlco.lib.nj.us/pinelands/cranber.shtml.

Craven, Wesley Frank. *New Jersey and the English Colonization of North America. The New Jersey Historical Series*, vol. 3. Princeton: D. Van Nostrand Company, 1964.

Cunningham, John T. *Made in New Jersey: The Industrial Story of a State*. New Brunswick: Rutgers University Press, 1954.

Cupolo, Diego. "A Place in the Sun: Jersey Building is First to Power Itself." *Newark Star-Ledger,* Nov. 28, 2007.

Curran, John. "An Ever-Evolving Casino Skyline." *Atlantic City magazine*, May 1998.

Dupont, Ronald J. *Images of America: Vernon Township*. Mount Pleasant: Arcadia Publishing, 2002.

Eastern Roads. "Garden State Parkway: Historic Overview." 2008. http://www.nycroads.com/roads/garden-state/.

E. I. du Pont de Nemours and Company. DuPont Heritage. "First Dynamite: 1880." http://heritage.dupont.com/touchpoints/tp_1880/overview.shtml.

Emporis. "The Beacon, a.k.a. Jersey City Medical Center." Emporis Corporation, 2008. http://www.emporis.com/en/wm/cx/?id=100394.

Federal Writers' Project. *New Jersey: A Guide to Its Present and Past*. New York: Hastings House, 1939.

Fortune on CNNMoney.com. "Fortune 500 2008, States: New Jersey." http://money.cnn.com/magazines/fortune/fortune500/2008/states/NJ.html.

Halgrim, Robert P. *The Thomas Edison, Henry Ford Winter Estates: Featuring Homes, Garden, Museum and Laboratory*. Kansas City, MO: Terrell Publishing Company, n.d.

Heston, Alfred M. *Jersey Waggon Jaunts*. Camden: Atlantic County Historical Society, 1926.

Hollow, Michele C. "This Way Up." *New Jersey Monthly Magazine,* May 2007.

Jennemann, Tom. "From Abandoned Factories to Sought-after Condos." Hoboken Reporter.com, Nov. 13, 2005. http://www.hudsonreporter.com/site/news.cfm?newsid=15574078&BRD=1291&PAG=461&dept_id=551343&rfi=6.

Jordan, Louis. "A Brief Outline of Dutch History and the Province of New Netherland." *The Coins of Colonial and Early America*. Notre Dame, IN: University of Notre Dame, Department of Special Collections, 1997. http://www.coins.nd.edu/ColCoin/ColCoinIntros/Netherlands.html.

Leiby, Adrian C. *The Early Dutch and Swedish Settlers of New Jersey. The New Jersey Historical Series,* vol. 10. Princeton: D. Van Nostrand Company, 1964.

Leuchtenburg, William E. *Franklin D. Roosevelt and the New Deal, 1932–1940*. New York: Harper & Row, 1963.

Lurie, Maxine N., and Marc Mappen, eds. *Encyclopedia of New Jersey*. New Brunswick: Rutgers University Press, 2004.

MacPherson, Kitta. "Hospital Embraces Future of Medicine with Stem Cell Bank." *Newark Star-Ledger,* March 7, 2007.

McCormick, Richard P. *New Jersey from Colony to State—1609–1789. The New Jersey Historical Series*, vol. 1. Princeton: D. Van Nostrand Company, 1964.

McDermott, Maura. "Private Tour of Xanadu Leaves Corzine 'Impressed,' Aide Says." *Newark Star-Ledger*, April 24, 2008.

McGlone, Peggy. "Newark's First New High-Rise Housing in Decades Rests on a Risk-Taker." *Newark Star-Ledger,* Jan. 20, 2008.

SELECTED BIBLIOGRAPHY

Meadowlands Developent. "Meadowlands Xanadu." The Mills Corporation. http://www.meadowlandsxanadu.com/static/node1305.jsp.

Monmouth Park Racetrack. Media Guide: "History." http://www.monmouth park.com/sharedimages/History(3).pdf.

Morris County Park Commission. "Historic Speedwell: Invention of the Telegraph." http://www.parks.morris.nj.us/speedwell/temp_index.htm.

Mysak, Joe, and Judith Schiffer. *Perpetual Motion: The Illustrated History of the Port Authority of New York & New Jersey.* Santa Monica, CA: General Publishing Group, 1997.

National Park Service. "Resorts & Recreation: An Historic Theme Study of the New Jersey Heritage Trail Route, Chapter II: Railroad Resorts." http://www.nps.gov/history/online_books/nj1/chap2.htm.

Newark Star-Ledger, "Sanofi Plans to Expand," Jan. 25, 2008.

New Jersey Commission on Science and Technology. "Grants & Initiatives." 2008. http://www.state.nj.us/scitech/programs.

New Jersey Department of Environmental Protection. "Brownfields: Revised Brownfield Development Area." http://www.state.nj.us/dep/srp/brownfields/bda/announce.htm.

New Jersey Department of Transportation. "New Jersey Future in Transportation." http://www.state.nj.us/transportation/works/njfit.

———. "Transit Village Initiative." http://www.state.nj.us/transportation/community/village.

New York Shipbuilding Company Historical Site. "A Brief History of the New York Shipbuilding Company." 2003. http://members.aol.com/nyship/history.html.

Niven, Felicia Lowenstein. "Centers of Health: Shore Memorial Hospital." *Casino Connection,* March 2007.

Office of Smart Growth. "New Jersey State Development and Redevelopment Plan." New Jersey Department of Community Affairs. http://www.state.nj.us/dca/osg/plan/.

Pierce, John R., and Arthur G. Tressler. *The Research State: A History of Science in New Jersey. The New Jersey Historical Series,* vol. 15. Princeton: D. Van Nostrand Company, 1964.

Project Administration Works, and Federal Writers' Project of the Works Pr. *The WPA Guide to 1930s New Jersey.* New Brunswick: Rutgers University Press, 1986.

Ramchandani, Dillip. "Benzodiazepines—How It All Started: Two Articles about Librium." Temple University Hospital Department of Psychiatry and Behavioral Science. http://www.benzo.org.uk/librium.htm.

Richman, Steven M. *The Bridges of New Jersey: Portraits of Garden State Crossings.* New Brunswick: Rutgers University Press, 2005.

Roman, Nyvia. "Newark's Pennsylvania Station." *The Newark Metro: Reports.* Rutgers University–Newark. http://www.newarkmetro.rutgers.edu/credits.php (accessed April 3, 2008).

Rutgers Business School News. "New Full-Time MBA Curriculum Announced," Rutgers Business School Newark and New Brunswick, Summer 2007.

Rutgers New Jersey Agricultural Experiment Station. "Natural Resources and the Environment: Biomass Energy Potential in New Jersey." Rutgers, the State University of New Jersey. http://www.njaes.rutgers.edu/bioenergy/.

Rutgers School of Business. "Camden: A Q&A with Dean Mitchell Koza." Rutgers, the State University of New Jersey. http://news.rutgers.edu/focus/issue.2008-01-22.1717181631/article.2008-01-22.7577706428 (Jan. 23, 2008).

Schmidt, George P. *Princeton and Rutgers—the Two Colonial Colleges of New Jersey. The New Jersey Historical Series,* vol. 5. Princeton: D. Van Nostrand Company, 1964.

South Jersey Transportation Authority. Atlantic City International Airport. "ACY Overview and History." http://www.sjta.com/acairport/about.asp.

State of New Jersey, Office of the Governor. "Governor Corzine Signs Legislation Authorizing $270 Million Investment in Stem Cell Research Centers." Press Release, Dec. 20, 2006. http://www.state.nj.us/governor/news/news/ approved/20061219b.html.

Strauss, Robert. "Briefing: Development; Garden State Park's Fate." New York and Region. *New York Times,* Aug. 12, 2001. http://query.nytimes.com/gst/fullpage.html?res=9505E1DB123FF931A2575BC0A9679C8B63.

———. "In Atlantic City, Hotels Plan for All Seasons." *New York Times,* Jan. 1, 2006.

Strum, Charles. "Our Towns: Investor's Dreams Rise From Decay." *New York Times,* Oct. 15, 1993. http://query.nytimes.com/gst/fullpage.html?res= 9F0CEED81731F936A25753C1A965958260 (accessed March 31, 2008).

Tropicana Casino and Resort. "Atlantic City Events Entertainment at the Quarter." www.tropicana.net/thequarter/.

Women's Project of New Jersey. *Past and Promise: Lives of New Jersey Women.* Syracuse, NY: Syracuse University Press, 1997.

The Web sites of the following organizations also were consulted:

Acrion Technologies, Bergen Community College, Berger Organization, Borgata Hotel Casino & Spa, Borough of Paramus, Campbell Soup Company, CentraState Medical Center, Cherry Hill Township, Cogswell Realty Group of New York, Coriell Institute for Medical Research, Crystal Springs Golf Resort, Delaware River and Bay Authority, Delaware River Joint Toll Bridge Commission, Delaware River Port Authority of Pennsylvania and New Jersey, Dranoff Properties, Essex County Airport, Gibbstown Fire Company, Goldman Sachs, Great Atlantic & Pacific Tea Company, Greater New Brunswick Innovation Zone, HealthCare Institute of New Jersey, Hoffmann-La Roche, Hudson-Bergen Light Rail, Institute for Advanced Study, L-3 Communication Systems, LifebankUSA, Meadowlands, National Association of Home Builders, National Starch and Chemical Company, Newark Bears, Newark City Subway, Newark Innovation Zone, New Jersey Business and Industry Association, New Jersey Business Portal, New Jersey Chamber of Commerce, New Jersey Coastal Heritage Trail Route, New Jersey Council of County Colleges, New Jersey Division of Travel and Tourism, New Jersey Economic Development Authority, New Jersey Future, New Jersey Historical Society, New Jersey Network, New Jersey Transit, New Jersey Turnpike Authority, Northwest New Jersey Skylands Guide, Pathmark, Port Authority of New York and New Jersey, Rutgers New Jersey Agricultural Experiment Station, Sanofi-Aventis, Somerset Medical Center, State of New Jersey Board of Public Utilities, Teterboro Airport, UBS, and Waterfront Technology Center at Camden.

INDEX

INDEX

PHOTO CREDITS

Page ii: © Tony Kurdzuk/
The Star-Ledger/Corbis
Page v: © Tony Kurdzuk/
The Star-Ledger/Corbis
Page vi: © Jeremy Edwards
Page viii, left: © Gail Mooney/Masterfile
Page viii, right: Courtesy, Trump Taj
Mahal, Atlantic City, NJ
Page ix: © Anne James
Page x: © Justin Lane/Corbis
Page xi, left: © Mike Booth/Alamy
Page xi, right: © David Zimmerman/
Masterfile
Page xii, left: © Andrew Shapiro
Page xii, right: © Najlah Feanny/Corbis
Page xiii: © Peter Mauss/Esto
Page xiv: © Serena A. Thaw
Page xv, left: © Eric Koppel
Page xv, right: © The Star-Ledger/
Corbis
Page xvii: © Steve Kelley
Page xx, left: © Bob Jagendorf
Page xx, right: © Najlah Feanny/Corbis
Page xxi: © Alan Schein Photography/
Corbis
Page xxii: © Paul Kist
Page xxiii, left: © Jeffrey Johnson
Page xxiii, right: © Dennis McDonald/
Getty Images
Page xxiv, left: © Bob Jagendorf
Page xxiv, right: © Leandro Karunungan
Page xxv: © Michael Longfellow
Page xxvi: © Steve Greer
Page xxvii, left: © Ruth Savitz
Page xxvii, right: © Tony Fischer
Page xxviii, left: © Matt Rainey/
The Star-Ledger/Corbis
Page xxviii, right: © PictureNet/Corbis

Page xxix: © Tyler Barrick/
The Star-Ledger/Corbis
Page xxx: © Steve Greer
Page 2, left: © Corbis
Page 2, right: Courtesy, New York
Public Library
Page 3, left: Courtesy, Library of
Congress
Page 3, right: Courtesy, Library of
Congress
Page 4, left: Courtesy, Special
Collections University Archives,
Rutgers University Libraries
Page 4, center: © Underwood &
Underwood/Corbis
Page 5, center: © Corbis
Page 5, right: © Bettman/Corbis
Page 6, left: © Hulton-Deutsch
Collection/Corbis
Page 6, center: © John Springer
Collection/Corbis
Page 6, right: © Hulton Archives/
Getty Images
Page 7, left: Courtesy, The National
Aeronautics and Space
Administration
Page 7, right: © Hulton-Deutsch
Collection/Corbis
Page 8, left: © Bettman/Corbis
Page 8, right: © AP Photo/Bill Kostroun
Page 9, left: © Trapper Frank/Corbis
Page 9, center: Courtesy, Johnson &
Johnson
Page 11: Courtesy, Library of Congress
Page 12: Courtesy, Library of Congress
Page 14, left: © Bettman/Corbis
Page 14, top right: Courtesy, New York
Public Library

Page 14, bottom right: © North Wind
Picture Archives
Page 15: © Corbis
Page 16: © North Wind Picture
Archives
Page 17, right: Public Domain
Page 18, left: Courtesy, New York
Public Library
Page 18, right: © Bettman/Corbis
Page 19: Courtesy, New York Public
Library
Page 20: Courtesy, New York Public
Library
Page 21: © Bettman/Corbis
Page 22, left: Courtesy, New York
Public Library
Page 22, right: Courtesy, New York
Public Library
Page 23, right: Courtesy, Library of
Congress
Page 24: Courtesy, New York Public
Library
Page 26, bottom left: © Bettman/
Corbis
Page 26, top right: Public Domain
Page 26, bottom right: © Bettman/
Corbis
Page 27: From the Collections of the
New Jersey Historical Society,
Newark, New Jersey
Page 28, left: Courtesy, Library of
Congress
Page 28, right: Courtesy, New York
Public Library
Page 29: © Bettman/Corbis
Page 30, left: From the Collections of
the New Jersey Historical Society,
Newark, New Jersey

Page 30, top center: Public Domain
Page 30, bottom center: © Bettman/
Corbis
Page 31, left: Courtesy, Library of
Congress
Page 31, right: © Bettman/Corbis
Page 32, bottom left: © Corbis
Page 32, top left: Courtesy, Victorian
Trade Card Collection, The
University of Iowa Libraries,
Iowa City, Iowa
Page 32, top right: Courtesy, Brandon
McKinney Collection/
www.whiteapplemultimedia.com/
history.html
Page 33: © Underwood & Underwood/
Corbis
Page 34, left: © Bettman/Corbis
Page 34, right: © Corbis
Page 35, left: Courtesy, Johnson &
Johnson
Page 35, right: Courtesy, Library of
Congress
Page 36: © Alinari Archives/Corbis
Page 38, bottom left: © AP Photo/
New Jersey Historical Society
Page 38, top left: © Bettman/Corbis
Page 38, top right: © Underwood &
Underwood/Corbis
Page 39, right: From *Greetings
from New Jersey: A Postcard Tour
of the Garden State* by Helen-
Chantal Pike
Page 40, left: © Corbis
Page 40, right: Courtesy, New Jersey
Historical Society
Page 41, left: © Bettman/Corbis
Page 41, right: Public Domain

cherbo publishing group, inc.

TYPOGRAPHY

Principal faces used: Aldus, designed by Hemann Zapf in 1954;
Helvetica, designed by Matthew Carter, Edouard Hoffmann,
and Max Miedinger in 1959;
Univers, designed by Adrian Frutiger in 1957

HARDWARE

Macintosh G5 desktops, digital color laser printing with Xerox Docucolor 250, digital
imaging with Creo EverSmart Supreme

SOFTWARE

QuarkXPress, Adobe Illustrator, Adobe Photoshop, Adobe Acrobat, Microsoft Word,
Eye-One Pro by Gretagmacbeth, Creo Oxygen, FlightCheck

PAPER

Text Paper: #80 Luna Matte

Bound in Rainbow® recycled content papers from
Ecological Fibers, Inc.

Dust Jacket: #100 Sterling-Litho Gloss